Fifty-Six

A New Novel

DANIEL MARUCCI

First Edition

NEWMAN SPRINGS PUBLISHING
320 Broad Street
Red Bank, NJ 07701

First originally published by Newman Springs Publishing 2024

ISBN 979-8-89061-906-8 (Paperback)
ISBN 979-8-89061-907-5 (Digital)

Printed in the United States of America

To Vincent Minelli and Donato Marucci;
Two men who met the challenge and won.

Special thanks to:
Anne Wesh
Gloria Bradley
Valerie Somma
Sue Humphrey

Introduction

In chapter 1, "Released 1983," we meet the novel's main character, Vince Donato.

Vince is a journeyman baseball player in the twilight of an exciting career. He's been a darling of the public, not for his ballplaying feats but for his life off the ballfield. For seventeen years, he has roamed with racketeers, slept with starlets, and generally boozed and brawled.

He's given his release from the Boston Red Sox only to be signed by the Jersey Riders, an expansion team playing in his home state of New Jersey. Vince is introduced to oil-rich Tex Hardin, who carries a wild reputation of his own, and is flown to Tex's ranch in Dallas for a few days so the two can get better acquainted.

Once in Dallas, Vince meets and quickly seduces Tex's playful wife, Roxanne, and shows Tex how he earned his reputation as a brawler by getting into a fight and pulverizing a man in the unlikely setting of a wild sex health club.

The chapter closes around a campfire on the Texas range with Vince about to tell his life story.

The next two chapters, "Memories" and "The Big Leagues," are told in the first person. Vince tells about his tough upbringing in the inner city and how "you had to hit first to survive." He introduces his family and closest friends, including Johnny "Midnight" Mezzanotte, a leader in the underworld.

Stories abound about his mischievous childhood, everything from throwing golf balls through the Lincoln Tunnel to stealing chickens from the local chickenyard.

He could have easily gone the way of his friends, a life of crime and deception, but a bad experience involving some strong arming over a gambling debt gave him no other choice than to contact the professional scout he had sent away numerous times and join the Chicago White Sox organization.

Sent to spring training in Sarasota, Florida, he promptly gets into a fight with three *rednecks* in a small diner. The seed of his reputation was planted in a greasy southern diner on a hot night.

He's sent to the Sox minor league team in El Paso, Texas, where he quickly takes charge of the team and is in the process of taking them to the Texas League pennant when he's brutally beaten by a team of hit men sent by a small time hood back home who was crossed by Vince prior to his leaving there.

The reputation took root in the minor league but fully blossomed once he hit the big time. Vince leaves no stone unturned as he tells about his nightclub brawls, beanball wars, and romances on the major league level. Stories range from going after the entire Yankee team in their clubhouse to getting into a nightclub brawl with a black Latin girl on his arm and a gun-toting gangster at his side.

At the end of the third chapter, it's tough to remain neutral about Vince Donato. You either like him or you don't.

The plot begins to develop in "The Gang's All Here." In this chapter, we go back to the narrative and meet the famous Walter "Hippity" Hop, the age-old, quick-witted vaudevillian manager of the Jersey Riders. His one-liners are magic, but they cannot help his struggling team on the field or at the gate.

Tex becomes worried that his team is losing money and very quietly and unsuspectingly starts to bait a so far-subdued Vince into exploding into the controversial player that he can be, fully knowing that an explosion from Vince would fill the press with headlines and his empty stadium with fans. To do this, Tex must be close to his team so he and Roxanne move from their Dallas home and take residence in a hotel close to the ballpark, where Roxanne quickly renews acquaintances with Vince.

Luellen Lee, the world-famous movie star and long-time companion of Vince, who was introduced in the previous chapter, also arrives on the scene. She's filming a movie in New York and, upon her arrival, tells Vince she is through being his lover. She wants to be his wife and gives him until the end of the season, which will coincide with the end of her movie, to make up his mind.

It's at this point that Vince starts to receive threatening letters and suspects it's a trick by Tex to get publicity to lure fans to the park. He confronts Tex with his theory, but Tex steadfastly denies he has anything to do with it and encourages Vince to take the letters to the police.

Vince ignores the police and turns to his close friend Johnny Midnight for help in tracking down the potential assassin. Johnny assigns his best man and long-time friend of Vince, "Red" Jones, to be Vince's personal bodyguard.

The screw is slowly starting to turn on Vince. In "The Long Hot Summer," we see that a number of events take place that show that Vince's patience and courage will be put to the test. Not only does Tex keep up his baiting by belittling the team in the press, but also now Vince must come to the aid of his sister Lucy who has fallen in love with another man and doesn't know what to do about it. Vince is shocked and angered when he finds out that the other man is Tex Hardin. Is this part of Tex's master plan for the explosion he needs from Vince, or does he truly love Lucy?

Vince is also having trouble juggling the two women in his life. He truly loves, respects, and admires Luellen, but he lusts for Roxanne who takes matters into her own hands by confronting Luellen with her affair and flaunting it in front of her. To make matters worse for Vince, Red is missing, and the assassin calls to say he has murdered him.

The chapter closes with a meeting of the five crime families of the New York metropolitan area. Johnny Midnight's under the gun for doing business outside his territory and barely escapes with his life. He must, in the near future, compensate the others with a *gift* from his many connections or his life will be worthless.

As the summer wears on, Vince is starting to bear pressure that no man should be expected to face. In Pressure, we see that Lucy still hasn't shaken her feelings for Tex and that Vince's other two sisters come to him with problems of their own.

Grace's husband is dying of cancer as she tells Vince they get no help from a wayward son, and Antoinette's husband has left her, leaving her in tears.

The assassin is still stalking him and teasing him with phone calls and letters, and Tex is still on Vince's back to *explode*, blaming Vince for the lack of attendance. If all that is not enough, Roxanne is constantly after him to leave Luellen and tell Tex of their affair.

The explosion from Vince that Tex has waited for all year finally comes when Vince tells Lucy that he'll settle her affairs with Tex his way. In a crowded clubhouse, Vince warns Tex to stay away from his sister or he'll break his legs. Tex is puzzled and plays innocent but erupts when Vince tells him of his affair with Roxanne. A fight quickly develops, and the two become the darlings of the media. Tex finally is getting the press he wanted.

The assassin is ready to make his kill but is thwarted by his interest in something that Vince is involved in. He has just gotten a hit in his twentieth straight game, and the assassin notifies Vince that when the streak stops, he dies. To live, Vince must continue his streak.

"The Streak" concerns the mass media pressure that falls on Vince as he runs the streak to twenty-five, thirty, thirty-five, forty, and fifty games to get closer every game to the great Joe DiMaggio's record of fifty-six (hence the name of the novel).

Tex is all smiles because he's finally drawing at the gate, but Vince, once a strong and sound man, has turned into a shaken, nervous wreck from the enormous pressures he has had to handle. He's bent but not broken.

Roxanne, still madly in love with Vince, even though he's long since left her, is constantly trying to break up Vince and Luellen. When all else fails, she leaves her senses and shoots Luellen three times, then puts the gun on herself.

Johnny, after months of searching, finally finds Vince's would-be assassin and is not surprised to learn that Tex is behind the whole plot, hiring the man that Vince beat up while in Dallas to come back and taunt him. Tex was going to break the news of the death threats to the papers for the publicity that it would bring, but their fight in the clubhouse and Vince's streak gave his team all the publicity Tex needed. Still, one of Johnny's men was murdered, and revenge was in order for both Tex and his man.

Both Johnny and Vince have a hand in avenging Red's death by brutally murdering the man who, for months, was the hunter only to be turned into the prey. Tex's retribution would come after the season, and the streak was over.

Things have lightened up on Vince considerably. His sisters' problems have all resolved themselves, his would-be assassin is dead, and Luellen will recover from her shooting. The only pressure left for him to bear is the pressure to get to fifty-six, and in "The Last Day," we see Vince as he approaches the last game—fifty-six.

The pressure on Vince becomes heavier than it's been all summer when Johnny sees this as a way to make amends with his rivals by asking Vince to take a dive, to purposely make out.

Vince doesn't understand but listens as Johnny tells him that he assured his rivals that the streak would stop and to bet the game accordingly.

"It was a sure thing," he said, "Vince will do it for me." Millions are involved through Las Vegas bookmakers and the locals. If Vince doesn't cooperate and gets a hit or even comes close to one, they'll think they were double-crossed, and both Vince and Johnny will be dead men.

Does the proud man take the dive to save his friend's neck? I'll leave it to you to read and find out.

Released 1983

1

A ray of sunlight woke him as it crossed his sleeping eyes. Face squinting like a prune, he jumped from the bed and drew the curtains. His naked body stood motionless as he held his head in one hand and the curtain cord in the other.

"Damn, my head hurts," he said in a confessional whisper. He turned to go back to bed and suddenly remembered he had a companion for the night. Looking at the top half of her nude body not covered by the sheets, his mind flashed back to the previous night. A redhead on a sofa coyly eating peanuts from a candy dish. An introduction. A drink, small talk, and then another drink. A slow, grinding dance. Still more drinks. He had no recollection of how he had landed back in his apartment nor of the act itself. Looking at her obvious huge proportions he embarrassingly said to himself I must've been shit-faced to wind up with this blimp. The girl was definitely not what he had been accustomed to.

Stumbling to the bathroom, he leaned over the vanity and looked into the mirror to see his morning face. "Maybe she was just as fucked up as you," he said, wishing he had not looked as bad the previous night. A cold shower and clean shave put him in better looks and spirits. A good full breakfast was just what he needed to fully erase the hangover of the night's party.

The smell of sausage frying reached her nostrils and awakened her. From the bed, she could peer out into the kitchen to watch Vince Donato, towel around his waist and fork in his hand, cooking at his stove. Quietly she slipped from bed, not bothering to put anything on, and as if walking on eggshells crept up and grabbed him from behind, putting one hand around his hairy chest and the other in his crotch.

"Good morning," she sang.

Again, he talked to himself, "This bitch is whacked-out. I just want some breakfast and to get the hell out." He turned and their eyes met.

"Now I know I was drunk," he said to himself.

"I'm making some sausage and eggs. A little toast, a little coffee, then you get dressed and go, okay?"

"I'm not hungry for eggs," she quickly answered back as her hand played with what she was hungry for.

Vince had gone through this type of scene a hundred times with young groupies that only wanted to bang a ballplayer, an actor, a politician, or anybody in the limelight. At times, it was an unexpected bonus, but other times, like this, it was a big pain.

"I'm hungry for Vince Donato, the gorgeous hunk of the Boston Red Sox. I'd much rather eat his sausage."

Vince laughed. He finally surmised that this leech was going to be a tough one to shake, and he didn't need this aggravation so early in the morning anyway. "You sure are something. I'll tell you what we'll do, it's now about ten. I have a very important meeting to go to at one. It looks like you're not going to leave until you get what you want." She nodded. "So we'll have some breakfast, some sex, and then we'll both go, okay?"

She dropped his towel. The sausage burnt, and the eggs were never fried.

2

"Do you know what time it is? You're forty-five fuckin' minutes late," said Frank Gilroy, General Manager for the Boston Red Sox, "forty-five fuckin' minutes!" he tensely yelled again, as the veins in his balding head showed a bulge. "You think because the season's over you can come and go as you please?"

"Relax, Frank," answered Vince as he placed his two hands out in a peaceful gesture. "Sit down, and I'll tell you all about it. No big deal. What's the problem? I'm here, aren't I?"

"The problem is," he nervously went on to say, "that we have a very important meeting with someone at two, and I wanted a little time to brief you in regards to what's going on."

Vince was puzzled, Frank Gilroy was not the nervous type—boisterous, arrogant, and cocky, definitely yes, but nervous, no. Vince sensed something was wrong. "Well, what is going on, Frank?"

The rotund general manager lit a cigar and finally sat down. "Well, if you were on time we'd have it all ironed out by now. By the way, why were you late?"

Vince looked him straight in the eye. "You know me, Frank. I never lie. I had a bitch up my place that wouldn't leave until I jammed her one more time."

Pointing his cigar, he replied, "I guess something like that would make you late. It would probably make me late too, but you're never going to learn are you?"

Vince smiled and shook his head. "Guess not." Sensing an air of normalcy between the two, the ballplayer asked his general manager, "So what is it, Frank?"

He put his cigar down and started. "You've always been straight with me, at least I think you always have, and I admire that in you.

That's why I'm going to be straight with you." He paused and nervously twirled the cigar in the ashtray before him. "The club is releasing you."

Vince's brown eyes darted around the room as a thousand thoughts passed through his mind.

The general manager continued, "You've given us seven solid years. You haven't made anyone forget Ted Williams, but then again there are a few people who'll remember Vince Donato, if not for your achievements on the field, then certainly for your off-the-field escapades. I don't think there's ever been a more controversial player in Boston than you. The fans seem to love you. They all seem to live or die wanting to know which starlet Vince Donato is banging or what club he hangs in. How about the time you were brought to the commissioner because of your ties with the rackets? You sure were a good copy for the papers too. Remember the year they ran the comic strip about you? You've made your mark here in Boston just as you did in Chicago and I guess anywhere else you've played ball. But, Vince, we put up with all that shit because you always put out on the field for us and the fact is you did draw the fans." He picked up his cigar and put it in his mouth as he leaned back in his chair. "Well, now you have to understand that baseball is a business. You're going to be thirty-seven next year, which is ancient for an athlete, and quite frankly your numbers haven't been getting any better the last few years have they, especially this past September."

Vince nodded in agreement. He knew that sooner or later this time would come. Like death, losing one's athletic skill is inevitable, but unlike death, an athlete still has a life to live. Vince had never prepared for retirement from the ballfield, and now as quick as a fastball, it had arrived.

The fat man continued, "I've got two studs on the farm that are too good to keep down there. The fact is if I took you to spring training next year, chances are you wouldn't even make the club. But"—he looked at his watch, it was 2:00 p.m., "there's a way out for you, and if I know anything, it'll be here any minute now."

As if taken on cue, Frank Gilroy's secretary buzzed, "Mr. Hardin is here to see you, Mr. Gilroy."

He looked at Vince. "Fuckin' guy must shit by the clock. Send him in."

The door immediately opened and, walking through, came a giant of a man standing six foot four and weighing at least two-thirty. Dressed entirely in Western wear, he kept his hat in one hand and extended the other. He had the bluest eyes and the biggest ears Vince had ever seen.

In a very Western accent, he spoke, "Frank, it's a pleasure to see you again and to be your guest here in Boston. This is indeed a very lovely town."

Ever the host, Gilroy replied with a wide smile, "Thank you very much. Have a seat, Tex. Can I get you a drink, cigar, a little something to eat perhaps?"

"Thank you. At two o'clock in the afternoon, all I'll have is a club soda." Then shifting in his chair, he turned to Vince and winked, "I don't do my drinking till the sun goes down."

All three laughed. Frank Gilroy then stood as if presiding at a corporate meeting. "Tex Hardin, I'd like you to meet Vince Donato."

The two shook hands. Vince had known the name of the Texas oilman but had never associated it with a young face. "I've heard of you, Tex," said the ballplayer as he pointed a finger at the huge rich Texan oilman, and you get around with the ladies too if I'm not mistaken."

The Texan replied, "Hell, Vince, if I fucked as many women as they say, I'd have to have a third pants leg for my prick, and then I'd have to go to your tailor to get those pants made." It brought a hearty laugh from Vince.

Vince thought that whatever Gilroy had up his sleeve for him involved Tex Hardin, and to be involved with a man with millions of dollars and hundreds of women couldn't be all that bad. All of a sudden, being released and subsequent retirement didn't look so bad to him.

"I've had seventeen years of this game. It's time to get out anyway," he said to himself.

Gilroy remained standing. "Vince, as I was saying, when Tex came in, we're giving you your release so you can play for Tex's club…"

Vince held his hand up like a traffic cop. "Hold it, Frank. I don't understand. One minute, I'm thinking release means retirement, and now you're telling me you're releasing me to play for Tex's club. I didn't even know Tex had a club. What's going on? Explain it to me."

The tall Texan spoke next, "Vince, I'm sure you know that next year, there will be a new team in the American League based in the New Jersey Meadowlands Sports Complex. Well, for certain reasons, I've kept it a secret long enough, but now it's out that I own that team and I want you to play for me."

Vince seemed very surprised. "No shit."

"I am a man who says what's on my mind, so listen to what I say, mull it over, then give me an answer. I may appear the country bumpkin, but I assure you I didn't get my wealth by playing bingo.

"You're probably wondering why I picked you as my first player. Well, I think you'd be good for my team for a lot of reasons. First place is you may be old, but I still believe you have a little sting left in your bat. Maybe a new environment closer to home, and it is only twenty minutes from the town you grew up in, can add a little extra something. It's true you've never been a superstar, but there's not a player in the league who'll have the balls to say you don't put out, and believe me I've asked, so I know. So in that respect, your attitude and desire should set a precedent for my team for years to come. I want you to know that I'm going up against the Yankees and Mets, two strong franchises, for the attendance in the Metropolitan area. I've got to draw the fans to land in the black, and with an expansion team, it'll be very hard to do until we become competitive.

"A player with the wild reputation you have can be a tremendous asset to my club. Every time you get into a barroom brawl, there'll be people at the park. Every time you're linked with some movie star in some scandalous gossip, there'll be people at the park. Every time you're seen with your quote mob friends, it'll create interest, and interest will bring people to the park. You're also a notorious streak hitter, and when you're going good, there's not a player in the game who can touch you, and that'll bring in people. I need you and what you can do both as a player and just by being yourself. Maybe a two-year deal, and then we'll find something else for you to do with the club, but I want you on my team. So is it a yes or no?"

Without hesitation, the solidly built ballplayer answered back, "I say I love the idea. It'd be great to finish my career so close to home, and I think it will have a very positive effect on my performance." Then looking at Frank Gilroy, he continued, "Frank, I don't know how I can ever pay you back. Right now, I'd just have to say thanks."

"Like I said before, Vince, you've given the club seven good solid years of baseball and seven good solid years of ulcers with the off-the-field shit. Regardless, we do have a reputation here of taking care of ballplayers who have busted their ass for us, and you certainly have done that, and this is our way of saying thanks."

"You're very welcome," added the ballplayer as he turned to speak to his new employer, "Tex, Frank will tell you I don't pass the bull when it comes to saying what's on my mind. So I'm going to tell you point-blank right up front that I'll try to be the best ballplayer I possibly can be at the age of thirty-seven. I'll give it all I can give, and that's all anyone can be expected to give. I truly would like to thank you for giving me the opportunity to show the baseball world that I can still rip it once in a while.

"But all that off-the-field shit worries me, and I'll tell you why. It's very true that I've been involved in my share of fights, gossip, and whatever else you want to throw in there, but I never planned it all to happen that way. I've somehow always been involved in something or other all my life. I have no control over all this. There may be months when I live the most normal life in the world, and if and when those months come, I don't want you up my ass, telling me to bang some broad or go hit an umpire just to create some press to put people in your ballpark, because if you do, then you and I will probably go at it, and that, I'm sure, isn't how you've planned it. So I'll accept your offer, but you've got to take me as I am, and if that's satisfactory to you, then it's satisfactory to me. I sign a contract, we shake hands, and then you get yourself a ballplayer"—he looked at Frank—"sound fair enough to you, Frank?"

Gilroy nodded in agreement. The tall Texan reached over and held Vince's arm. "Sounds very fair to me. Why don't we talk contract back in Dallas? You and Frank can be my guests for a few days at my place. It'll give you some time to get to know me a little better just to see if you'd want to work for a rich oil baron who technically has no baseball background at all. We'll have a few laughs, see a few sights, do some things, and generally have a nice little mini vacation all on me. Now I think that's a good idea." He then smiled and added, "And I might add that the girls in Dallas are the most beautiful in God's country."

It was an offer that both Vince and Frank Gilroy could not turn down. It had been a long hard season for the Boston Red Sox. Going into September, they had held a two-game lead over the hated Yankees, but in the first two weeks of the month, they lost five of six to the New Yorkers, then lost their last six games of the season to finish in third place, seven games behind the Yanks. Vince batted only .204 for the month and an almost sure 100 RBI season going into September with eighty-six saw him finish the year with ninety. For the first time in seven years of playing for the Boston Red Sox, Vince Donato heard the boos of the Fenway faithful.

Frank Gilroy heard the boos as well. Noted as a true genius in the handling and moving of players, the sixty-two-year-old general manager let Tinker Morgan, an aging two-time National League MVP, clear waivers only to be picked up by the Yankees and help beat the Red Sox three straight games in Boston. After the sweep, Gilroy, whose team had needed a second baseman all season long and was soundly thrashed both in the field and at the plate by second baseman Morgan, stated to the press that his scouts advised him, after seeing Morgan the last two weeks in August, that Morgan was just playing out the string. The reports said he had lost his bat speed, his arm was weak, and he looked as if he was just riding out the year getting ready to call it quits.

However, there appeared a story in the *Boston Globe* that one of the scouts, when questioned about Morgan, told Gilroy, "He could be just what we need for a September run. Sure, he looks tired, but that's only because his team is twenty-nine games out of first. Put him in a pennant race and you'll see some of the old Tinker Morgan. He'll make things happen." Once that story hit the papers, it became headlines, especially after a Morgan two-runner homer beat the Sox in the last inning in one of the games in Fenway.

They both could use a little time off for some well-deserved rest. Tex made all the proper arrangements.

3

The big D. Dallas is a phenomenon that burst on the scene in the seventies probably more through its professional football team than anything else, even though it is a prime example of American wealth and ingenuity. It has no major port nor does it boast of a major railroad line, yet more money is generated out of Dallas than any other American city except New York.

Mercedes Benzs line its streets, designer clothes live on its storefront mannequins, and its tall buildings glisten like bright icicles on a sunny winter day. Everything about Dallas is clean, healthy, and above all, wealthy. It's been likened to Beverly Hills West. It was here where Tex Hardin, ex-SMU football All-American, ex-academic All-American, and valedictorian of his class made his millions in oil, as an independent buyer of crude; and it was here, where Tex Hardin, the new owner of a professional baseball team, would entertain his first player and try to get to know him a little better.

Tex's limousine was at the airport to meet the three tired travelers. They cruised through Dallas drinking cocktails, all except Tex who stuck by his creed of never drinking 'till the sun went down, and talking of the soon-to-be-played playoffs. Tex was very anxious to hear what professional baseball men had to say about the ultimate objective in their chosen field. However, he was disappointed when Vince told him the Yankees would win because they always do.

"Hell, I could say that just as easily as you did, and I'm not in the game at all."

"You want the inside stuff? The stuff all us baseball people know?" toyed Frank Gilroy as Tex now was all wide-eyed and excited as a little boy let loose in a toy store. "Their pitchers are all lowball pitchers, and their infielders gobble up groundballs like a vacuum cleaner gobbles up dirt. It's strange, but the four teams involved in the postseason all play on natural grass, so you'll see no *astroturf* groundballs going through the infield for hits. Ninety-five percent of all groundballs will be outs. All the ballparks involved are big stadiums, and the Yankees are the only team that has the big bats that can jack it out. The White Sox is a highball pitching team that feeds right into the Yankees' style of hitting. Also, the White Sox was winless in the stadium this year, and three games will be played there. It really doesn't matter who the Yankees play in the Series because neither San Diego nor the Mets have a catcher who can throw, and their pitchers are very poor at keeping runners on base, so you might say the Yanks could very easily win this World Series with the stolen base. Plus Tinker Morgan hit over .400 against each team this year while he was in the National League and has a lot of firsthand knowledge about the pitchers that he can pass on. Is that deep enough for you?"

The big Texan smiled. "You sure know your baseball."

"How about the fact that in the last two weeks of the season, when the chips were down and the money on the line, the Yankee bullpen had not allowed a run and had stranded eleven runners on third base with less than two outs. They also threw fourteen double play balls to the twenty batters they faced immediately out of the pen. You can't beat pitching like that. As for me knowing baseball, well, that's my job," the general manager concluded.

Tex was very excited now. "I just can't wait to get that team of mine going."

The experience of Frank Gilroy spoke again, "You know it won't be all cake. Just because you have a team doesn't mean you're not going to have lots of problems. An expansion team, especially in the New York area, can't afford to make stupid mistakes. Sure, people will realize the kids are young and the older players have more or less seen their day, but you're up against two teams that are in postseason play, and if you don't make the game interesting, the people will just as soon go see the Yankees and Mets, and your stadium will be like a ghost town. Plus, New York is a very big town with a thousand other things to do besides going to a ballgame. A lot of people would rather go to the Jersey shore, the racetrack right next to your stadium, or a

Broadway play rather than watch your team get their ass kicked day after day. I hope you understand, I really do."

"Everything you say is certainly the gospel truth, but I think I can handle any tough situation that comes along. I believe the most important thing is to be competitive right away. Like you say, nobody will show up day after day if we're getting killed ten nothing all the time. I'm going to mold a winning attitude in my team from the first day of spring training. I don't want anybody who will accept losing because we're an expansion team, and expansion teams are supposed to lose. I know Vince Donato won't, and in that respect, he'll pave the way for the others. My manager will be one tough son of a bitch who won't stand for it either. We'll be competitive all right, you can bet your ass on that, and with a few promotion days that I have planned, I feel very confident that we'll do okay."

"Who is the manager going to be?" asked Vince, as he read the sign that said, "Welcome to Tex's Texas Ranch."

"That's my secret for now," was the answer as he winked an eye at Vince, "enough baseball." He pointed to the wide open range. "Everything you see for miles is on my land. I should've built my stadium right here, but I don't think the commissioner would like that very much. We've got about two miles before we reach the house," he continued as he changed the subject, "I've a little party planned tonight. They'll be a few friends around, some Dallas sports fans, and of course, some Dallas women."

"Looking very forward to that," chimed in the ballplayer.

"Maybe tomorrow I'll take you on a little tour of the city, some dinner, then maybe we'll hit a few nightspots. We can go to a football game, camp out on the range, whatever you want to do just let me know. You two are my guests, and your wish is my command."

The itinerary sounded very good, and Vince couldn't wait to get to some of the Dallas cowgirls. He had spent some time in Texas in the minors and fully remembered how hospitable the blond-haired blue-eyed Texan girls can be. As for touring the city, Vince was always eager to learn about new places, and Dallas was one city he had heard so much about in recent years but had never had the opportunity to visit, now he had.

The limo finally reached the main house, a tall two-storied plantation type that looked like it came from the set of a civil war movie rather than belonging on a Texas ranch.

Vince looked at it, and it immediately brought back memories of the apartment house he grew up in, a four-room apartment in a six-family house. "Some house you got here, Tex."

"Recognize it?"

"Should I?" replied Vince.

"Frank?"

The general manager's face was deep in thought. "This house does look very familiar."

"Hell, it's Tara, the house in *Gone with the Wind.* I had it specially built because my wife loved it so much."

"Your wife?" quizzed Vince, "you do all that fuckin' around and you got a wife? Tex Hardin, you do have brass balls."

Tex convincingly answered back, "Every man must have some kind of an outside diversion to keep his marriage from getting stale, and chasing women is mine. Ah, here comes Roxanne now."

Coming through the door, dressed in tight jeans and a plaid top, was one of the most put-together women whom Vince Donato, world-famous womanizer, had ever laid eyes on. She had long shoulder-length brown hair, jade-green eyes, glass-smooth skin, curled up nose, snow-white teeth, and the prettiest smile Vince had seen in a long, long time. Standing little more than five feet, Mrs. Hardin had one of the biggest busts for her size woman that Vince had laid eyes on. It made his knees weak with a lust that he had not felt in some time.

"Like you to meet my wife Roxanne. Roxanne, this is Frank Gilroy and Vince Donato. Vince will be playing for my baseball team and hopefully"—looking at Frank—"we can persuade Frank to come to work with us too."

The voice fit the woman, silently sweet, "It's a pleasure to have you here as our guests. Mr. Gilroy, I'm afraid, is a new name to me, but what woman hasn't heard of Vince Donato."

Vince put out a hand and turned on the Italian charm. As a rule, Vince never went after another man's wife, hadn't done it since he was caught with a teammate's wife years ago, which embarrassed him more than anything else, even though the player was separated from her.

But after taking one look at Mrs. Tex Hardin, Vince knew he had to have her. "The pleasure is indeed all mine to have such a beautiful hostess as yourself, Mrs. Hardin."

She took his hand firmly. "I can certainly see why all the ladies go after you, and I understand you let very few of them go by too. I have to go to town to get a few things. Sorry, we can't talk more. Perhaps tonight we can sit and talk about Tex's team and get to know each other a little better."

Vince was flattered that this beautiful woman had apparently taken some time to read up on him, and he privately hoped her interest wasn't purely of a professional nature. Anyway, he thought Tex Hardin was an asshole to play the gigolo with that prime cut sitting at home. If Tex wanted to screw around with other women, then who was screwing with his own?

Tex's get-acquainted party was pure Texas through and through. Everything was done up to the hilt. The affair was held in the back patio under the Western sky and catered by the most exclusive caterer in Dallas. It featured everything from caviar to Rocky Mountain oysters and had plenty of everything to go around. A large pig was roasted on an open fire in the back, and the booze flowed all night long.

Tex's few friends and acquaintances turned out to be well over two hundred, and it seemed that every one of them wanted to meet his ballplayer. Vince loved the limelight and thrived at the center stage. Dressed in navy slacks, a white blazer, and a rose-colored shirt, Vince was indeed the center of attention, not only to the many male sports fans who were guests but also to the many females who seemed to look at this handsome man endlessly. "The toughest pitcher I ever faced throughout my career was Jim Palmer. The best park to hit is Fenway Park in Boston, although I've had success in Tiger Stadium too. The best player I ever saw was George Brett in 1980, the year he hit three-ninety." And so it went on and on for what seemed like hours.

"What does Vince Donato think of Dallas and the Dallas women?" a voice came out from behind two men.

"Excuse me, miss, I didn't hear the question too well."

Roxanne Hardin emerged from behind the two men, looking splendidly beautiful in a white silk dress, revealing a deep cleavage and bare shoulders. "I said what does Vince Donato think of Dallas and the Dallas women?"

He quickly thought to himself how he'd like to bury himself in that cleavage and kiss every inch of her body and how he'd love to just hold her near him right then at that very moment, but he was a guest in front of many people, the time to play on Mrs. Hardin would come, and when it did, he'd make the most of it. "Everything I've seen so far is very, very beautiful. I feel for Texas, Mrs. Hardin, I really do. I spent some time here during my minor league days, and it was time well spent. Texas to me is like a very sensuous woman."

"Oh, how's that?" She quizzed as the conversation now seemed to narrow down to the ballplayer and his boss's wife.

"Well, you may sleep with her one night and leave the next, not seeing her again for years, yet that deep sexual drive will always come back when you do see her again."

"And you have that sexual drive now?"

"Moreso than ever." The eyes told the message that Vince wanted to convey.

"That's quite an analogy," she said as she sipped some wine, "do you always compare places and things to your sexual experiences? If so, Lord knows you have a lot of comparing to do." She ended her sentence with a smile that seemed to Vince to be an invitation to take the conversation further.

The game had begun, Vince thought, *this woman probably does it at home as much as Tex does when he's away, and now she's putting the bait on the hook for me and wants to reel me in.*

He had intentionally ignored her all evening, figuring the less attention paid her the more receptive she would become when the time came. Vince had caught her glancing all night, and now it was Vince who seemed to have her baited on his hook, and he was the one ready to do the reeling.

"Not often. Just the ones that make it very tough to forget, and lately they've been too far and in between."

"Perhaps you'd like me to show you the rest of the house." Her eyes were inviting. The tip of her tongue put on a show for Vince as it lipped the rim of her wine glass. She held his hand and immediately felt his heavy vibrations. Her pulse was high, and her legs went weak. It had been a while since she had another man, and she vowed not to do it again, but this man seemed so masculine, so experienced, and so confident that she had to have him between her legs. They started to walk away when Tex spotted them.

"Hey, Vince!" he yelled, approaching the two, "where're you going?"

"I was going to show him the rest of the house and the outside grounds," the wife answered back as she had planned the route to end in the empty servant's house.

"Hell, there's plenty of time for that, honey. Vince, I want you to meet an old football friend of mine who's been a fan of yours for years. Come on, he's right over here. Excuse us, honey."

Anger immediately flowed through Roxanne Hardin. She had planned this very carefully all the way into Dallas on her afternoon trip, and now it was spoiled by some football jock who wanted to talk to a baseball player. *There'll be another time; she'd make sure of it.*

Vince looked at Roxanne's face, and it told the story, he understood. "I'll be here for four or five days. They'll be plenty of time, Mrs. Hardin."

She watched as they walked away.

The sooner the better, she thought, *the sooner the better.*

Breakfast the following morning was served out on the back veranda overlooking the magnificent Texas plains. There was small talk about the night's party, and Tex, minus Roxanne, was amazed at how comfortably Vince fit in with new people, even joking to Vince to try politics when his playing days were over.

"A little leaguer would have more of a chance against a major league fastball than I would ever have in politics. I've got more stories out about me than you have dollar bills in your bank account, and that's a lot." It brought a laugh to everyone at the table.

After breakfast, the three men jumped into Tex's Mercedes and rode off to Dallas for a day and night on the town.

"Got the day all planned," said Tex as he injected a country and Western cartridge into the cassette tape player. "I'm going to let you visit my office, just to let you see how we operate. I have some business to attend to for an hour or so, but in the meantime, there's a health lounge in the building, weights, whirlpool, steam, sauna, the whole bit. You can relax there for a while until lunch. After lunch, I'll give you the tour of the city, then we'll have some dinner and later visit a few of Dallas' nightspots."

Vince smiled. "Bet you know every little cathouse in this town." His loins still ached for Roxanne.

"Hell, what do you expect? And I bet you know every little thing that'll spread its legs in Boston and Jersey, and when we get to the Garden State, I fully expect you to return the favor."

Vince nodded. "You got yourself a deal." Silently he said to himself, "Just bring your wife and leave the rest to me."

Dallas was busy. The early morning traffic was down to an ebb, but the streets were still very congested. It was Vince's first visit, but Frank Gilroy had visited many times before. "The thing I like most about Dallas is that it's always so clean. Boston is nice, but it somehow reminds me of an unshuffled deck of cards. Dallas seems to me to be shuffled, stacked, and ready to deal."

"What about the women in Dallas as opposed to the women in Boston? We sure do have some mighty fine flesh here," Tex boasted as he turned in the driver's seat to look at Frank.

"I can't argue that fact Tex, but a pretty woman is a pretty woman no matter where she's from."

"Amen to that."

"Me, I'll take the first thing that comes along with big tits whether she's from Dallas, Boston, or Timbuktu," added the ballplayer.

"Hell, then you must really go for Roxanne." Tex's smile was one that revealed a proud face as if to say there's one woman you'll never get because she's all mine.

Vince wasn't too surprised by his boss' behavior; it only made him want to plow Roxanne more. "Come to think of it, Tex, I am attracted to her, but she's so beautiful. What American-born man wouldn't be? Besides, I made a promise years ago never to fuck around with another man's wife. It's just not the manly thing to do. None of my family ever did it, none of my crowd does it, and I'll never do it. I'll be content to look and not touch." Vince also had learned years ago to keep his friends close, but his enemies closer, and in this case, Tex Hardin was indeed the enemy, and Vince was leading him on with his truthful recital of the Vince Donato code of ethics.

Once in his office and at his desk, Tex Hardin was all business. No longer a baseball owner or womanizer, Tex Hardin was the owner and operating president of Mustang Oil, a company whose sole purpose was to buy crude and sell it to the various oil companies for refining. Terminal on, his fingers on the keys, Tex worked steady and effortlessly as he edited a draft letter to the president of a bank, interpreted three graphs and their outgoing effect on the next quarter's business, and charted the salary structure for ten of his field supervisors.

"These fuckin' things are the greatest invention since the pill. I can run my whole operation just by programming any function of Mustang Oil that I want. While you were browsin' around, I wrote a letter to a West German bank, figured my next quarter's worth in the Mexican market, and adjusted ten salaries according to next quarter's profits."

"What is it that you exactly do here?" asked Frank.

"Trying to keep it simple, what we do here is buy crude oil, then sell it to oil companies for refining. It's a very convincing cut-throat business, but I wouldn't have it any other way. I was working for one of the big oil companies, only out of college for three or four years when the oil embargo came in seventy-three. I saw an immediate demand for oil, and I knew who had it and for what price. Acting independently, I made a few deals, some legitimate and some not, but the results were what mattered. After I saw what could be done with a little guile and some good old American know-how, I told the oil company to go fuck themselves, and I started Mustang Oil. It was hard at first, but I have a knack for making the right connections in the right places, and we just took off. Now the oil company I once worked for is buying crude from me for their refineries. Funny how things work out, isn't it? I made my first million in seven months, and the rest just flowed in."

"Only in America," said a very impressed Vince. He wondered when the corporate Tex Hardin would come out and reveal himself, and now he had just made a stellar performance. It would be that much more challenging for Vince to seduce the wife of such a cunning man as Tex Hardin.

"Exactly right. This is God's country indeed and such a beautiful one. Now if you'll excuse me for a few hours, I have a meeting to attend. If you take the elevator to the lobby and turn right, it'll take you right down to our health club. When you get there, ask for Sam. He's the attendant there, and he's been instructed to give you the full nine yards. So go down and have a good time."

Vince noticed a twinkle in Tex's eye and couldn't help but feel that Tex knew something that the two of them did not. He was sure that whatever it was, he'd find out in the health club.

Sam was an aging old black man with a head of pure white hair. He seemed very happy to meet a real live major-league ballplayer.

"Iz so glad to meet ya, Mista Danata. Ain't neva meet a real ballplaya before," his accent was deep south, he continued. "Ther be a lotta football playas that come here, but we ain't gots no ball team and baseball and me got a long real good when I was younga. I even played 'gainst ol' Sartchel Paige hisself one day. "Course ol' Satch struck me out few times but I didn't mind none. Was an hona to be struck out by Satch. Anyways, Mr. Hardin 'rainged fa everything. Yawl gots gym clothers in his locka and his privat masseuse be along in a while ta take care o' yawl. So yawl have a good time and if yawl need anything just hollar fo' Ol' Sam and I'll be glad ta take car o' whateva it is. Mista Danata it's been a real pleasa." He smiled and extended his hand.

Vince returned the smile and told Sam he'd arrange it for Sam and a friend to be flown to Jersey for the home opener, all expenses paid on him.

Sam embraced the ballplayer and said, "God bless ya, Vince Danata, God bless ya."

Vince laughed. "He'd better."

The two men were led into the locker room and changed into their gym clothes. Vince, always conscious of his body, immediately started to work on the various machines in the gym. Frank, not conscious of his body, and it showed, strolled around, and talked to the other patrons who were there. After Vince's workout, the two went in the sauna, steam, then into the Turkish plunge, cold water designed to quickly shut open pours left open from the steam room, then relaxed in the warmth of the whirlpool. When they were ready for their massage, Sam instructed Vince to enter the massage room first, and Frank went to the club lounge to have a fruit drink and wait.

This massage room was none like Vince had ever been in before. The walls were a dark purple velvet and there was a deep red velvet couch and chair. In one corner of the room was a small bar and in the middle of the room was the rubbing table. Of course, it, too, was a deep-dark-red velvet. On the side of the room opposite the bar was another door. Vince thought that it was a bathroom and was all set to walk in to relieve himself when from the door appeared a large extremely well-built blond in a string bikini. Vince immediately remembered the twinkle in Tex's eye when they left his office, and now he knew the reason why.

"Hi, my name is Linda."

"Vince Donato."

"It's a pleasure, Vince," she said as she walked to the bar. "Can I get you a drink before we start?"

"No, thanks. I was just going to the john when you came in."

She waved her hand. "Ho ahead. When you come out, I'll have everything ready to go."

Vince's organ was hard, and it made it very difficult to pass his liquid, but he finally got it all out after bending over and holding it firm with his hand. He always had this problem early in the morning, and he had turned into an expert in the art of urinating with an erection.

When he returned, he realized that Linda had dimmed the lights and had the stereo playing a record of soft moans in a female voice. Incense was burning, and the whole scene reminded him of an orgy he once attended in Milwaukee. Linda instructed Vince to lay his stomach down on the rubbing table. His organ was very noticeable as he approached it.

She laughed. "That's why I said stomach down."

She started to rub his back. Her fingers were very strong yet very delicate as they worked the shoulders of the well-built ballplayer. "Mr. Hardin told me to give you a first-class job. I guess you must be a very important client or something because he doesn't call me for just anybody."

Vince turned over to one side and faced her. "I'll be doing some work for him." His face was right in her cleavage.

"Do you like them?" she asked as she removed the top of her bikini.

"They are simply adorable," he answered as his hands began to roam.

"Now, now," she said as she gently pushed Vince back down on the table, this time stomach up. She removed his towel and ever so gently started to rub the inside of his thighs and down his legs. She turned and put oil on her hands and started to rub his organ, first softly then with hard strokes as she reached its head.

"How's all that feel, Vince?" she asked as for the first time she admired the athletic build of her client. She privately though that Tex Hardin had thrown away two-hundred dollars and that she'd gladly screw this guy for nothing.

"Feels real good, Lin. I'd like a chance to do it to you." He reached down, moistened his hand with oil, and started to caress her nipple. The passion felt between the two could no longer be held down. Linda started to kiss his body as Vince's fingers found their way under her bikini bottom and into her. Her mouth found his rod, and Vince immediately lifted her on the table and began to feast in her private stock. The table started to tip and rolled over. The position had not been broken. The moans on the stereo were being replaced by the real thing as Vince reversed his position and entered her with full force. The excitement was electric as position after position the moans grew louder until it was Vince's moan that ended the play. The final position had Linda face-to-face with the ballplayer.

"Mister, anytime you're within a hundred miles of Dallas, I want to hear from you. You got that?"

"Lin, I want you to know I haven't had a fuck like that since God knows when. I'd be more than happy to visit this town again, and when I do, you have my word we'll definitely get together."

"Christ, you were in there a fuckin' long time," complained Frank as Vince entered the lounge.

"Frank, best fuckin' rubdown you'll every get. Take my word for it. Enjoy."

The fat balding general manager entered the room clothed only in his towel. His look was one of total surprise as he saw the beauty stand to greet him as he walked in. Linda eyed her client and said privately to herself, "I'll earn my pay here."

"Hi, I'm Linda."

An hour later, Frank emerged from the session, looking more like he had just run a marathon race rather than enjoying the comforts of a private massage. His hair was messed with, and a slight strain lived over his forehead.

"Enjoying the rubdown, Frank?" quizzed Vince.

"You fuck!" yelled Frank, "Why didn't you tell me what was going on? I wasn't totally prepared in the mind to fuck that bitch."

"You mean you didn't whack her?"

"I mean I tried. Jes, I tried. But at my age, I have to sort of get myself up to whack a broad. In my younger days, I'd give you a run for your money, but now it's a lot harder to keep it up and get it going. Know what I mean?"

Vince's comic looks turned to one of understanding. He put a hand on Frank's shoulder. "Next time, ask Tex what he has in store for us. I figured he'd have something like this going. Anyway, if it ever happens again, I'll be sure to give you plenty of time to make a game plan, okay?"

He pointed a finger and assuringly stated, "If you don't, I'll spread the rumor that you're dripping, and you'll never get laid again." They both laughed.

The two dressed and went back upstairs to meet Tex for lunch. Standing true to a gentlemen's code, Vince said nothing of Frank's misadventure with Linda, instead, boasting that Frank had stayed with her a lot longer than he had. Tex was very amused at it all and told a story of how he was once trying to win a large account and tried everything to make a deal, but all his efforts had seemed to fall through. "Finally, I learned that the guy had a hard-on for big tits. Well, I just met Linda through an acquaintance of mine, and I figured that this was the right time to try her out. Within two days, I had this guy locked up and delivered. Linda is one of my most important employees, and it might flatter you to know I only use her for my most important business deals. Of course, she was a little treat for you two, but how'd you like her?"

Neither man had a complaint, Frank even going as far as to ask to see her again before they left Dallas. "Just let him know ahead of time, Tex, otherwise Frank could get homesick and fly back to Boston and leave us flat," asked Vince, hoping to get Frank an advanced notice of his next encounter with Linda.

"I'll be sure to do that. Now let's have some lunch, and then I'll take you on a tour of our beautiful city."

Lunch was served in one of Dallas' most exclusive restaurants, and Tex saw to it that nothing was held back for his two guests as he had fresh Boston clam chowder expressly flown in just for them. The drinks were plentiful and conversation roamed from the playoffs to a problem that Tex had run across in the morning meeting, resulting in Tex firing one of his junior executives. "The boy was bright and energetic, full of enthusiasm, but he never fully learned that this is my game, and we play by my rules. Anyway, he'll have no trouble finding another job, so I'm not too concerned about him."

Vince wondered if, in fact, Tex wasn't laying down his ground rules by telling him of this firing incident. It was a good point for Vince to remember.

Tex seemed very proud as he cruised through the streets of Dallas.

"You know Dallas is the second largest city in the state? Believe it or not, we do more business in cotton than any other city in the entire southwest. We're the leading printing, publishing, and advertising center as well."

His ride took them to the Trinity River, which runs through Dallas. "Someday we'll make this river navigable to go all the way to the Gulf, then you'll see some dollars fly from this city. As a matter of fact, we're working on a little something right now along those lines. Maybe when it's done, they'll call it the Tex Hardin Waterway or something like that. That'd be real nice."

The next stop was the campus of Southern Methodist University, Tex's alma mater. "I'm still a big man on campus here, only now for different reasons. I head the athletic alumni foundation for grants and aid for athletic scholarships. You know, see that a recruit gets a car for graduation and things like that. It's underhanded, true, but everybody does it, and truthfully if you want to compete on a big-time level, it's absolutely necessary. Even used Linda once or twice."

They next stopped at the Cotton Bowl and Tex's voice was very reminiscent. "I put a lot of blood on that field. Three varsity years. All-American senior year, All-Southwest Conference my sophomore and junior year. We could never beat Texas though. God, I hated them and their fuckin' hook-em-horns. I tore my shoulder up on the last play of my senior year, the fuckin' last play, and that ruined me for a pro career. Probably just as well as I don't think I'd have accomplished as much in as quick a time as I did in the oil business."

Six Flags Park is Dallas' version of Disneyland where one can trace the history of Texas under the flags of Spain, France, Mexico, Texas Republic, and the US Confederacy. "Not many people recognize the Confederacy as a country, but they were. Right here in Dallas was the main supply line for the whole Southern Army. It was stockpiled here and issued out to wherever it had to go. The section on the Alamo is my favorite," continued Tex. "You know ol' Davy Crockett never died with the rest of them? He hid under a cot in one of the barracks and was later executed after they found him. It's a whole different version from John Wayne going down in a cloud of dust, isn't it?"

The tour continued through the fashionable areas of Highland Park, University Park, Irving, Grand Prairie, and Mesquite. "If you want to break it up, Dallas has its poor section in the South of town and on out in what they call Little Mexico in the Western part of town. Naturally, the suburbs are a little more fashionable to live in. The far North section of Dallas is the most exclusive, though. Lots of bucks to live there."

The ride moved on out to the East Texas oil field where Tex explained the operations of more than thirty companies associated with the fields. "And of course, Mustang Oil has a lot to do with these fields as well. If these fields ever went dry it would cause a major catastrophe in the economy not only of Dallas but of the whole country. Gentlemen, you're looking at a major source of your country's wealth in those wells. Thank God for oil."

4

The evening food was as bountiful and succulent as the afternoon lunch. The drinks were abundant and the laughs many. Everywhere the trio went people seemed to know Tex and always sent drinks their way.

The first stop was a new nightclub that had recently opened with the help of an influential word from Tex to a banker in town. The club was aptly named Texas. It wasn't packed with patrons probably because it was a midweek night, but there still were plenty of beautiful Texas women ready to be taken for Tex and his friends. Tex was ever the host, introducing Vince and Frank to whoever came over or sent over drinks. The music was country and Western, not Vince's style, but with a few drinks in him, Vince Donato, the tough city boy, could turn into Vince Donato, the country farmer, very easily. Throughout it all, Vince seemed to be having a very good time, and he was starting to become very fond of Tex Hardin.

On the other hand, Frank Gilroy sat quietly and seemed to be having a terrible time, even though he stated time and time again that he was enjoying himself like he had never had before. Vince knew better. The afternoon mishap with Linda was still on Frank's mind, and Vince knew it. Poor Frank. Old age for Frank had come down to psyching himself up to have sex. If someone had told Frank thirty years before he'd have to do it that way, Frank would've laughed in their face. He was Frank Gilroy, the virile son of Tommy Gilroy, the Irish middleweight of the forties who challenged the champions of his time. He loved them and left them, the Vince Donato of his day; he never dreamed it would come down to this.

Vince sensed the mood and whispered into Tex's ear, "You know that ol' son-of-a-bitch Frank whacked that broad twice today, and he's still looking for more. Didn't I read somewhere that there's a new controversial sex club that opened up in town somewhere? I think Frank would enjoy that very much, Tex."

"You mean Hells Hole." Tex smiled back. "I was there the night they opened. I really didn't care for it too much, I like my women one at a time, and they had this one room where everybody was fuckin' everybody. If Frank's still horny, then that's the place to go."

The drive was a short one as Hells Hole was in the same general neighborhood as where they were. In the car, Vince was kidding Frank. "Frank, get yourself mentally prepared. Tex has a place that's going to knock your balls off. Think women, Frank, two, three at a time, all sucking that rod of yours. Think of them all over your body licking it and sucking it. Oh weee!"

Gilroy was full of sexual anticipation. "Holy shit!"

"Yes, sir, boys, here it is," said Tex as the car approached what looked to be an old abandoned warehouse. "We enter through the side door, then go down a flight of stairs to the Hole."

In the warehouse, they walked. Tex, Vince (a little wobbly due to the night's drink), and Frank in eager anticipation to make up for the afternoon's embarrassment. The warehouse was dimly lit and damp. A door with a red light over it showed them the way. Tex opened it, and in single file, they walked down a long flight of stairs. The walls along the stairway were peeling, and the stairway smelled of a nasty stench.

"Reminds me of some apartments I've been to in New York when I was younger," said Vince.

"Bet you were fuckin' then too," added Tex.

At the bottom of the steps, behind a counter, was a very old-looking woman painted with too much makeup trying to bring back some of her youthful vigor. Her figure was stout and her tone of voice deep, "Howdy, Tex."

"Marsha."

"See you brought some friends tonight. Gentlemen, you come to the right place if a little lovin' is what you need. There are plenty of women in there, and they're all ready to roll. Tex, that'll be one-fifty. Tell the boys they can change in the locker or go in fully clothed"—

she looked at Vince and added—"I'll see you later," putting the emphasis on the word you.

They decided to change and enter the club in body towels. The locker room had a mildew smell to it. The attendant was an old man dressed in a workout suit. The three checked their valuables and were assigned lockers.

"Hope that old bitch didn't mean what she said about seeing me later. I'd have to be pretty drunk to bed down with her for the night," said Vince, a little fright in his voice.

"Hell, old Marsha be the best piece you'll have in a long time. She's an ex-madam from one of the biggest cat houses that used to be in Dallas. In her day, she was saved only for the most important people around. I bet she still has a few good wiggles left in her body."

"Maybe Frank will try her and let us know." Vince laughed.

The general manager turned red. "Maybe Frank won't try her. Maybe Frank will be involved with somebody else when old Marsha decides to strut on in. Anyway, none of us are going to get involved with anybody if we bullshit in here all night."

"Frank, you're right. Let's get going."

The three entered the club to hear loud up-beat music and see people three deep at the bar. Vince looked around. To his left, the bar could hardly be seen behind the people, some dressed in clothes, some in towels, and some totally nude. Ahead of him was a crowded dance floor, and to his right was a large buffet table, and beyond that, a long dark hallway dimly lit with different colors.

"I've heard about these clubs," warned Frank, "you can catch a lot of different things in one of these places."

"You getting scared, Frank?" asked Tex. "Hell, sex is sex." He quickly reached to Frank and ripped his body towel from him. "Now ain't nothing funny about that, is it, Frank?"

The three laughed. Frank seemed very at ease standing in the nude in the middle of the club. After all, he was far from home so he didn't have to fear about being seen here, and he did blend in with the clientele. Almost immediately a woman approached the three. She was tall and thin and wearing absolutely nothing at all. Her breasts were small but erect, and her nipples were hard.

"Hi. I'm Cheryl. Some other woman might take the tall, dark handsome one"—she looked at Vince—"or the rich one," pointing to Tex, "but I simply go ape over little fat men."

"No shit. Go get her, Frank." Vince laughed.

"Un fuckin' real," exclaimed Tex, "can you imagine that? Ol' Frank didn't say one fuckin' word."

"Just body chemistry, that's all there is to it, Tex. She likes little short fat men. Me, I like big tits and a tight ass, and I see one right over there."

Vince approached a fully dressed blond helping herself to the treats on the buffet table. Her hair was short, and her eyes light. She wore tight-fitting jeans and a tighter pink sweater that made her mounds protrude. Her plate was loaded with food.

"You feeding an army or is all that food for yourself?" was Vince's line.

The blond laughed. "I'm so hungry. I haven't eaten all day, and I'm starved."

"Well, what's good here?" he said as he overlooked the table pretending to be interested in the food. "I'm starved too."

She quickly showed him what was good and what was not and helped Vince load his plate. The two then went to a table in the far corner and started to eat their food.

Tex stood there watching Vince make his move. That guy has a lot of class.

"A lot of charm. He's real smooth," he said to himself.

The party was going on all around Tex, and he finally decided to get involved. This club was really not his style, but he had to be the gracious host and get involved in whatever his guests were doing so he stood tall and erect, stripped himself of his body towel, and stood proud as a peacock. This place is like a fishing hole, all these women are the fish, and my thing is the bait. It's just a matter of time, he reasoned. No sooner did Tex have his line in the water when a little Mexican girl approached him and started a conversation. The two quickly exchanged small talk, then went down the long dimly lit hallway.

As Vince was sitting and talking, he was also watching the show that Tex had put on. He was amazed at Tex's gall, just standing there with his thing hung waiting for any Maryjane to come along and grab it. Vince's first impression of Tex Hardin was one of the old-fashioned country boys who happened to make good, but now his opinion had changed drastically. The man was a self-made millionaire and Vince had admired him for that. He was world-known, could buy anything he wanted, and was definitely not affected by his wealth. The man had a cunning sort of attitude and a riverboat gambler's nerve. He would screw anybody, anywhere, even in Dallas in his wife's hometown, and he would take on the Yankees and the Mets in their backyard. Some kind of nerve.

"Ready for dessert?" the girl said to Vince.

"Sure," answered Vince, half expecting what was to come. After all, it was a sex club.

The girl stood up and removed her top to reveal two firm and erect breasts. She reached and held Vince's hand and led him down the long hallway where Tex had just previously walked.

Vince and the girl entered the hallway full of erotic excitement. She detoured them into a large room full of wild moans and groans. In the room, Vince could make out about twenty people all over each other in every position imagined. He wondered which one was Tex and if Frank was in there. The girl removed Vince's towel and then her pants. The two fell into each other's arms and down to the floor.

Everywhere Vince licked and kissed her body, the girl licked and kissed him back. He went down on her and she on him. Another girl rolled off her partner and joined Vince's lovemaking. Vince loved it. He motioned for the new girl to position herself so that her pleasure was in his face while the other girl was still down on him. It lasted on and on. Vince went from one partner to the next like a pinball bouncing from bumper to bumper. He was in a small lightly skinned black woman when a voice came from next to him.

"Oh God, help me come one more time."

"Frank, is that you?"

"Vince?" A voice came from the other side. It was Tex.

"You're here too. Holy shit, all three of us are lined up here fuckin' our asses off."

An angry voice followed, "Why don't yawl have your fuckin' reunion someplace else you jerkoffs"

"Who said that!" Vince Donato's voice rang out in the dark.

Tex was excited. This was the Vince Donato he had heard so much about, and now it appeared it was the Vince Donato he was going to see.

A mountain of a man stood up and silhouetted himself against what light there was. "I said it, and when I fuck, I don't like to have any fuckin' high school reunions going on. Now who wanted to know who I was?'

Vince rose, a little weak from his past pleasure. He was surely the underdog to the huge man. Nevertheless, size was never a determining factor for Vince. He approached the man and started to answer as he walked over a few bodies. "It was me, you sick motherfucker." With that, Vince unleashed a long swift hard kick in the man's groin. It doubled him over. Vince followed with a quick left hook to the side of his face that threw the man across a couple deep in erotic pleasures totally unaware of the fight that had just started. People jumped up and scattered and screams were everywhere. The man rose to one knee, and Vince let loose with a powerful right uppercut that put the giant flat on his back, again across the same couple. The man's partner, a short chubby woman, next went after the ballplayer. Not knowing who this running shadow was, Vince dropped her with a straight right.

The lights were turned on and suddenly four bouncers, all bodybuilders, ran in and straight toward Vince. One immediately tackled the ballplayer while another assisted in pinning him down to the ground. The third bouncer comforted the knocked-out woman, who was just starting to regain consciousness while the fourth went to aide the fallen victim of Vince's barrage. Half the room was up and standing in an embarrassing sort of way so as not to expose themselves in the light.

Vince was still swinging under the two massive hulks. After pleading with him to calm down and getting assurance that he would, the two bouncers let Vince up. Once again, all eyes were on the ballplayer as he stood tall and walked toward his victim, who was standing and rocking on very wobbly legs. His nose was dripping blood, and the left side of his face swelled to twice its size.

The man looked at Vince with a killing stare, then said, "I don't know who you are or where you come from, but you'll pay for this. As sure as shit stinks, you'll pay for this."

Vince seemed to start to boil again. "My name is Vincent Donato. I'll be around Dallas for a couple more days, staying with Tex Hardin. If you want to look me up when I leave, I'm going to a town in New Jersey called Orange." His voice was now approaching a strong rage. "I kicked your ass in Dallas, and I'll kick your ass in Orange." His finger was pointing directly at the man's face, and his own face had become red with rage.

The gall of this fuckin' hick to threaten me after I just gave him a beating he'll never forget, Vince thought to himself, and that infuriated him even more.

Two bouncers quickly stepped between the two as Vince almost took another swing but took it back.

"Okay, okay I'm all right," assured Vince as the two men held him back. He turned his back and started to look for his friends when Vince heard the man say one more time. "You'll pay for this."

He had walked away but not that far away where he couldn't turn and throw a quick punch. Vince quickly spun and shot out a long looping right that caught its target flush on the chin. The man dropped instantly and landed with his back up against the wall and in a sitting position. Such a huge boisterous man was now relegated to a beaten pulp of knocked-out flesh being held up by a wall.

At that moment, two uniformed policemen entered the room looking for action. Vince had visions of spending the night in jail rather than in Tex's home, but Tex had other ideas. The Texas millionaire immediately approached one of the officers and talked to him quietly and to the side for a few minutes. After the conversation, the policeman asked the bouncers if everything was under control and then turned to the beaten man who was shaking his head to clear it. "You need a doctor partner?"

With glassy eyes, the man answered no.

"You better be more careful next time you open your mouth to somebody, hear?"

The policeman next turned to Vince. "Want to press charges?"

Vince was totally shocked. He had been in many a brawl but had never seen it taken care of so efficiently and quickly as this one apparently had been. Whatever Tex had told the policeman must've been as serious as death.

"No. I'll let it go this time."

"All right. Party's over. Go back to whatever it was you were doing," ordered the policeman. Immediately the people who were entwined with each other just moments before started to go at it one more time. Tex grabbed Vince by the arm and ushered him to the locker.

"I think it's best if we get out of here now. That fuckin' cowboy could come back with a gun for all we know. Where's Frank?"

Vince was starting to get dressed. "Beats me. Maybe he's still in there fucking. I told you once you get him started he couldn't stop."

Tex went to look for his newfound friend, leaving Vince alone in the locker room. The smell was dingy, and the lockers were very dirty. Vince was tired and drained and couldn't wait to get in a nice comfortable bed. He put on his shirt and happened to turn toward the shower and look in. There, emerging in a steam of hot water, was the man Vince had just pulverized. He turned off the shower and started walking in toward the lockers and Vince. It was just the two of them.

"Don't start with me, mister. I don't want any more trouble, and you don't need any more of it either," Vince's voice was sincere and serious.

The man looked hesitant and afraid. "Now is not the time, but there will come a time, and maybe the outcome will be different."

Just at that moment, Tex and Frank came walking in. "Found this son of a bitch knee-deep in beaver!" yelled Tex. He paused to see the two staring each other in the eye. "Now let's not go through all this again. Mister, you better keep your distance. My Lord, your face is beat now, don't let him add to it."

The man answered back, not taking his eyes off Vince, "It's all over for tonight, but there'll be another time." He then looked at all three one at a time. "They'll be another time." Then walked away.

Frank eased up next to Vince, "Vince, that fucker scares me. He's got hate in his eyes.

"Frank, if I had a nickel for every guy I hit that said he's going to get even I'd have a fuckin' million dollars. He's just talk, ignore him. Would you come back for more if I gave you the beating I gave him?"

"But I'm not him. Just be careful while we're still here, o.k.?"

"Hell. Tomorrow I'll find out all about that rascal and see if he really is dangerous or not. Come on, let's get dressed, and get the fuck out of here," added Tex.

The ride home was full of laughs as the three were each telling their versions of the night's actions. "I didn't want to go in that room at all. They have private rooms there too. Why didn't I go to one of those? Frank, if you didn't scream out loud, 'I'm cumming, I'm cumming,' all of this would've never happened in the first place. Shit, can't you fuck without yelling it out?" asked the ballplayer.

"Fuck you, that was the best head I had in a long time. I've got a right to yell if I want," retorted Frank. "Besides, nobody told you to get up and take on King Kong."

"Hell, that sure was exciting. Vince, you see why I got you for my team? If this happened in New York, I'd get a couple of thousand more fans out to the ballpark the next day. God, you're an exciting man. I heard all the stories and never believed half of them, now I'm in one. I can't wait to get the season started."

"Hold on now, partner. I didn't plan for this to happen. It just happened. As I told you before, these things happen. I may go a year without another incident like this."

"I'll take my chances."

"Anyway, what did you tell those cops? I never saw anything like that before."

"It pays to be rich. I told that fucker who I was, and that if he let you alone, there'd be five hundred in it for him and his partner. It's simple."

"Tex, you're one hell of a man."

FIFTY-SIX

Once again, breakfast was served out on the back veranda overlooking the beautiful Texas morning. To Vince's delight, Roxanne accompanied them, clothed only in a pink robe. Riley French, one of Tex's business associates, was the fifth member of the party. The breakfast was all country, steak and eggs.

"So how, you boys, like Dallas last night?" the pretty one spoke, her eyes never leaving Vince.

"This rascal has more balls than a herd of bulls. He beat the shit out of a man twice his size. Yes sir, that Vince Donato is truly a man not to toy with," interrupted Tex.

"Oh, where was this? Did anybody get hurt?"

Tex spoke first, "It was at dinner, and the man just wouldn't leave Vince alone. Vince told him three or four times that he'd be happy to talk to him at the bar after dinner, but that son of a bitch wouldn't leave. Then he started to become loud and obnoxious and pushed Vince so Vince had to sort of push back."

Vince was amused at the lie his host had to think of at a moment's notice, although he was sure Tex had probably planned this too.

"Sounds like an exciting evening. You're not hurt at all, are you?" Her concern was genuine.

Vince smiled coyly. "My hand's just a little sore, that's all. I'm kind of sorry the whole thing happened. I never ask for trouble, but somehow it always manages to find me. I guess sometimes I can turn the other cheek and walk away, but at times I just go into another world and get crazy."

"That doesn't sound like the Vince I've come to know," she answered. His verbal description of his wild personality was making her aroused.

"It sounds pretty barbaric to me that two men can't sit down and talk out their problems like gentlemen." Riley French, a tall, lean, and frail accountant with thin blond hair and pinkish skin looked at Vince as he spoke.

Vince didn't like him from the start, his handshake was too frail and his manners too feminine. "Tell me what you know about things like that. I bet you get picked on quite a bit, which cheek do you turn?" asked Vince.

The reply was quick and to the point, "Whichever one I have to to avoid a confrontation."

Vince was direct and also out of line, "I'll bet you spread them once or twice too."

"Try it sometime, you might like it."

"Now let's not get out of hand here," said Tex, fully aware of how Vince was liable to fly off the handle at any time and not wanting a scene in front of his wife. "Vince, French here is the best accountant I have, and his sexual persuasions are no reflection on his work, which is excellent, so let's just drop it and let it go at that."

"No problem, Tex, but French shouldn't comment on things he knows nothing about."

"Well, anyway enough is enough. Honey, French, and I are going to Dallas for a morning appointment, we'll be back for lunch. Yesterday I showed you the sights of Dallas, and today I'll show you the ranch. We'll ride out on the range and camp for the night, the four of us. In the meantime, feel free to do anything you want, the house is yours. If there's something you want just ask Roxanne and she'll get it for you."

Vince immediately thought of himself all alone with Roxanne for the morning, "Sounds good to me, Tex."

"How far do we have to ride horses?" hesitantly asked Frank, not too enthused to go riding for miles on a bumpy animal.

"Frank, you should jump at every opportunity that comes along to do something different. Hell, if it's your ass you're worried about, I have a custom-made cushion soft saddle you can use, okay?"

Vince shook his head, "is there anything you don't have?"

"Your nerve, but if I stick around you long enough I'm sure some of it will rub off on me," Tex answered with a smile.

Silently the ballplayer thought to himself. This nervy bastard. Here he makes oil deals in the millions, whacks broads right here in his backyard in Dallas, and he says he wants my nerve! "Tex," he paused, trying to think of something to come back with but coming up empty, "go to Dallas."

5

Roxanne reentered the house after sending off her husband. She had changed into a pair of cut-off jeans and a light-blue sweater, going barefooted through the house. As soon as her husband said that he'd be away for the morning her thoughts were the same as Vince's. As she showered after breakfast, she had been especially efficient in shaving her legs and armpits. She wanted her lover to stroke smooth skin. The sheer anticipation of her knowing that today would be the day that it would happen forced her to explore her own body, and the pleasure of it was too great for her to bear. She found herself moaning in the shower and quickly put a halt to the procedure, reassuring herself that soon she would get the real thing.

In the guest room, Vince was practically going through the same motions. He shaved to a clean close finish, taking extra precaution under his chin, always a sensitive spot. His jet-black hair was neatly put in place, not a hair askew. The full mustache was trimmed with the care that a landscaper takes on a row of hedges. His nails were cleaned and polished. He dressed in robin egg blue slacks and a pink sweater, his tan body contrasting perfectly with the pink. He finished his picture with a gold bracelet, chain, and pinky ring. The shark was out for the kill.

The first agenda of his program was to get rid of Frank, but how?

"Hey, Frank," he called through the party bath, "why don't you go down to the pool and start figuring up my contract? You would know better than me the fine print and shit like that. I'll join you later."

"What about your agent?"

"Look, I trust you. We've always been fair with each other. Draft up something, and then we'll show it to the cowboy and see what he says. If he likes it, we'll take it back to Tommy and let him finalize the deal."

"That'll take a couple of hours." He then walked through the bath and into Vince's room. "What'll you be doing?"

"Tex's wife wanted to show me the grounds, so I think we'll take a stroll."

Frank held his arm firm. "Vince, I know she's prime cut. I've been around you too long not to know what's going on in your mind. It's trouble. Tex Hardin is not the kind of guy to fuck with, especially through his wife."

"Relax, Frank. Do you think I'd take advantage of Tex like that? Especially after he's been so hospitable to us? And why would I want to screw the guy who's giving me a chance to finally play at home? Come on, have some sense. Besides, you know I don't fuck around with other guy's wives. It's not ethical. So relax. Mrs. Tex Hardin is perfectly safe with me." If they ever hand out academy awards to ballplayers, I definitely should get one for that speech he told himself. The sincerity in his speech and the sense in what he said convinced Frank.

"Okay, I'll work on a contract and expect you at the pool in an hour or so."

After leaving Frank at the poolside, Roxanne and her guest began their stroll. It commenced with a walk through her garden, with hundreds of flowers in full bloom. The different fragrances started her spark, and she reached and gently held Vince's arm. Through the garden, they walked to the stables, where Tex housed twelve quarter-horses he kept on the ranch and twelve riding horses. They leaned on the corral fence and watched as the horses lazily strolled about their area. A large gelding walked by them, and Roxanne noted it.

"It's a crime they did that to that poor horse. If they ever did that to me"—he turned and faced her—"I think I'd die."

"I don't think it'll ever happen to you. They can't be that big that they throw you off stride when you run, can they?" her question was direct.

"Not as big as a horse," Vince replied, wondering if this was the moment that the move should be made.

She answered his question for him as she grabbed his arm and took him off the fence, "Come on, let me show you the servant's quarters."

It was a small little farm-type house, all white with a railed front porch. They walked right up to the front door and right into the living room. The furniture was plain. There was a Winchester over the fireplace and fresh logs to its side.

"You just barge in like that? What if they were at it right here on the living room couch? It'd be pretty embarrassing." Vince wasn't embarrassed at all; he just played the role.

She laughed. "I sent them to Dallas to shop. They wouldn't be back for hours."

Vince quickly jumped at the invitation and reached for her shoulders in his hands. There was no resistance. Her smell was still of the garden, her perfume outlasting the smell of the horses, and the scent aroused him. Their eyes met, and they kissed, at first brief pecks but then a full embrace and then long wet kisses. She immediately felt him grow, and she yearned for it.

With one hand, she ran her fingers through his smooth hair, and with the other, she held his crotch. She unzipped him and quickly fell to her knees. She then unbuttoned his jeans and threw him back on the couch, taking them off in the process, then continued her work.

Vince looked down at her and caught her looking up at him.

"I love it," she said. "It's the hardest, biggest thing I've ever had. Oh god, how I love it."

Vince leaned back and laughed.

They got up and went to the bedroom where Vince toyed with her for hours. His method of making love was new to her. She never had a man who kissed her everywhere, who entered her everywhere, who was in complete control throughout. Tears would come to her eyes as she would plead him to do it, only to have him take her to further heights before doing so. She pleased him in every way she knew how, and she loved every moment of it. Her capacity to make love was just as strong as Vince's, and after a few hours, they both fell asleep in each other's arms.

After their nap, they showered together, got dressed, and were ready to leave. Before they were ready to go, she assured her lover, "Tex is good, but you are in another league. Whenever you want me, honey, you can stick that Italian rod in me whenever you want."

Vince had suddenly become excited again. The knowledge that she was his for the asking made him rise one more time. "Like now?"

Once again, they divulged, only to be interrupted by the sound of a car approaching. Vince had risen to peek out the window to see Tex's silver Mercedes passing by on its way to the main house. It seemed they had only left, but the clock on the mantlepiece said one thirty. His whole morning was an exotic interlude that made them forget the time.

"What'll we do now?"

"Why don't we invite Tex in, and you take us both on?" he joked while pulling up his pants.

"I'm a little scared, really. If he ever catches us," her voice was firm, "you don't know how he can be sometimes."

"Don't worry. He's in the main house, which is around the corral and behind the barn. He can't see this house. We'll come from the corral area and say we're returning from our walk. He'll never suspect a thing."

"Don't underestimate my husband," she warned, "somehow that man knows more than he should."

"I never underestimate anybody. Now come on, if you daddle any more, he'll surely start looking for us." He held her hand and out the back door they went, circling through the barn to wind up on the corral fence one more time.

Out of nowhere, Tex appeared, "Where have you been?"

"Strolling," answered Vince. "Roxanne took me on a tour of the whole ranch, and we've been standing here, talking and looking at your horses. Say, which one's mine?" Vince Donato could talk a turtle out of its shell. Though he infrequently lied, preferring always to speak the truth, no matter who it hurt, he could always sound very convincing whenever he had to. He had won over Tex.

"Anyone you want. I got Frank coming over now, and as soon as we all saddle up, I figure we got four or five more hours of daylight left before we camp out."

Vince chose a big black stallion and suggested Frank ride a pony. Tex was on his favorite mount, a white charger named King, and Roxanne, her mons hurting, rode sidesaddle on a gray mare. After a very quick riding lesson given to Frank, the four left, accompanied by an old pack mule.

The Texas countryside was like a painted picture. Vince described it to Tex as a paradise that every person should have the pleasure of seeing. "Pure poetry. This land is so dry and hot yet as wet as an ocean in its naturalistic beauty. It's untouched by the human conglomerate that we call civilization. Now I know how a bird must feel when he takes off and flies away. It's a thing of beauty, Tex, it really is."

Tex showed a look of surprise. "Vince, that's pretty deep."

"Well, you said you're not the country bumpkin that you appear to be, and I'm not the dumb ballplayer that I may appear to be. Actually, I could've gone to just about any college that I wanted to. My marks were very good, and I even did a lot of writing, if you can believe it. Fortunately or unfortunately, depending on how you look at it, it never worked out that I should go to college.

"Any regrets?"

Remembering his most enjoyable afternoon and many just like it and realizing that they would have never happened under any other circumstances, Vince denied any regrets.

As they continued to ride, Tex did most of the talking, telling about a movie that was made on his ranch, the danger of snakes on the open range, the old cattle drives, and his collection of old six-shooters.

They camped near a cool stream, and Roxanne started to prepare dinner while the three men walked in the brush.

"Tex, I think you're an anachronism. You talk like you should've been born in the 1830s so you could've gone on a cattle drive, fought Indians, and gunned down Billy the Kid." Frank laughed.

"Don't laugh," Tex answered as they started to walk back toward the smell of fresh stew being cooked on an open fire. "I've been there many times before. I've tasted the dust of a cattle drive, I've smelt the shit on an open range, and I've been afraid of an Indian's howl." He was very serious as he continued, "I tell you as sure as my name is Tex Hardin, I've been there."

"You're pretty deep yourself," said Vince.

"Even the most fun-loving people have their serious moments. When I talk business and the old west, I'm very serious they both mean a lot to me."

They walked into camp and commenced to eat the hot stew, served from a big black kettle.

"Gabby Hayes never looked so good for the cow drives, did he, Vince?" asked Tex, his mouth full of beef.

"Gabby Hayes never looked like Roxanne."

"If he did, those cows would've never made it to Texas 'cause all those drovers would be after the cook!" They all laughed.

After dinner, Tex broke out a bottle of Mexican tequila, salt, and lemon. "Ever do tequila before?"

Frank smiled. "I've seen it done, but I've never tried it."

"Tex, you seem to forget I played minor league ball in Texas, and what youngster in Texas has never done tequila?"

"Good. Well, right now I think is as good a time as any to start talking dollars and cents. First, I'll teach Frank to do tequila, then we'll talk contract."

Vince nodded in agreement then watched as Tex and Roxanne shook salt from a shaker to the side of their hand, licked it, took a shot of tequila, then sucked on a wedge of lemon. It was all demonstrated step by step and looked to Frank to be very simple. Frank followed the instructions to a tee. It tasted very good. All four followed at once and then they all had one more.

"We going to finish the whole bottle?" asked the ballplayer, the taste lingering in his mouth.

"Well, we have no TV, no radio, no newspapers. Our only entertainment is ourselves and this tequila. So I think it'd be a very good idea to finish it, don't you Frank?"

All ready lightheaded, Frank agreed.

"Now let's get right to the point Vince. How much do you want to play for my team?"

Vince was always reluctant to talk money. He was not an economic genius or corporate lawyer. His agent had always handled his contract negotiations and had always handled them well. But they were in the middle of the Texas prairie, and Tex Hardin wanted an answer at that moment.

"Well, I had Frank draw something up this afternoon. He's a lot better at these things than I am and…"

Tex interrupted, "Look, I'll make it easy. You just finished playing this year for $325,000. It also says in your contract that the team you retire from will be responsible for paying you $50,000 a year for the next ten years after you retire. It also says that at the end of those ten years, the said ball club is to offer you a job at the average salary for the job offered, and it is your decision to accept the job or not. Throw in a few incidentals and I'd say you have a pretty smart agent that took care of you.

"Frank, I think Vince got the best of the Red Sox all these years. You had to pay for his housing, give him a new car every year, a private room on the road, and be responsible for two endorsements a year.

"Vince, let's face it. If you don't play for me next year, this past year was probably be your last. At your age and coming off that shit September you just had, I doubt very much if somebody will pick you up, but I'll take the chance because I know you have some sting left, and I think the conditions are right with my team.

"A home atmosphere will pump you up, and I think you and I have gotten to know each other well in this short time, and I think you'll play your ass off for me. So I'm going to offer you a two-year contract at the same price." He paused and poured more tequila for all.

"I'll keep the ten-year clause. I don't want to argue with your agent on that, but the new car every year and free housing and that endorsement shit goes. You can buy your own cars, have a roommate, and negotiate your own endorsements. In place of that, I'll give you and a guest a two-week vacation anywhere in the country, all expenses paid. Let's call it a signing bonus. So do we have a deal?"

Vince took another shot of tequila. "I like you, Tex. I really do. I was raised a poor boy, who never had much money. I have no wife, no kids, that I know of anyway, and not that many financial responsibilities other than to myself. Money never really mattered that much to me. In the beginning, I'd play ball for free, and getting paid for it was the icing on the cake. What you say about my career is probably true. If you didn't offer me this, I'd probably retire before spring training. It all makes sense to me, so it's okay with me, and I'll tell my agent we have a deal. Is this deal just about what you had in mind, Frank?"

The general manager shook his head. "Right about the same lines. I think what Tex offers is fair and very reasonable. If Tommy goes for it—and I see no reason why he shouldn't—it's a deal."

"Hell, you're just happy to get out of that retirement clause of the contract. Now tell me, Frank, what would it take to lure you out of Boston?"

"Tex, I appreciate the offer, whatever it may be, but I've been in Boston all of my life, and I don't think I could ever leave under any circumstances, so I'd have to say no."

"Well, listen to me first, then decide. I know you only make $80,000. That's shit for a man with your experience and knowledge in the game. You have no incentives or bonuses. I'll double your salary and give you 5 percent of the club. That's an offer that you can't refuse."

"Tex, thank you, but I'd still have to say no."

"Tex Hardin never chases anybody. No hard feelings. Let's have another drink with my new ballplayer." Once again, they passed around the tequila. For the fifth time, they poured it down, and spirits were getting high.

"Now that we have the contract thing over with, why don't you tell us about yourself, Vince? From what I've found out about you, you're a very interesting person with a very revealing past. I think the Vince Donato story would be a very leisurely way to finish our tequila and spend the evening," said Tex as he leaned back on his saddle, bottle in hand.

Vince smiled. "I'm flattered. With all the shit in my life, I'll have you all up the night. I hope you have another bottle of tequila."

Out from a saddlebag, Roxanne pulled out two more bottles.

Fully knowing a lot of the stories that were to come, Frank interjected, "Let's keep it sort of respectable. After all, there's a lady present."

Roxanne quickly answered back, "Shit, Vince, let it all hang out."

"Well, here goes, but before I started, I forgot one thing."

"What's that?"

"I promised old Sam at the health club that he and a guest can get a free ride to the season opener. Any problem there?"

"None at all."

"Well, here comes the Vince Donato story."

Memories

Italy, during the turn of the century, was a very poor country, especially in the south where my people came from. there was no steady work to be had, just poor tenant farming. Donato's had lots of kids, and a lot of mouths to feed. There had to be a better way Must've been hard to pack up and leave home, but it was probably out of necessity that they left. Like any other immigrant family, America was a hope, a dream, a new world, and a new life.

I remember my grandfather, a little bit of a man with grey hair and the smallest nose I ever saw, and how he used to rave about this country. "America iza the best country ina the world." I guess coming from a place where goats and chickens were steady guests in your house even a cold water flat looked like a palace.

The Donato family settled in a small city in Jersey outside of Newark called Orange. It seemed that all the people from Alberona and surrounding villages wound up there. So it was like old homecoming week when Americo Donato and his family arrived at the home of his cousin. As is any other era of immigration before or since, the Italians, who at the time were the most recent, seemed to be the poorest and lived in the worst conditions and my father's family was no exception.

Once they got settled in their little place, they crowded seven people in four rooms, with no cold water, a black stove for heat, and a bathroom shared by three other families, which was at the end of a hallway. It was tough living conditions, but they were bearable as long as there was a will and a way.

My grandfather's job started to be a pretty good one. He was working for the city stable and with all the horses around in those days he kept pretty busy shoeing and attending to the city equipment that needed his touch. As the years passed by, so did his trade, and the horse-drawn wagons were replaced by the automobile. Eventually, he was let go. Blacksmithing was the only thing he knew how to do. His father had been one and his father's father had been one all the way down the line. Imagine how he must've felt; an immigrant barely able to speak the language, with seven mouths to feed, and no job. Some paradise.

He wasn't qualified for anything else except manual labor, so he took whatever work he could. He dug ditches, hauled coal, carried lumber, you name it he did it. He was too proud and determined a man to give in to his adversity. Whatever it took to put food on the table that's what he did. You have to admire a man like Americo Donato, he faced the challenge and won. He survived.

That pride and determination naturally were handed down to the sons. They had it just as hard being the first generation as the parents did in the beginning. None of the sons were formerly educated, even though their father's wish was to send at least one to college, and yet in many ways they are all successful. One unfortunately was killed at Pearl Harbor. He was the oldest. The middle three were all in the landscaping business and did quite well for themselves. My father went into the construction business as a trained carpenter and did well for himself too.

My father is a tough son of a bitch. He still works to this day and he's pushing seventy! I don't think he knows what it is to take a break. In the winters, when he had no work, he used to haul coal for the same man that his father hauled for years before. He'd also do a few jobs on the side for contractors who needed a fine woodworking touch. Don't forget, there was no collecting unemployment in those days, a man worked when he could find it, and believe me, in the winter, my father went out and found it. Now in the spring and summer, he works for his nephews on a few lawns and flower gardens for their select customers.

My father's story is like millions of others during that era. Immigrant family, tightly knit, strong father type, sons make good. My mother's story is very different. Her story is one of fear and death. Her story should be in the movies. My mother came here from Sicily a few years after my father arrived. Where Americo Donato came here for a better life, Rosetta Maganella came here to escape death. You see, the Sicily of her time, and even today, is ruled by the underworld. In Sicily, people live for vengeance, to get even. A vendetta is a way of life.

Well, my mother's father had somehow gotten on the wrong side of the local big shot and was murdered. Naturally, they went after the remaining members of the family thinking that whoever they are they are capable of fulfilling the vendetta and avenging the death of the father. They killed her mother and brother but somehow she managed to escape and run into the mountains. She was only six. There was a mass search for the only living descendant of Fortuno Manganella. Fortunately, friends found her first and shipped her to America.

She came to New York, lived with a family who took her in while on the boat, and was raised in Brooklyn. She met my father a few years later at a local feast and was married at eighteen. It took her years before she finally overcame her fear that they'd get her. Mama is your typical Italian mother. First, she's subservient to my father, always. She's always in the kitchen cooking and is forever prompting you to eat more. There were more statues of saints in my house than you'll find in any church. Her children could do no wrong and everybody was a beautiful baby. In short, my mother is such a good person there's no doubt in my mind that when her time comes she's going straight to God, no stops on the way.

I'm the youngest in a family of four. My father wanted a very large family but after delivering me my mother had complications and that was it for the family, we stayed at four. If that hadn't happened I guess they would've had seven or eight kids because my father always talked of having as many sons as daughters, and being that his first three were girls, I guess he would've had to go to at least seven or eight to get even.

My sisters. They're very beautiful women, always were, and always will be. I'm not just saying that because they're my sisters, but everyone is as attractive and beautiful as any other woman you could name; movie stars included. They had a lot of guys after them throughout the years, a lot of guys. It seemed that every night the phone was tied up for hours by guys calling so much. Finally, my father had to put a stop to it and only accept calls at certain hours; if calls came after those hours he would answer each call and tell the poor guy to call the next day at the allotted time. It was a shame, but the calls got to the point where something like that had to be done.

Grace is the oldest in the family. She's forty-seven now and still as attractive as she's ever been. Olive skin, big brown eyes, attractive shape. Gracie still has it all. She married a butcher. A local guy and a very nice guy. He works very hard, and he's a good provider. They have a boy and a girl, and I guess I've always been partial to the little girl because I'm her godfather. They have a house, white picket fence, dog, station wagon, the whole bit. Gracie and Sal have a happy marriage, and we have no complaints about them at all.

Antionette is a carbon copy of Grace, both in looks and mannerisms, and they both take after my mother so much that you'd think all three of them were raised together. They cook, clean, and raise children. That's the Italian way. Truthfully though, I wish these two sisters had made something more of their lives. Gracie is a terrific organizer, and I could see her in the business world, and Antionette is a very talented artist, but unfortunately, she's never done anything with it, never wanted to. Yet they're happy in their way and besides, who am I to judge another person's life? Antionette's husband is a purchasing agent for a pharmaceutical company and is the black sheep of the family because he happens to be Jewish. When Antionette brought Marvin home, my father walked out when he walked in. It wasn't right, but his daughter had to marry an Italian or nothing at all.

For myself, I don't particularly care for the guy but not for the same reasons that my father has. Marvin is very weak and very easy to manipulate. Just once I'd love it if he stood up and told my sister to shut up, but he doesn't have the backbone for it. I just can't warm up to a man who gets that manipulated by a woman. Still, all in all, he's not such a bad guy, and if Antionett's happy, then I'm happy.

Lucy is the youngest daughter and only two years older than me and probably is my best friend. I'm as close to her as I've been to anyone in my life. I've told Lucy things that were deep in me, true feelings that a man of my reputation and background would be ashamed to tell, yet she's understood everything. Lucy is a lot like me in the way that she presents herself. She's very up-front, tell you off in a second, then run and hug you in her next breath. Lucy has visited me in Chicago, Boston, and a lot of other cities around the country. She's always ready to jump and go whenever the impulse grabs her.

But Lucy drastically changed when she met her husband. She took a cruise on an Italian liner and fell in love with one of the stewards. She came home in another world. All she did was talk about her Domenic for months until he came back our way from another cruise. Domenic barely spoke English, and my parents thought that was just fine and dandy. They all got along like bread and butter. However, Dom carried a lot of the old-fashioned ways with him in terms of "I'm the man and you're the woman and you obey." He was the complete opposite of Marvin, already my brother-in-law.

One day in the summer, when we were playing in New York and I was home, I noticed a giant hand mark on Lucy's leg. It could only have been put there by an act of aggression. I knew it because I'd seen it on a number of girls before. It's put there by a hard slap and then a tight clasping hold. Well, I had to have a little talk with Mr. Domenic Forte and tell him that this wasn't the old country. I gave him the beating of his life. Lucy knew it was coming and had warned him, but since then, we've been very good friends, and he's become a lot more gentler with my sister.

Domenic has a small restaurant that he runs with his brother and my sister. It's very neighborly and comfortable. You'll see no fancy table setting or expensive prices, but the food is as good as any I've eaten in any restaurant in the country. Lucy is the one who holds that restaurant together. She keeps the books, pays the bills, sometimes tends the bar, is the hostess, and whatever else she has to do to make it a success. Domenic doesn't have the head for the business aspect of it, but he sure can cook. You have to hand it to my sister, she runs that restaurant, runs the house, looks after three kids, and still, whenever I'm in town, is always ready to party.

My family is very close. To me, there's nothing as binding as love in a family. I would die for any of them, and I'm sure they'd do the same for me. If anybody ever hurt any of them, whoever it was had better look out because I'd be after them. I gave Domenic the money to start the restaurant. I bought Antionette a house for her wedding present, and I carried Sal and Grace for a year when my brother-in-law was sick and couldn't work. I asked for nothing in return. It's my responsibility. I know they'd do it for me.

My father, on the other hand, hasn't taken a thing from me. I don't know if you'd call him proud or stupid. I bought him a house when I made the big leagues. At the time, Antionette and Lucy weren't married, and my grandfather living in the house with us made six more in a four-room apartment, and they needed a house. He wouldn't take it. He just wouldn't take it. He said if he couldn't buy a house for his family, then nobody else could. So I had to sell a house that I had just bought. He did break down though and accept a trip to Italy that I have him one Christmas. He had tears in his eyes when he opened the envelope and took out the travel brochure. He hugged me very tightly; didn't say anything, just hugged me.

Family life was very strict. My father was and still is a strict disciplinarian, so that meant laying down the law whenever he saw fit, which was quite often. Many a time I'd catch a backhand to the face and then a stern reprimand after. The girls, they got it too. But through it all, I guess he was a fair man through all of this discipline. There were many times when we'd see a lighter side of him, and those times were fun.

It was the girls, however, who suffered more than me. Every guy who came by had to go through the mill. Where do you live? What do you do? Where are your people from? What are your intentions? Where are you going? I mean if I had to put up with all that bullshit, it would've driven me nuts. Throw in his timed phone calls and you can see that life wasn't easy for the Donato girls.

We had to eat together at every meal, and my father had to be the first one served, and he was the only one who got a linen napkin. There were times when I'd miss a meal, and I'd catch a backhand and no food. I made it my business to be there when the food was served. I always had to wear a shirt at the table. T-shirts were not allowed.

Sundays meant that the whole family attended Mass, and everyone received communion. I didn't mind that too much because I always felt a certain closeness to God, and going to church made me feel good. I can't say I've been a model Catholic all my life. God knows I've done some things that'll shame the devil, but I have always tried to do what's right and not go out and purposely hurt anyone. I still go to church every Sunday, believe it or not, and when I do, I pray that when my mother and father die, they die without any pain and that God judges them in a fair way.

I pray for the rest of the family, that they have good health and success, for peace in this world and for all the sick and handicapped. I never pray for myself. I think God gave me enough spunk to take care of myself, and I've been doing a fair job of it. If people knew how I was with religion, they'd be shocked. It's definitely not the image I have, but there's always something different behind the image, isn't there?

But getting back to homelife and my father. I was the only one to rebel against his ways and that didn't happen until I was about sixteen. I think to explain it, you'd have to know a little bit about the environment that I grew up in and the people I hung out with. Orange is a city, not your clean Maple Drive suburb, but your tough, rough, dirty little city that you'd imagine the dead-end kids to come from. It's more back alleys and railroad tracks than green grass and trees. It wasn't always that way, but that's how it was when I lived there. The ethnic makeup was about half black and half lower-middle-class whites, who were mostly Italian. The code was hit first and ask questions later, if you didn't you'd be the one that got hit. It's a town where you can very easily get stepped on, and it didn't matter who did the stepping on, white or black. If you were that low to get stepped on, you were a free game for anybody. If you're not street-smart, you're not not smart at all in Orange. I think by now you get the picture. In Orange, only the strong survived.

I was very fortunate. If you want to call it that because I learned the ways of the street at a young age, and it helped me immensely in later years. My father always told me never to look for a fight, but when you think one is coming and you can't get out of it, swing like hell and hope for the best. God knows how many times I used that as an excuse. "I tried to talk him out of it, but he just wouldn't listen, so I had to hit him before he hit me." I quickly developed a reputation as a tough guy not to mess with, and once you get that, it stays with you for a long time. However, there always comes a time when you have to prove yourself all over, and for me, that happened during my freshman year in high school.

I was always fair-sized for my age, and as a freshman, I'd have to say that I was bigger than the average fourteen or fifteen-year-old kid. Still, Orange High School was a jungle, and every day was a day of survival. As big as I was, I went to school scared. I could see every day how the bigger upperclassmen would pick on the smaller underclassmen. Everything from shaking them down for their money to stripping them in the gym locker room and throwing their clothes in the showers. Even though I had close friends who were older than me, there still would have to come a time when I'd have to prove myself, and I knew it. Even knew where and how it would happen. Every day at lunch there was a big black guy who'd shake down all the scared little white kids for their quarters. They were the ones getting stepped on, see what I meant? He always bypassed me though. I don't know if it was my size, even though he was bigger than me, or the way I looked or what, but he never tried to shake me down.

Truthfully, I was scared shit of him, but I wouldn't let anybody know it. Then came the day when he finally did ask me for a quarter. "Gimme a quarter." I had often wondered what I'd do in that situation, and I always gave him the quarter, but it's funny that sometimes you just don't do what you think you'd do. I looked him eye to eye and didn't say a word. "Gimme a fuckin' quarter punk." I had a ham sandwich in my hand, and I shoved it in his face and jumped him. It was a good fight while it lasted, and I'd have to say I got the best of him. It started a confrontation between the whites and blacks that lasted a few days. This particular guy and I went at it a few days later, and I left no doubt as to the victor in that one. That was the only fight I had in Orange High School, and that probably made my reputation for the rest of my school years.

All my life, I guess I've always been getting into some kind of trouble, either fighting or childish mischief. We lived in a very congested part of town with project housing across the street from us filled with blacks. After we fought them, like kids are prone to do, we became good friends. I remember a time when I had it out with Winfred Thomas behind the school. He said something about Lucy and we had as big a fight as fourth graders can have. After school, we were friends again, and we stole a chicken from Spinelli's chicken yard to give to Winfred's mother because they were a little low on food. God knows how many chickens were stolen from old man Spinelli.

I had a lot of laughs when I was a kid. I can recall another time when the traveling circus came to town. It was a real big event for Orange. My god, it seemed like every night there'd be thousands of people there. We made that circus our home. We'd go there early in the morning on the way to school, spend our lunch hour there, and spend the whole night there. They had a clown that sat on a board over a big barrel of water. The idea was for the clown to entice people through insults, so they'd buy three balls for a quarter to hit a bull's eye that would open the plank, and the clown would fall into the barrel of water.

For three nights, we spent all our money going after that clown. We hated him! Finally, I got him, and into the water, he fell. He came up laughing. "It took you three days to get me wet, and I bet you it'll take you another three days to do it again." We threw some barbs back at him, and then the insults between us became more offensive and personal. One night, we planned to get him real good. It was the end of June and near July 4, and everybody had fireworks, so what we did was sneak around his cage and throw lit cherry bombs in the water. You talk about being scared. That clown jumped a mile off his plank and lay submerged under the water for what seemed like an hour. It was wrong, I know, but at thirteen, I thought it was hilarious.

I can recall another time when we used to steal fruit from the freight trains that used to stop in the yards. One time, we slid open a door and jumped in, and the next thing, we knew somebody had closed the door shut. We wound up in Buffalo, New York. Needless to say, I caught the beating of my life.

My early teen years were the most fun. It was a lot of childhood mischief, summer playground romances, and baseball. I had my first piece when I was sixteen from Carla Testa. I guess the first time is the time you'll never forget, and I haven't forgotten mine. We had gone on a summer day trip with the playground up to Swartwood Lake in North Jersey, something they always did to get the kids out of the city. Carla had always liked me, and I had always liked her, but I'd never tell her. I was too tough to get involved with girls. If Carla hadn't been the aggressive one, I don't think we'd have ever gotten together. While we were wading in the water, she reached down and grabbed my pecker. I loved it. We made plans to wander off into the woods, and we did it on a picnic table. Crude as it was, it was beautiful, and I haven't stopped doing it to this day.

They say it's rare when a man has one good reliable friend that he can count on through thick and thin. Well, I go beyond that because I've been blessed with four of the best friends that any guy can ever have. They've been my best friends my entire life. Now how many people that you know can say that?

In my building, there were five other families, and three of them happened to have sons in my age bracket. Directly across the hall from us lived Frank Lupo. We called him the wolf because in Italian that's what lupo means. Frankie was a year older than me, but Frankie started working when he was eleven or twelve. He always had a job, sometimes two jobs at one time. I don't know what it was with him, but he was always a workaholic. Frankie was a lot of laughs too. If ever you needed to know a joke or a funny story, Frankie had one to tell. I think he should've been a comedian instead of a dock worker in Port Newark. I'd say next to me, and I'll say it modestly, Frankie managed to get his share of the women. He was tall, dark, and handsome, but he had that Italian beak nose. Still, he married a pretty woman and has a couple of kids. Frankie is a hard worker and a good and loyal friend.

Tommy Dara was always the brains of the gang. Tommy lived downstairs on the first floor and was two years older than me. All through grammar school, high school, and college, all Tommy got were As, but for a guy as smart as he was, he sure got in his share of trouble like the rest of us. He was always the class clown, but he knew just how far to go to still maintain his A average. Tommy went to college locally and became a lawyer. Unfortunately for him, he got tied up with the wrong firm, and things just didn't work out. He seems to think that his ties to our next friend had plenty to do with it, and he's probably right. Now he still practices law, but he's a private lawyer for only one person, and that one person is Johnny Mezzanotte. I should also add that Tommy is my agent.

Johnny "Midnight," again we used the Italian translation, has become famous in his own right. I'll tell you more about him as the story goes on. Johnny lived above us. He was the oldest of the group, four years older than me, and everyone looked up and followed him no matter what it was, that is everyone but me. There was always a difference between the two of us. I liked him and respected him, but I wasn't one of his *boys* like the others were.

If I wanted to go along, I went, and if I didn't, I didn't. There were many times when I stood up to him throughout the years and to be perfectly honest, if it were any of the others, they'd catch a beating, but the bond was strong between Johnny and me. I think he respected the fact that I stood up to him and sort of let me do my own thing. But make no mistake about it, when Johnny "Midnight" really wanted you for something, and you didn't go along, you'd better be prepared to pay the consequences because he is the toughest son of a bitch that I know. I'd fight anybody and almost be sure that I'd win, but if I ever had to tangle with Johnny, more than likely I'd come out of the short end.

The fifth member of our gang lived across the street in the projects. "Red" Jones was the nicest guy you'd ever want to meet. He was a perfect gentleman at all times, but you didn't want to rile him either because Red is about six feet and two and two hundred pounds. Red complimented the group in a lot of ways. First of all, he was the athlete that everybody admired. He was All-State in football and basketball. He went to the University of Kentucky on a dual scholarship but tore his knee up on the first day of football practice so badly that to this day, he still can't walk right. He came home immediately after that and started down on the docks with Frankie.

Red got his nickname. His real name is Therow due to the fact that his pumpkin pie skin is brown, sort of reddish. Red and I were very close, and it was me who sort of brought him into our gang. One day in school, I saw a key on the ground and picked it up. I was only in the third or fourth grade at the time. It turned out that Red was looking for that key. He had dropped it during lunch break, and his mother would've really laid into him if she found out he lost the apartment key. He saw me pick it up and very politely asked if I could see it. I showed it to him, and when he found out, it was his key he became so happy he hugged me and took me to the corner store and stole me a candy bar. We've been good friends ever since.

As for myself, I was always the lady killer. I had more girls asking my friends about me than there were snowflakes in a storm. I guess it's just chemistry, but I've never had any problems getting girls. If Johnny was the vocal leader of the group, then I was the silent leader. As I said before, I always did what I wanted whenever I wanted regardless of what anyone said, Johnny included. If the rest of them came along, they were welcome if they didn't, then I went ahead anyway. We clashed more than once, but things always worked out.

I was the hotheaded guy of the bunch too. There were many times when I got everybody in a fight simply because I wouldn't look the other way. I was the tough guy, and I'd take on all comers who even looked at me the wrong way. I've calmed down a lot from what I used to be, but there still are times when I'll go a little berserk. I guess if I'd have gotten a good beatin' years ago, I would've calmed down, trouble was there was nobody that could do it, except Johnny, and we were best of friends.

It wasn't till we all were in our late to early teens that we began to take our paths in life. Where we were headed wasn't a good path. We were headed for a lot of trouble, bad trouble!

I suppose it all started when we began hanging in a little candy store on the other side of the projects. It was owned and operated by a guy named Tony Sasso, who was a short, fat, balding, slick-ass small timer from Newark. But to us kids, he was a big shot. I never saw a wod of hundreds until Tony, I never drove in a Cadillac until I drove in Tony's, I never saw a diamond pinky ring until I saw Tony's. I mean the guy lived a fast life. He was always on the phone with guys from all over. He had rich-looking ladies. He was an influence on us, and it wasn't long before he started to break us into his world.

Although he turned out to be a real prick, Tony was a funny guy. I remember one time in particular when we were down at his Italian club in Newark, and we were heavy into drinking Sambuca. Tony had just started taking up golf and was bragging about how far he could drive a golf ball. I forgot exactly how it came up, but somebody challenged Tony that he couldn't throw, not hit but throw, a golf ball through the Lincoln Tunnel. Tony put down a bet of two hundred and off we went to the Lincoln Tunnel. It was about two thirty in the morning, and the tunnel traffic was very low. We dropped Tony off at the Jersey side with five golf balls and told him to give us five minutes to get to the New York side and then throw them through.

If any came through, we'd get them, then drive back and pick him up. You have to understand that we were almost as drunk as Tony, not quite, but almost. Well, we drove through and pulled over and waited while Red and Frankie stood in the tunnel, waiting for the balls to come through; naturally, they didn't. We waited about a half hour, then went back through to the Jersey side to pick up Tony. He wasn't there. He had gotten himself arrested. Not only did he lose himself two hundred on his bet, but also the fine was two-fifty plus court charges. That was a very expensive night for him, and a lot of laughs afterward just thinking about it.

My introduction to Tony Sasso's world came when I was fifteen. One day he asked Red and me to take a walk over to Mike's Route 66 gas station, get a bag from Mike, and bring it back to him. I knew where the station was, it was on the other side of town, and I knew Mike, the owner, as a guy who played cards with my father in his club. But I didn't understand all this business about a bag. Red and I took the walk over, picked up a brown paper bag, and started to walk back. Mike and Tony both told us not to open it, so naturally, we did.

In the bag were about a hundred little slips of paper with names and numbers on them and a big roll of money. We were afraid to unravel the roll and count it, but we both were excited about carrying all that money. We didn't understand what it was all about, but we knew it wasn't on the up and up.

When we gave it to Tony, he was all smiles. "Didn't peek in, did ya?" We assured him we didn't, but he knew better. He gave us five bucks a piece and told us to scram and to keep our mouths shut about this to our parents. We didn't tell our parents, but we told Johnny and the rest of the guys, Johnny explained that we had just run numbers and explained to us the whole thing about the last three digits in the race track total and how people bet on them. That was my baptismal.

It wasn't long after that that we were constantly doing his running around for him. Johnny and Tommy were both driving, and the rest of us looked young and innocent enough to do certain things with no questions asked. We all had special assignments to do, but it was Johnny who seemed the most intrigued by the whole scene, and it wasn't long before Johnny started doing his own thing. You might say that Tony created his downfall because in a year or so, Johnny was practically running Sasso's whole operation, and he was only twenty. That's how smart Johnny is in this thing, show him something once, and he's got it down pat, and he really had the operation down pat.

The rest of us naturally were with Johnny, although we knew that Tony was the boss. But as long as everything went smoothly, and there were no problems we didn't really care who ran the show, and we all knew that Tony took orders himself anyway.

Football season was the time when we made the most money. Tony had us working two phones, one in the back of the store and another down in Newark, taking down bets. A guy would call up and identify himself with a codename. We'd give him the day's line, then take his action. On any given Saturday and Sunday, there'd be sixty or seventy thousand dollars of bets on the line. More times than not, Tony would win, and on Thursday, he'd go around to all the winners and losers and payoff or collect. He never welched; I got to hand him that. A good bookie pays out all winners, he's got to if he wants a good name for himself. I've got to say that Tony was a good book. Guys that stuck him he'd take care of in his way. We found out later, and it wasn't pretty.

There was always action on the horses too, although we didn't see too much of it because those bets were placed mostly during the day for the day races or the upcoming night races. The few times that Tony did let us in on some of the action was when he'd give us a thousand and tell us to drive to Roosevelt or Yonkers and place it all on one certain horse in a race and only that horse. He told us never to collect the money but to bring the winning tickets to him and he'd bring them to somebody else. Every time we took that ride the horses came in. Finally, we realized what was going on, the horses we were betting on were fixed to win the races. From then on, whenever we went there, we placed our bets and collected ourselves plus the fifty that Tony gave us.

One night we were at Roosevelt, and we had just bet twenty-four hundred on a horse called Fast Mike. We had split up all the money between the five of us, and we all went to different windows. We had bet six hundred of our own money on this horse as well, and we were just waiting for the finish so we could collect. Fast Mike went off at odds of five to one, a twelve-dollar horse. We stood to win over thirty-five hundred, and Tony's man stood to win over twenty thousand. Well, wouldn't you know it, but Fast Mike breaks stride and comes in last. We were pissed. When we got back home and told Tony what happened he was furious. On our next trip, there we saw that same rider with a broken arm. Think there was a connection? We didn't want to bet anymore after that, and after a while, we stopped going to the track for him altogether.

Tony also took a lot of action on baseball. He'd lay six to five that you couldn't pick any three players that on any particular day would get six or more hits between them. He'd also take a lot of action on the Yankees and Mets, the local teams, and clean up. People don't know how to bet on baseball. When an overpowering pitcher is on the mound, sure he's favored to win, but are you willing to give the long odds that he will? Too many people do and all it takes is for one of those games to go the bookway, and he covers five winning bets. Tony always wondered if there was a way he could fix a baseball game. We talked about it many times and agreed you'd have to have the plate umpire and a pitcher. I honestly think that he tried a few times, but I don't know for sure if he ever did or not, I know later it happened, and I'll tell you about that when the 'time comes.

Although it was all of us that were involved in this gambling thing it was Johnny that was Tony's boy. He took Johnny everywhere with him, to New York, to his club in Newark, out to eat with his New York friends, and they even went to Chicago together for something, although we never found out. Johnny loved every minute of it. It seemed he lived for the action.

One day Johnny came back from a ride to Staten Island with Tony to visit Tony's boss. Johnny said his house was huge and there were guard dogs all around and guards at the front gate. He talked like a little kid who had just sat on Santa's lap. That's the day I figured that Johnny would stay in it for good. I wasn't wrong. As for myself I could take it or leave it. The money was good, and the times were high, but at eighteen, who knew what was to lie ahead?

I made my decision on a cold December night in a little gas station in Newark. It was a Friday night, and we were having a few in Tony's club getting ready to go out. It was about ten-thirty, and we were ready to leave when Tony called Johnny back and took him into the backroom. That night, Frankie was working, so it was the four of us, and we were really sharp, new clothes, clean shave, cologne, the whole bit. A new club had opened and we were ready to score, how I wish we had made it there instead of what happened.

We got in Johnny's car and took off. I had the feeling that something was coming down. "There's a guy that owes Tony thirty-five hundred and is stickin' him for it. Tony wants us to go over there and scare him a little. Tony'll take care of us later. This guy owns his station. What we'll do is wait until the lights go out, and he's checking the pumps, then pull up, get out of the car, and maybe throw him down or something. I don't want to hurt the guy just scare him." Johnny laid out the plans like a general before a battle. I wasn't too sure about this. I didn't get a good feeling.

FIFTY-SIX

When we got to the station, the lights were already out, and the guy apparently had just finished checking the pumps because he was on his way back to the garage. Johnny pulled in quickly and jumped out in front of him. I was riding a shotgun and jumped out on the other side. Red and Tommy came out from the back seats, and we quickly had the guy surrounded. He was a big man, well over six feet, and he wasn't as old as I had visioned, more in his early thirties. It probably would take all four of us to "throw him down or something" as Johnny suggested.

Johnny told him that Tony had asked us to come over and remind him about the thrity-five hundred, or there'd be trouble. "Tell asshole Sasso to send some men over, not boys, next time he wants to scare me." The guy had brass balls. He was outnumbered four to one, and we weren't exactly small, and he was coming on with the wisecracks. Johnny remained cool and slid his hand into his coat pocket and pointed it like he had a gun in there like they did in the old gangster movies. "Let's talk about it in the back." That's all Johnny said and the guy sort of changed his tune a little. "Calm down kid, sure we'll talk." We took the guy around the back of the garage, and as soon as we turned the corner, Johnny hauled off and hit the guy. He fell, and Red and Tommy picked him up and held him. Johnny was still cool. "Let's make it easy on you. When can I tell Tony he'll get his money?" The guy was bleeding from his nose and started to rant and rave, cursing Sasso and us in every breath. He started kicking and swearing to God he'd get us. Johnny threw another punch that landed on the side of his head. I know that hurt his hand, on a cold night like that you don't want to punch anything as hard as a skull, it's like punching solid ice. Johnny gave a quick *goddamn* and suddenly turned raging mad. His eyes were fire, and I'd say if he had a gun, he might've used it right there.

Standing next to us was a barrel of oil. It was probably drained from the cars and waiting to be recycled, but Johnny "Midnight" had other ideas for it. He motioned "Red" and Tommy to bring him nearer to the barrel and when they did Johnny grabbed the guy's arm and dunked it in the oil. He took out his lighter and flicked it on. "I'll burn your fuckin' hand off if I don't get an answer." I can't tell you how scared I was. I didn't know whether to stop him or let him go; fortunately, the decision was made for me. The guy suddenly broke loose and reached for the nearest thing he could find, it happened to be a tire iron. He swung at Johnny and laid him out cold with one shot across his head.

I reacted in a second and hit that guy with the best shot I ever tagged anybody in my life. I guess he forgot I was there, and he didn't seem to be aware of me as he seemed more intent on going after Red and Tommy and left himself open to me. He flew right over that oil barrel and was out like a log. Unfortunately so was Johnny. We were about as nervous as anybody could get. Johnny was shaking on the ground, blood all over his head and the other guy stayed still. At first, Tommy thought the guy was dead, maybe hitting his head when he fell. He ran to him and felt his heart, it was pumping. I took control. "Pick up, Johnny, and let's get out of here. Leave him alone. He'll come to."

We put Johnny in the car and took off, but to where? Johnny was totally out of it and covered with blood. The tire iron caught him on the top of the head down through his forehead and across his face. It was an ugly sight, and I've seen some ugly sights. It was obvious that he needed medical attention, but how would we explain it? We figured we'd make something up at the hospital, but Johnny had to go.

We took him to Columbus Hospital in Newark, only two or three blocks from where it happened. We said that we had gotten into a fight with some guys in the parking lot of the club we were going to and one guy hit Johnny with a tire iron. All the people we told the story to believe it, even the police, who had been called. Johnny was in an emergency for a couple of hours when a doctor finally came out and wanted to get in touch with his parents. That's when I knew it was bad. Johnny had slipped into a coma. I knew Johnny's father wasn't home. On Friday, he always played cards at his Italian club with my father, so I called him there. The two of them were at the hospital in twenty minutes. It was a long vigil and lasted into the next day, but Johnny pulled out of it. He'd have stitches and headaches for a while, but at least he was alive. When we all heard the good news, we went home for some breakfast and rest.

Saturday afternoon, we went to see Tony in the store. He hadn't heard what happened, and his opening comment showed it, "You guys did a helluva job last night. I got a call first thing this morning. My money is on the way." He pulled out a hundred-dollar bill and gave it to me.

I was pissed. "Keep your fuckin" money. Johnny almost got his head taken off from that guy and you smile and hand us a hundred. Next time go get your own money. I walked out in a rage leaving Tommy and Red there to explain what had happened. Tony had no idea. The guy said that one of his men fractured his cheek and that if a young man did that, then he didn't want any part of Tony's pros. I guess at another time I would've been flattered, but I had had enough, and later that night I told Johnny while I visited him.

When I walked into his room, there was a huge wreath of flowers standing next to his bed. His face was swelled and half covered with bandages but his features were recognizable. I looked at the flowers and asked if they were from Tony. "Mr. Battita, Tony's boss from Staten Island." Johnny was hurt real bad, but all he could talk about were those flowers and Battita. I thought hundred to split four ways. Is your head worth twenty-five bucks? Tony's bad people. For the first time in five years, I see it, and I'm getting out now while I can and so should you."

Johnny was always a very stubborn person. "I'm in it, I like it, and I'll stay in it."

I can see that my efforts were fruitless, so I said goodbye and left. I was a very confused young man. I was watching my best friends all starting to travel a very dangerous road. It seemed that they were all caught up with this thing and loved every minute of it. There was nothing I could do about it.

I came home and sulked around the apartment. Lucy sensed something wrong and tried to get it out of me, but for the first and only time in my life, I just couldn't confide in her. I was embarrassed to tell my sister what I had become and how I was going to handle it. We were in the kitchen when I got a call. It was Frankie telling me he wanted to go out that night, he finally had a night off, and mentioning if I heard the news that Sasso had some guys coming from New York to get the guy that hit Johnny. That really got me riled. Hadn't we all had enough of this?

On Saturday nights, Tony hung out at his club down in Newark. I raced down there not knowing what I was going to do, to hit him and let loose all my frustration, or try to talk him out of busting up that guy. After all, wasn't his cheek fractured? And didn't Tony get his money? So what was the reasoning?

I walked in and saw fat ass Sasso stuffing himself with a slice of tomato pie. "Tony, we got to talk."

He wiped his mouth and motioned me to his back room. "I hope you calmed down from this afternoon. You shouldn't talk to me that way." I could've hit him there, but I didn't. "Answer me yes or no, did you send out some goons after the guy that hit Johnny?" My voice was straight and calm.

He tried to lay a guilt trip on me. "You guys are the ones that should be after him. If he hit my friend in the fuckin' head with a tire iron, I'd had his arms broken by now. I swear to Christ sometimes you, guys, remind me of little girls."

I still remained calm, although it was harder to do. "Don't pull that shit with me fat man. My friend got his head broke for you last night, and you got your fuckin' money, and your guy got a fractured cheek, and now let's just say that the case is closed and leave it at that." As I talked, my rage became more obvious, and my finger was pointing in his face. I waited for him to make a move; the time was right to act. Tony Sasso was a lot of things, but he wasn't a fool. He knew he was no match for me, and he quickly changed his tune.

"Okay, I'll call them off just this once. But, Vinnie, from now on, don't let our paths cross because one of us might get hurt."

The place was full of his men, so I didn't press my luck, although that threat would be taken care of at a later date. I left quickly, got in the car, and sped off. Where I was going, I didn't know. I just knew I had to go and think.

I guess it's times like that when you need a little divine help and that's where I got mine from. Here I was, a lonely confused young man trying to swim upstream. I had my friends on my mind. I could see the wrong in it. Why couldn't they? I was a block away from home and stopped at a red light. I just happened to be stopped in front of our church. I figured it would do me some good to go in and sit down and think a little.

I was sitting there for about a half hour when from behind the altar came Father Virgilio. The short little white-haired priest had always been my favorite from the days when I was an altar boy, and he'd give me some of his cherries from the brandy. He was just what I needed at that time.

He said he had been watching me and sensed that there was something wrong. I explained to him what was going on. I was always a smart boy and a good athlete, but what was I doing with what God gave me? I was taking books and beating up guys for money. Was this the life that God had planned for me?

Father was very patient and practical. You see he came from the same environment as me, only in New York, and he understood everything I was going through. "Vinnie, God gave you something else. He gave you the freedom to choose. To choose what is right and to choose what is wrong. He gave you common sense to help you make those choices. He gave them to everyone so everyone must make their own choice. You must choose for Vince Donato, and Tom, John, Frank, and the colored boy must choose for themselves. It's their choice to make by themselves, not by you. Just as you have now made your decision they must make theirs. If they don't choose with you, you can't let it hold you back. You're a fine young man with a sound mind and a good family. God will show you the path to take, and when he does, it'll be up to you to walk it.

I felt a whole lot better after my talk with Father Virgilio. Somehow he took the weight of being everybody's savior off my back. I don't think I've ever talked to anyone who made more sense than he did on that day. I knew then what I had to do.

The next night, we all got together at Johnny's. He had been released that day and was under orders to just rest up a little. He really recovered very quickly from his ordeal. All his signs were normal, and the swelling had subsided in his face. His head still hurt a little but the doctor said that was to be expected. If his face wasn't bandaged up you'd swear that nothing had happened to him, he really looked good. We were all in his room just passing the time, listening to the radio, and singing along a little bit. I was half-heartedly into it. My mind was on other things. Finally, I had to get it off my chest. "Don't you all know that if you keep this shit with Sasso, you're all headed for trouble. We're all better than that. We don't need Sasso or his connections. There are plenty of ways of making a living here. We don't have to flirt with the law to make a few bucks. I'm not going around beating up guys for twenty-five dollars the rest of my life. I'm too good for that."

Tommy always had something to say, "Shit, Vin, you've done it all your fuckin' life for nothing. Don't you think it's about time you made some money out of it?"

I couldn't believe him. Here was the smartest guy going, and he was making jokes about the whole thing. The cause was lost, but I gave it one more try. "Go ahead and laugh, but the joke may very well be on you the next time. Maybe the next guy will pull out a gun, then what?"

"Come on, brother. Tony wouldn't send us out if he knew the guy was carryin' a piece."

"Like I told you yesterday, Vince, it's all part of the game. The guy knew what he was gettin' into. Besides, Tony don't go after nobody that doesn't deserve it, and that guy deserved it."

"And he got it too."

"Tony's goons broke the guy's arms." I was fit to be tied. "That fat fuckin' shit lied to me." I had it. "I want you guys to know that I love you all like my family, but as of right now, I'm washing my hands of everything. We'll still hang out together, that won't change, but don't ever get me associated with any of Sasso's shit again, ever. Because if you do I'll go right after Tony, kick his ass good, then I'll go after whichever one of you got me involved and kick ass again and I swear to Jesus Christ that's the truth." I never saw my four friends so silent in all my life. I think I shocked them.

Johnny was the one who answered for them, "I think I speak for all of us when I say that if that's the way you want it then so be it. But listen to me and listen to me good, one day our paths are going to cross and a decision will have to be made. I pray that you'll make the right one, for your sake." I didn't know what he was talking about, but the way he said it sort of put a tingling feeling through my body. Johnny "Midnight" had a way of putting across a point that could be as subtle as a punch in the mouth.

Once again, a blanket of silence fell on the room, and once again, Johnny lifted it, "So what will you do for yourself?"

"I'm going to give baseball a shot."

Frankie laughed. "That scout don't want you no more. You sent him out of here like a dried-up pussy last year. He ain't coming back for you."

Frankie was right. I was very fortunate to even have a professional scout looking at me. Orange High School had never been noted for its baseball teams. In my three varsity seasons, we won only seven games. No scouts look at teams that are that bad. Nevertheless, I was a diamond on a beach of sand. When I was a sophomore, I hit close to four hundred, improved it to exactly five hundred as a junior, and stayed there as a senior. My teammates were so bad that there were some games when I'd be intentionally walked with nobody on base just to get to the other guys so they wouldn't have to pitch to me. I got a few letters from scouts who happened to see me while scouting other players, but there was only one who showed more than the usual casual interest and started to follow me at the end of my senior year.

I thank God for a man like Jimmy Kushner. As many times as he showed up and talked to me after games, that's how many times I told him that I wasn't interested. He sent me tickets one time to see the White Sox at the Stadium, and I never went, I sold them instead. I loved the competition, and I'll always love that, but I just didn't want to play baseball. All I wanted to do was hang with the guys, bang the broads, go to clubs, and do the Sasso thing. Finally, Kushner went above my head and went to my father. He told him that I had potential and could possibly be a big-league ballplayer. He didn't promise anything; he told it like it was. He said the White Sox would pay me two thousand to sign and offer me a minor league contract of four hundred a month. My father wasn't too impressed. He never followed sports so the whole thing didn't matter to him. He did want me off the streets, and we had numerous arguments about that, so from that standpoint, he was for it. But my father wanted me home. A good Italian son never leaves the home until he gets married, and that's that. Still, he left it up to me. I turned Kushner down. Before he left, he gave me his card and told me if I changed my mind in a year or so to give him a call. I was very lucky that I saved that card.

I could see the smile on Kushner's face when I called him on the phone. His happiness just came through that wire, and he couldn't come out quick enough to sign the papers. I was to report to a minor league camp at the end of February. I'd be playing class D ball in El Paso in the Texas League. Kushner told me that with a little luck, I could make the big leagues in three or four years. I figured more like two or three.

The guys were real happy for me. They had made their choice, and I had made mine, and there wasn't any reason why we still couldn't be as tight as ever. They gave me a terrific send-off party, lots of broads and lots of booze. That was the first night that I ever had two girls at one time. Leave it to Johnny to swing something like that.

The party was great as all parties are when friends, booze, and broads all get together, but it seems all parties in Orange must have a fight and mine was no exception. After my family and most of the other people left, there were just a few of my closest friends there and Lucy. Sasso was there against my wishes, but I let Johnny talk me into it. They had become a lot closer since Johnny's accident. The booze was flowing, and I was really having a good time until I saw Sasso whispering something in Lucy's ear. I went about the business that had to be done in a different way than I would normally have done it. "Hey, Tony, whatever happened to that guy and the thirty-five hundred?"

"What guy?" He was stuffing his face with his third or fourth meatball sandwich.

"The guy that hit Johnny."

"Oh, him. He had a little accident. Broke both his arms." I hated his laugh that followed.

I smiled back. "You didn't have anything to do with it, did you?"

He could see where I was coming from. "What you gettin' at?"

"You lied to me, you fat fuck. You said you were going to let it go." My friends knew how hot-tempered I was and knew how I felt about Tony, so Red jumped between us right away before anything could happen. "It's okay, Red. I just want him to know that I know he lied to me. I'm not as dumb as you look, Tony. I'm going to make something of myself and get out of this stinkin' city, and I want you to know it." I was really playing a good act. I had everybody thinking that I had had a little too much to drink and was just blowing off some steam.

I yelled from the top of my lungs, "I'm going to make it!" It was Academy Award material.

His frightened face turned to one of confidence. He probably figured he could handle any drunk kid. "Vince, nobody wants you to make it more than me honestly. Let's shake and let bygones be bygones."

"Go ahead and shake. Tony's not such a bad guy. Go ahead."

Tony stood there with his right hand extended and his left hand holding his sandwich. I shuffled my feet and looked down like a little boy who got his hand caught in the cookie jar. I went to shake hands and instead kicked him where it would hurt him the most, in his fat-loaded stomach. He fell to his knees and started gasping for air. Suddenly all his food came rushing out, and he started to roll all over in it. I went to the buffet table and picked up the pot of meatballs and sauce and poured it all over him. Then I started once again. I was the hot-tempered fighter that my friends knew, "Don't ever lie to me again, you fat ass, and if I ever catch you near my sister again, I'll cut out your tongue and shove it up your ass." I went to kick him, but Red grabbed me and, with Tommy's help, took me outside.

I was calm. They were all running around like chickens with their heads cut off. After a while, Johnny came out, and he was very serious. "Vince, you're in deep."

I teased him as if I was scared, "Am I going to get my arms broken?

Why did you do that?"

I was mad. "He had it coming if not from me then from that guy in the gas station."

"Let me put it to you like this. I don't know if I can hold him off. Tony's a very vengeful man with a lot of connections. You got yourself in some very hot water tonight."

It was then that I realized that everything Johnny had just told me was true. I quickly became timid and started to shake a little.

Johnny continued, "Look, you're taking off in a couple of days. I doubt if he'll do anything in that short a time, but man be careful out in Texas. Tony Sasso is a dangerous man, and if he wants you, he'll find a way to get you. Just ask that guy in the station. If I hear of anything, I'll let you know. Now go with Red and Tommy. They got a little surprise for you. I'll take care of Lucy. Don't worry." My surprise was waiting for me at a motel; it was the two women.

After Mass the next day, I stopped to say goodbye to Father Virgilio. After all, if it wasn't for his advice I'd probably never have done what I did, so I felt I had to stop by and thank him one more time. Once again his words of wisdom rang true.

"Vince," he said, "God gave you the ability to play baseball well. Use it. Use all of it, not half of it or 95 percent of it but all of it. If you don't, it's cheating, and you don't ever want to cheat God."

Throughout my whole career, I've done what Father Virgilio instructed me to do that day. I've never cheated God when it came to using the talent He gave me. Some days, after long nights, I just wasn't up to par, but still, I gave it my all on those days, and I feel confident that God knows I've never cheated Him.

The apartment was like a balloon slowly filling up with air. One by one, people started coming over to say goodbye. First, it was my high school coach, then a few of my mother's friends. Zia Petroneilla, my mother's closest friend whom we all called Aunt Helen, came and gave me her rosary beads. Zizza the baker gave me a loaf of bread and some cookies to eat on the plane. By the time we were ready to start Sunday dinner, the normal seating of seven swelled to twelve or thirteen, but my mother didn't mind. All she did was throw in another pound of macaroni and tell Zizza to bring up a few more loaves of bread, and we were set.

After dinner, the guys came up and that packed the apartment even more. But the more, the merrier, and we were like one big happy family anyway. We had a hell of a good time listening to the old Italian stories from Aunt Helen and Zizza the baker. Even Red got a kick out of them. Later on, we cleared the table, and the men played cards while the women did the desert dishes and sat and talked in the kitchen. I can't recall a more enjoyable time with my family than that day. Then it was time to leave. What a drawn-out affair that turned out to be. You'd have thought that I was off to war. My mother and the other ladies all cried, and my sisters, except Lucy, joined in. My father shook my hand and told me not to embarrass the Donato name, in other words, to stay out of trouble. Lucy gave me a hug and couldn't wait till she had some time so she could visit me, she seemed to be the only one who didn't take me leaving too seriously.

The guys drove me to the airport, and even that was kind of sad. This was the first time in my life that I was going to be away from my family and friends, and at the airport was the first time that it hit me. I was scared. I was going to a place I knew nothing about, alone, and not knowing anybody once I got there. It was frightening, but the macho in me wouldn't let on to my friends. It would be something I'd have to deal with when I got there. The five of us all embraced, and off I went with Johnny's warning clear in my mind, "He's mad as hell. Be careful."

My plans called for me to work with the Class D and C teams in Sarasota, Florida, until the season began, then we'd go to El Paso. When I was to arrive in Sarasota, I was to check in with my manager, Art Mannigan, at a small hotel outside of Sarasota.

Art Mannigan was a man I'll never forget. He was huge; six feet five and weighed at least two-forty. His dark skin accentuated his blue eyes. He had a tough-looking face but a very gentle attitude about himself. I immediately took a liking to him. "Kushner told me you could be one hell of a ballplayer if you stayed out of trouble. Well let's talk man to man, you do what you're supposed to do, and you and I will get along fine. You don't and you'll wish you never left, New Jersey because I'll have my foot up your ass every day. Can we shake on it?"

"I understand you perfectly." We shook. I wanted no part of that giant man after me. Later he took me to my room and told me I'd be rooming with a pitcher from Iowa. I waited for my roommate to show up. I had always gotten along with other people, and I tried to convince myself that there was no difference, but what did I know about Iowa? I couldn't even remember where it was. What would a farm boy and a city kid have in common? We'd soon find out.

The door opened and in walked the tallest, skinniest, freckled-faced kid I'd ever seen. He'd have lasted two days in Orange High before he'd have his bell rung. He stuck out his hand in a slow drawl and introduced himself, "Paul Tannen, pitcher." The kid was pure Americana. I was waiting for him to unpack an apple pie and hang up a picture of George Washington. We exchanged small talk for about an hour and turned it in. I was beginning to doubt my decision. I was thinking about what the guys were doing and how I'd miss the clubs on Friday nights and my mother's cooking and my father's growling. My stomach was getting a wheezing feeling when I heard crying coming from the next bed.

"I'm afraid," he said. "This is my first time away from home, and I'm afraid I won't make it, and I'll have to go back and tell my pa." Shit, it was the first time away from home for me too, and I was just as afraid. I didn't need that shit at that time.

I got out of bed and faced him. "Look, it's the first time out for all of us. We're all in the same boat. Sooner or later, you'd have to leave home anyway, so it's now rather than later." I put a hand on his shoulder, and it seemed to settle him down a little. I tried to be convincing and, at the same time, convince myself of the same doubts. "Come on, get dressed, and we'll have a little something to eat." We both got dressed and walked down the road to a little diner about half a mile from the hotel.

It was a very small place. As soon as we walked in, we faced the counter, and to each side of the door were three booths. The smell of grease was everywhere, and I wondered just how good the food would be. But then I figured how bad could they mess up a hamburger and coke. It turned out to be pretty bad. That was the first time that I had ever heard soda called pop, and I really had a ball with it. To me, it was hilarious the way Paul said it.

At the counter were three guys, and in the booth next to us was a black guy. I had noticed that the black guy had a trim athletic build and thought that he must've been with the White Sox too. We exchanged brief hellos, and I asked him if he was a ballplayer, "Shit yea." We asked him to join us.

He was from Philadelphia, and for the first time all day, I genuinely felt I had something in common with somebody. He was from the city, and so was I, so I knew we'd get along. He'd have to like the same things as me. He introduced himself as Jerry Alexander, and he played center field. He'd been assigned to the El Paso team, which meant we were all teammates. I was starting to feel good when all hell started to break loose.

The three guys at the counter were starting to get a little loud and abusive toward Jerry. Don't forget that Florida is the South, and this was almost twenty years ago. Prejudice runs high in certain places, and it seemed to be running very high that night in that little diner.

I heard about the Klu Klux Klan and what they did to blacks, and it made me shiver. Now I didn't know if those guys were the Klan or not, but the way they were talking, and their tone of voice sure could've convinced me. If I was scared, imagine how Jerry must've felt. Here he was a black kid from Philly having to hear this abuse his first night in camp.

Sooner or later, I figured that if the verbal abuse kept up either Jerry or myself was going to explode. I was frightened, but being frightened never stopped me from giving it to somebody who deserved it, and those three had it coming. I didn't count much on Paul, but it was Paul who started it. "Excuse me, sir," he said to the big fat one with the long sideburns and scraggly beard, "don't you know that it's not God's way to talk about other people the way you're doing?"

I thought if he was going to start it he could've started it with a better line than that.

The fat one turned on his stool. "Is that right? Well, it just so happens, Mr. Farmboy, that me and my friends hate them black ass niggers, and we even hate the white trash that sits and eats with 'em." After he said that, the three of them got off their stools and blocked off our booth. The fat one started again, "You hear what I say, boy?" He was looking straight at Jerry.

I could see that Jerry was turning white, who wouldn't? He probably had visions of being tarred and feathered. If only I had a few of the guys with me, we'd tear the place up, but I didn't. All I had was Jerry and Paul, and I figured soon enough we'd see what they were made of. It was time for some action. "Why don't you just leave us alone and let us eat."

That ticked off the fat one. He grabbed me by my shirt and lifted me straight up. God that guy was strong. I backed off and punched him square in the nose, and blood splattered like a rain shower. One of the others jumped and wrestled me down to the floor. I could see Jerry going at it as I figured he would, but Paul was just standing there, waving his arms, saying to break it up. I finally managed to get this guy in a headlock, and I took him out with a good shot, but in the meantime, ol' broken nose had recovered and laid one into me good that sent me flying down the aisle. I stood up really woozy and on shaky legs. I dodged his next punch but fell into another booth in doing it. I seemed to be at the mercy of this madman. He took off his belt and started whipping me with his buckle as I was sprawled out across the seat. I was beat. It was the first time in years that I had got a good beating, but I have to say it took two guys to do it, and I didn't go down without doing damage to both of them. As for Jerry, he took his lumps too. They not only beat him and whipped him, but they also kicked him in his ribs. Paul finally tried to throw a punch, but the fat guy laid him out with a smack, of all things.

When it all was over, the three guys took off and left us sprawled out all over the place. When the police came, they questioned us and then brought us straight to Mannigan.

We were pretty beat up, especially Jerry, and I expected a lecture or a reprimand from the coach, but instead, he bawled into the policemen. He screamed at them that they should be out trying to find those three bastards who beat up his *boys* rather than wasting time at the hotel. If I were one of those cops, I would've arrested him right there on the spot, but I guess they understood his reasoning, and they finally left us to go track down those three men.

After we told the story to Mannigan, he became very fatherly to us. Jerry was taken to the hospital for x-rays on his ribs, which proved to be just bruised rather than broken. I had about five or six welts from that belt buckle, and Paul had a giant hand mark on the right side of his face from the slap. Mannigan told us if anything like that happened again, he'd personally knock out the guy's teeth and then drag him to the nearest police station. He sat with us most of the night until we were too tired to stay up and listen to him. I got the impression that he somehow felt responsible for the incident and was trying to make up for it in some way.

Well, that's how my first day in organized baseball went. I met my two closest friends that I made playing ball, and for the first time in my life, I began to realize that there was another world outside of Orange, New Jersey. One thing that I have regretted even to this day is that they never found those guys who beat us up. I'd like to have another go at it with that fat one. If I ever saw him again, I'd get even for that whipping. You can make a book on it.

The following day, we were excused from the morning practice, but Paul and I were in good enough shape to go through it anyway, only Jerry had to miss a few days because of his ribs. Word of the night's incident had filtered through the camp, and we three were treated like celebrities. We practiced along with the class C teams on our separate field away from the big team and the higher minor leaguers, but all day long, players filtered over to ask questions and find out what happened.

Ol' Hungry Janks himself, reputedly the meanest man in the league, even came over and had a few words to say. In a menacing growl, he said, "If you ever see those three fuckin' guys again, let me know. I'll have one each for breakfast, lunch, and supper." He wasn't kidding. Bob Janks got his nickname of Hungry because of a fight he once got into in Chicago. It seems he wasn't satisfied just beating up somebody, he went and bit the poor guy's ear off.

Jerry and I quickly became the closest of friends. Most of the guys on our squad were farm boys from the Midwest or South. Jerry was the only black, which was fine by me, and our city backgrounds just seemed to draw us together. To me, everybody else seemed to talk funny with their accents and all. I mean it was pop for soda, and Mom and Dad instead of Ma and Da, the movies was the show. I had a lot of trouble adjusting to them, so it was just natural that the two city kids got along. We'd bring Paul along with us wherever we went because we felt a bond with him because of the fight, and besides, Paul Tannen was a lot of laughs.

I was holding my own on the field. I hadn't played ball in over a year, but my batting eye was still sharp, my arm as strong as ever, and my competitive desire as dominant as it always was. The way I saw our team shaping up was around Jerry and myself. Jerry had so much natural talent it was scary. He could hit, hit with power, run, catch, and throw. He was without a doubt the best pure athlete on our team. I likened him a lot with Red before Red's knee injury. If Jerry was the best in the club, then I thought that I wasn't that far behind. I didn't have Jerry's natural swing, but I had just as much power if not more. His arm was stronger than mine but not by that much, and in a race, he'd only beat me by half a stride.

We caught the ball about the same, but Jerry's range was a little more than mine. That's why he played center field, and I was in left. We two were definite starters, but the rest of the positions were up for grabs. I felt that all the other players were good but equally talented. Nobody stood out like Jerry and me. In fact, there was talk that we two were going to the class D team, but that was nixed when Mannigan stepped in and said we should start at the bottom and work up. If we were that good, we'd find our way up there soon enough.

Paul, being a pitcher, I'd have to judge differently. His curve was natural. With those long thin fingers of his, it was easy for him to break it off and make the ball drop down and away. He threw his curve over the top and sidearm and when he threw it sidearm it was murder on a right-handed hitter. That ball looked like it would plant itself right in your ear, then it'd break down and out and catch the outside corner for a strike. His fastball was decent. I guess it was average for his level of ball. The older and stronger he got, it would improve, and it did. But Paul's biggest asset was that he knew the philosophy behind pitching, and he understood it even at eighteen years old.

Every pitch he threw had a purpose; one would set up the next and still another one would set up one more in the sequence. He threw inside, and he threw outside, high and low. He'd throw two fastballs, then throw off your timing with a slow curve. Just when you'd figured he'd throw that curve, he'd come with a fastball. He always outguessed the batter. As he grew older, he became a master at the pitching game, and at eighteen, you could just see that Paul Tannen was going to be one hell of a big-league pitcher, and he was. I'd call eight straight twenty-win seasons great, wouldn't you?

But that Paul was a funny guy. He was so nieve about things that it just made you laugh, especially about women and sex. I can't help but laugh whenever I think about the first time Paul got laid. You see all during that month in camp, Paul was looking at every girl there was, and Lord knows there were plenty. A major league baseball camp is like a big jar of honey, and boy, does it draw the bees. I was never shy with women, and Jerry turned out to be pretty good too, but all Paul did was look. He never opened his mouth to speak, and when he did, it was all jibber jabber anyway, stuff that never made any sense. It was a shame because all he'd have to do was say he was with the White Sox, and he'd get over like a fat rat, but he was so shy it was a crime.

Well, Paul could talk about nothing except a little blond whose girlfriend I happened to be hitting on, but Paul didn't know that I was hitting on his blond beauty too, and so was Jerry. As a matter of fact, this cute little blond that Paul had eyes for was about the biggest nymph in camp. She loved her sex. She'd find five or six guys every spring and rotate two on different nights. She was like a machine.

One night, both Jerry and I were with her, and we're banging away having a grand old time. She loved Jerry because he's hung like a horse. Jerry suddenly had a brilliant idea. "You think this is big? You should get a hold of Paul Tannens'. Paint it yellow, and you'd mistake it for an ear of corn." She lit up like a neon sign. She couldn't wait for the next day. The following day after practice, she walks right up to him and asks him out for that night. Paul was so tongue-tied he couldn't even say yes. He just nodded.

Paul was as excited as a kid at Christmas. I mean you couldn't shut him up. He asked Jerry and I a million questions. Should I hold her hand? How should I kiss her good night? Should I extend my arm for her to take it? All sorts of questions that I hadn't thought of in years. We kidded him back. "She just might grab your pecker right off the bat and forget all the formalities. I hear she loves to ball and loves to give head."

"She better leave my head alone," Paul answered back. He was just unreal.

Finally, eight o'clock came, and a knock on the door. Paul wasn't ready. We had had a late meeting, and he was still in the shower. She walked in, and I could see she was a little jittery. "All I've been thinking about all day was that ear of corn." She was really into it. I've got to hand it to her.

Jerry said, "As long as Paul's still in the shower, why don't you surprise him and go scrub his back?"

In a flash, she stripped and ran in. I never heard anyone scream that loud in my life. Paul came running out with a towel half wrapped around him, and she was right behind him with one hand in his crotch. Jerry and I were hysterical, and we laughed ourselves out of there and closed the door behind us. We waited about three hours and came back; she was still in there. We went out and came back again, and she had finally left. Paul was in the middle of his bed, stark naked with sheets and blankets sprawled all over the place. He had the look of a man that just broke the bank of Monte Carlo. "Best head I ever had." We laughed so hard we peed our pants.

We were in camp for about a month when it was time to break and head our way. The big team flew first class to Chicago, and the high minors flew first class to their destinations as well. The class C and D teams flew charter. We waited in that airport for over four hours for that charter flight to El Paso. I envied the big leaguers. Everything they got seemed like carte blanch. They stayed in the best hotels, ate at the best restaurants, dressed in the finest clothes, and had the best women. I wanted it all. I made a vow in that airport that I'd have it all in two years at the most, and I'd do anything to get it.

El Paso is a little town right on the Mexican border in Southwest Texas. It's a cowboy town and has a history that dates back a long time to the Old West. Whenever I think of my days in El Paso, I think of how warm the people were and how hot it always was.

When I arrived, the first thing on the agenda was to find lodging for the three of us. When you're with a minor league team, they don't foot any bills. It's up to you to find a place to live and a place to eat. The club supplies you with names and a number of local residents who'll put you up for the season, but we wanted rooms for three, and that was going to be hard.

We did a lot of looking around with little success. It seemed that we found plenty of places for two players but nothing for three. I think too that the fact that Jerry was black might've had something to do with it. Nevertheless, on our third day and the day before our first game, we found a place in the Mexican side of town.

It was a grand old house with eleven rooms owned by an old couple whose family roots were in the area for over two hundred years. Mr. Guzman was a tall well-built elderly man with dark features and had recently retired from the maintenance department of nearby Fort Bliss. Mrs. Guzman was a small plumpy woman with a big gold front tooth. She was always smiling and was a very pleasant person. He had four sons who all went to the big cities of the north to find a better way, so he had plenty of space for us, and living on a fixed income meant he certainly could've used the extra money. We made the deal for fifty dollars a month each with breakfast included.

My first season is still very clear in my mind. Jerry batted third, and I followed by batting fourth. We both hit a homer, and Paul pitched a shutout in our first game. We filled our stadium with soldiers from the base and a lot of locals. At that time, the ball in El

Paso was new. It was the third year for the franchise, and the previous two years were very bad, both on the field and at the gate. This year was very pivotal in terms of El Paso keeping and supporting a minor league franchise.

The El Paso Pokes took off like a bullet from a gun. We won seven of our first eight games with Jerry and myself doing most of the damage. There was a game where Jerry had four stolen bases and a homerun and made the greatest catch that I have ever seen. I had a two-homer game, and Paul had three wins. Mannigan was the toast of the town, and everything seemed to be coming up aces. Then we hit the road.

Those bus rides, I'll never forget them. All we did was drive hours and hours all over the state of Texas. We'd all get stiff and bored. We'd play cards, word games, and anything else to keep our minds fresh, and we'd play for hours, and we'd still be miles away from our destination. When it was hot, and it was always hot, that bus was like a sauna. We'd stop for some roadside food, a burger, and a coke, then stop an hour later to shit it out. The motels we stayed in were old, dusty, and roach-infested. El Paso sure wasn't heaven, but coming home from a road trip, it sure was the next best thing.

We lost three straight to the Val Verde Rattlers. I made my first error that cost us a game. There was a runner on second in the ninth with the score tied at three. The batter hit a sharp single to left, and I charged it quickly, fully knowing that the runner on second was going to give it a shot to score. I fielded the ball smoothly and came up throwing. The runner had just rounded third and was headed home. A decent throw would have nailed him with no problem; the only thing was my throw landed in the stands behind home plate. The ball just got away from me. I never embarrassed myself that way before. I felt two inches tall. Jerry and Paul tried to console me, but it was Mannigan who gave me fatherly advice that I needed.

"Vince, there'll be plenty more errors down the line. There's not a ballplayer in this game that hasn't made an error. As long as your errors are physical and not mental, don't worry about a thing. Just think about it, you gave a fan a souvenir and something to talk about for a long time." That talk made me feel a little better.

FIFTY-SIX

The Del Rio Diablos were next on our schedule and we lost two more there, making it five in a row. We cooled off. From Del Rio, we traveled north to Abilene for a weekend series. This is where a lot of my troubles had their beginning, and the reputation was born. We stayed at a nice motel for a change. Why? I don't know, but I suspect it was because Mannigan was hitting the proprietor. She ran up to him and greeted him with a great big kiss and hug, and then she took him to a side room, and we didn't see him again until game time.

The Friday night game was a close, action-packed barn burner for nine innings. The house was full, and the closeness of the game made tensions high. My competitive desire was flowing like a river. The score was tied in the top of the tenth inning at six. My game had been so-so up until then. I had doubled in two runs in the first but was later thrown out at the plate on a play I absolutely know I was safe on. I came up from my slide ready to go at it with the umpire, but I thought better of it and ran into the dugout, swearing every step of the way.

All through the game, I was getting bad calls from that plate umpire, and when I did hit the ball, I hit three line drives right at the fielders for outs. It was a frustrating game for me, but now in the tenth inning with runners on first and third with two outs, I had a chance to show my stuff. The umpire called me out on a third strike that was at least six inches outside. I blew my cool. That call was the proverbial straw that broke the camel's back. I ranted and raved like a madman, cursing the umpire to his face every second. You can take the kid out of the city, but you can't take the city out of the kid. Mannigan came out and held me back but argued my cause as furious as I had been doing.

Poor Art, he had no idea how I was when I lost my cool. He figured we'd blow off some steam and retreat to the dugout, satisfied that we gave it our all in the argument. He wished it was that easy. In a rage, I went after the umpire. Fortunately for him, I had to go by Art to do it. That big guy had all he could do to handle me, but he did with the help of other coaches and some of my teammates. I swear I would've clawed that umpire to death if I ever got a hold of him that day. Naturally, I was thrown out of the game. We lost the game, and afterward, Mannigan was fuming. He said if I ever acted like that again, he'd personally beat me blue and send me back to Orange so fast I wouldn't have time to wipe my ass after a shit. I got the message.

After the game, we went out for a few drinks. I had to unwind. Mannigan was right. A good ballplayer doesn't blow his cool like that. If he becomes upset, he can't concentrate on what he's doing, and if he can't concentrate on baseball, he's no good to the team. We hit a few bars and landed in a little cafe that the Abilene players frequented. Why we were in the other teams' hangout, I don't know, but it was evident as soon as we walked in that, we should have never gone there. The first player to talk was the catcher. He was a big brawny type. The kind you envision as a high school wrestler, crew cut and all. He was a wise guy too.

"You put on some show for those people tonight. We should have a packed house tomorrow to see if you hit that umpire or not." It was a little funny, the way he said it, and I thought he was only joking around until he started to needle me. "You know that pitch caught the corner. You were so embarrassed that you choked in that situation you had to take it out on somebody." If Mannigan's words weren't fresh on my mind, I would've hit him right there, but I had to keep my cool. We finished our beers and quietly left as they laughed at our calm exit. Jerry started to say something, but I shut him up quickly. They must've thought we were pushovers because we didn't do anything regarding their comments. All my life, I had never been humiliated and made fun of like I was that night and not be able to do anything about it. I felt like a wild horse confined to a plow.

The next day, my picture was on the front page of the morning sports. It showed me with clenched fists trying to fly over Mannigan and get at the umpire. I was told later that that picture appeared in the Chicago papers; the reputation was building.

Paul was ready for the next game, and we needed a win like a fish needs water. We had gone downhill real fast from our quick start. If anybody could bring us around, it had to be Paul. The game began, and I came up in the first with Jerry on second from a double. They had a big crowd that night, about five thousand, and most of them either booed or cheered, very few were neutral. Naturally, the catcher had a few things to say about my manhood in the bar, and that didn't make it any easier. I wanted to rip one good, but instead, I hit a weak grounder too short.

On the way out to the field, I had to pass the umpire from the argument. He looked at me and laughed. "Is that all you could do?" I could've done more if Mannigan had let me, but I put my head down and ran out to take my position.

I took a lot of flack from the crowd too. There was one guy behind the plate who just wouldn't let up. I had him zeroed in too. Needless to say, things weren't too rosy at that time. I could've very easily hit the umpire and the catcher, then went into the stands after that fan, but common sense prevailed. If I was ever going to make it in the big leagues and fly that first-class plane, I'd have to get through this, and that's just what I intended to do.

This was another close game, and going into the ninth the score was tied just like it was the previous night, only this time at one. Paul had a two-hitter going, and I felt confident that if we got just one more run in the ninth, we'd wrap it up. Jerry got up with two outs and singled. The crowd once again cheered and booed as I stepped up. I had a lousy game, oh, for three, up to that point, I was ready to redeem myself. The catcher said, "Gonna' choke again?" I wanted him so badly, but a hit was more important.

I concentrated and bore down on the pitcher. The pitch was a fastball away, and I took it for a ball, but Jerry had broken with the pitch and was stealing second! The throw down there was close, and the umpire, that same umpire, called him out. From where I was standing, Jerry looked safe, and Jerry must've thought so too. He was too calm a guy to argue the way he did. Mannigan shot from the dugout and came running out like a wild buffalo. He tore up the place. He ripped his cap, kicked the dirt, then picked up second base, and threw it into center field. Of course, he got thumbed, but before he left the field, he got the last word in, "You're donkey shit. Next call we get that goes against us. I'll let Donato have you for supper, and I'll finish you for dessert." Now he was talking. A perfect suicide squeeze in the last inning gave us our seventh loss in a row.

The Sunday paper ran a picture of Mannigan with a second base in his arms next to the picture of me they ran Saturday with the caption, "Who Will It Be Today?" Before the game, you could see that Mannigan was still hot. The whole thing was starting to get to me too. I couldn't wait till we left Abilene, or I hit that catcher, the umpire, the guy in the stand, or we won a game. I'd take any of them. It's amazing how things can get to you when you're losing. If we had won seven straight, I doubt if any of those other things would've bothered me very much, but losing tends to get under your skin. It itches like a scratch that won't go away and the only cure is a win. We'd die for a win on that day.

In our pregame meeting, Mannigan told everybody to keep their cool. Play like it's the first game of the season. He told us not to be intimidated by the umpire, and to leave him to the coaching staff. After he dismissed everybody he took me aside. He put his arm around me and walked out on the field. "Jerry and Paul told me about your meeting with that catcher the other night. He's been on you the whole series hasn't he?" I nodded. "As a matter of fact, everybody has been on you this whole series. I'm proud of you for keeping your cool, but there's so much a man can take. We need somebody to lead us out of this streak. I think you can do it." He looked me in the eye. I read it perfectly. "Now go out and have a good game." I felt like a hundred-pound weight was off my back. I couldn't wait for the game to start.

It happened in the fourth inning. My first time at bat I had popped up. I heard a few laughs from the Abilene side, but I knew my time would come. They seemed like they were having a picnic with us. Well, it was about time the ants came. That pitch looked as big as a basketball. I swung, and I knew from the moment of contact that it was gone. The only question was how far was it going to go. Trotting down to first, I couldn't keep my eyes off the umpire. I was just waiting for him to do any little thing, and he'd get it. He didn't.

After I crossed the plate, the catcher made a remark. Truthfully, I can't even recall what it was. All I know is that I ran back and jumped him and squished his face in the dirt. Immediately both benches cleared, and we had an old-fashioned baseball fight. Everybody stood around and held each other until it got cleared up. After we all calmed down, I went to the stands and asked that fan if he wanted any. He shut up and backed up a few rows, then I took off my cap and tipped it to the fans. They ate it up and gave me a standing ovation. I was ejected from the game, but my little incident was the spark that we needed to get us back on track. No longer would we be intimidated by umpires, opposing players, or opposing fans.

We wound up in a very tight race with Abilene all summer long for first place. We would go up by two or three games, then they'd catch us, then we'd catch them and start all over.

The tight race and the exciting brand of ball we were playing had El Paso alive and buzzing. Jerry was the best player in the Texas League and every game he played brought more thrills than the next. He was leading the league in average, hits, doubles, and stolen bases. He was a shoo-in for league MVP. I wasn't doing too bad myself. I was leading the league in runs batted in and was second in homers, and Paul was the dominant pitcher in the league. He was sixteen and five going into the last week of play, and that's an unbelievable amount of wins for a minor league, considering we only played one hundred and twenty games.

All this notoriety made us celebrities, and we were the toast of the town. We did local promotions and public appearances and got paid pretty well for it. Women were all over us wherever we went. We were all getting it three and four times a week. It seemed like heaven.

I'd keep in touch with home by a letter and a phone call once a week. I'd send my clippings to Lucy, who was putting together a nice scrapbook, and my year was being followed very closely by the Orange Transcript. Everybody in Orange knew how many homers I had. Lucy told me I was the talk of the town wherever she went. It made me feel good to hear that.

The guys would write once in a while, but mostly I'd get a Sunday morning phone call. Johnny had broken off with Sasso and had gone off on his own, backed by Battita in Staten Island. Naturally, Tommy, Frankie, and Red all went with him. I don't know how it affected Sasso, but he'd have to be hurting to lose a guy with Johnny's loyalty and know-how. Tommy had managed to contact the crabs, Frankie and Red had gotten a steady job on the docks, thanks to a friend of Johnny, and Red had a baby but no wife to go with it.

All in all, it was an interesting first season and an interesting first time away from home. There was a time in the beginning when I got very homesick and called Lucy and practically cried to her. Everybody was so different from what I had been accustomed to. Nobody got dressed up sharp to go out; they all wore blue jeans and flannel shirts. Their hair was all long and not styled like mine was. I couldn't find good Italian food anywhere. How I missed my macaroni. Lucy was very understanding and told me to face up to it and try it out for a while, and things would work themselves out, and they did. I love my sister Lucy.

Going into the final week, we were in a tie for first place with Abilene on the last Monday of the schedule. They were coming to El Paso to finish the year with a four-game series on the weekend, but first, they had to play lowly Del Rio three games before they arrived. We were scheduled to play Amarillo, who was just as bad, so it looked like the tie would stand up for the weekend.

On Tuesday night, I received a call from Johnny. I got scared. I thought that something was wrong at home. I wish that it was. Johnny came right to the point. "You remember you kicked Sasso's ass, embarrassed him in front of everybody, and he swore he'd get you."

"Yeah, I remember."

"Well, he's got two goons out there now, scouting you out. They've been out there about a week. I don't know who they are, what they look like, or how they're planning to get you. I just found all this out, and I'm calling as quickly as I can. Be careful. Don't go anywhere without your buddies. We'll be out as soon as we can. We've got some business that needs attending to. If I find out anything else, I'll call as soon as I can."

For the first time in my life, I started to shake from fright. It's one thing to get in a fight in a bar or on a ballfield, but it's quite a different story when you have to fight off two professional hitmen. I was tough, but could I stand up to two pros?

FIFTY-SIX

I kept it a secret but I was a different person. Everywhere I went I was constantly on the lookout. I didn't know who they were or where they'd come from and that was the worst part of it, the waiting.

The week went good for the club. We won all four games from Amarillo, and we were a hot ballclub when Abilene came in for Friday night's game. It also meant that there were only three more days left for them to make their move. I was on pins and needles.

Paul started Friday's game before a packed house. Our stadium held about forty-five hundred, but that night there must've been about five thousand squeezed in. The game was over in the first two innings. Jerry hit a three-run homer in the first, and I hit one in the second. After two innings, we had eight runs and ten hits. The final was twelve to one.

After the game, we were all in a joyous mood. We were rolling, and nothing was going to stop us. My mind wandered away from my two preditors and was on other things like wine, women, and song. We stopped for a few at our regular places and finally landed in our favorite spot, a cozy little Mexican place that served great food. That night we were more interested in the booze rather than the food and parked ourselves at the bar.

It was about one o'clock when they came in, and I didn't even notice them. Jerry was blasted, and Paul could just about stand, and I was feeling no pain either. We were just about to order one more for the road when I felt a tap on my shoulder. He was solidly built, about five feet ten and two hundred, and had a crew cut. He resembled a Marine drill sergeant.

"Is this the guy?" he asked to a busty blond standing next to him. She nodded.

"What you talking about?" I didn't expect it to happen like this.

"Why'd you pinch her ass when she went by you?"

"I didn't even see her."

"Yes, he did. He pinched it and rubbed it." She was naturally lying. The first punch was the one that I felt. It was a left hook to my right side. I took all the air out of my lungs. The second punch was a right to my face and left me on straw legs. Another right to my side and a follow-up hook put me to the floor. The other guy held back Jerry and Paul and threw them aside. In their condition, they couldn't do much anyway. I was later told the guy gave me a kick goodbye and yelled at me to keep my hands off his wife. Nobody saw where they went. They seemed to disappear. I guess that's why they were pros.

I was unconscious for two days. My parents flew in the next day, and I was even given last rights by a priest. I had four broken ribs, two on each side, a punctured lung, eye damage, a fractured cheek, and a concussion that had me in a coma for two days. The following day, Johnny and the guys flew in with my sisters. It was a long vigil for all of them.

The papers had a ball with them. By this time, I was a local celebrity, and this barroom brawl over a mysterious blond made headlines for days. Chicago papers also played it up, calling me the minor league terror of the Texas League. I don't think any of them cared if I lived or died. To them what happened was news, that's all, and their job was to report it and sell papers.

The remaining three games were lost. The team just didn't have any spunk to them no matter how hard Mannigan tried to get them up. He even told them those guys were hired by the Abilene club to get me, but it didn't work. We finished second place.

That was the end of August. I stayed in the hospital till the end of September. My sisters and father flew back as soon as they knew I'd make it, they had jobs to go to, but my mother stayed the whole month, living with the Guzman's. I finally got my bowl of macaroni. Johnny and the guys also stayed for a few days after they knew I'd make it, and then they left too. Paul and Jerry felt so bad. They stayed with me the whole month when they could've been home. Those are dedicated friends. I didn't blame them. They had no idea what we were up against, even if they did, I doubt that it would've mattered. Mannigan was another one that came every day. He even went so far as to call the FBI into the case. That's how mad he was, but naturally, it wasn't a federal offense, so they could do nothing about it. No, the only guy that could do something about it was Johnny, and before he left, he swore to me that he'd get even. Somehow I knew that he would.

FIFTY-SIX

When I came home, I was treated like a king. Even my father gave me the royal treatment, and that was very rare. Anything I wanted, it seemed I could have, although there wasn't much they could give. Still, my mother made me all my favorite dishes, and my sisters were just great to me in every way.

It didn't take me long to get associated with Johnny and the guys again. I would only be home for five or six months, so getting a steady job was out of the question. Who'd hire somebody for only five months? Johnny had a smooth operation going. He opened a little social club, called it Club Alberona, and had the Italian old-timers out front while his operations went on in the back room. He took action on all the games and the horses.

Two nights a week, he ran card games that he'd take ten percent each hand. He also made connections with a guy in Port Newark to fence stolen property. He was starting to deal with some drugs too, against his own intuition, but the money was too good to pass up. All told he was doing close to two grand a week for himself, and that was after payoffs to the police and Batitta. Not bad for a twenty-three-year-old guy. He knew I was looking for something to do, so he offered me a job. No beating up guys or running drugs, just light stuff. I'd work the phones on the football games like I used to do for Sasso, moderate the card games, put bets in at the track, drive with him to Staten Island and the port, and in general just help out whenever needed. For that, he'd give me two hundred a week. Christ, that was more than my father made!

I accepted the offer on a few conditions. I didn't want to beat up anybody unless I had to, and I wanted nothing to do with drugs. The rest of the stuff to me are victimless crimes that I could live with, but not the other things. My second condition was that I first take a week's vacation. I had just been through a lot, and I needed a little time to get away and relax. Johnny assured me there'd be no rough stuff and suggested we all take a vacation. So off to the Carribean, we went, Johnny, Frankie, and myself. Johnny left the business to Tommy and Red. It was in very good hands.

We went to Club Paradise, one of those places where you throw away the clock, newspaper, TV, and radio and just have a good time for a week. For two days, it was kind of boring. During the day, there was a lot of activity, plenty of sun, a beach, and organized activities, but the night was the pits. After dinner, in which the whole club ate at one time, there was a cabaret show and then a nightclub. After two nights of that, I was ready to go back to Orange. There was just nothing happening that kept my interest, although the ladies were lovely. But on the third day, I received one of the surprises in my life in the day and met my angel at night.

The surprise of the day happened on the beach. The three of us were just relaxing and checking out the ladies. All of a sudden, Johnny turned and said, "We'll have no more trouble from Sasso." I had thought about him often and kept on thinking just how I'd get back at him, but Johnny beat me to it.

"What do you mean?"

"We got rid of him," he said as calm as an afternoon breeze.

"You killed him?" I couldn't believe what I was hearing.

Johnny said it straight out he had no apologies or remorse in his voice. "He had it coming. He was getting out of hand in his business with some of the things he was up to, and he had no permission from Batitta to do to you what he did. He's been missing, and nobody's even asking for him."

I didn't care if Sasso lived or died, but I did care that my friends were involved. "Did you do it personally?"

Johnny rolled on his stomach to let the sun hit his back. "Let's just say it's done, and I don't want to hear any more about it."

I understood and fully knew that Johnny "Midnight" and the rest of the guys had now gone the whole route. They were no longer on the road to trouble, they had arrived.

We were in the nightclub just playing the role that tough guys play. Standing there looking cool, all decked out, drink in the hand, just waiting to be gobbled up. Like I said there were a lot of ladies but nobody had caught my eye yet until that moment. At first, I thought she was French. She had a European look about her, and after all, the island was a French colony. She had a perfect shape for me. She was heavy up top and trimmed at the bottom. In the dimly lit club, I couldn't see her face that well, but from what I did see, she was very beautiful. I approached her and asked her if she'd like to dance. She politely turned me down. Very few girls had ever turned me down, and that was a blow to my ego, but that made it more of a challenge, and I love challenges.

"Maybe some other time," I said, and I walked away.

A couple of hours went by, and we crossed paths again. "Got your dancing shoes on now?" She smiled, held my hand, and led me to the dance floor. In the light, I could clearly see her face. She was absolutely the most beautiful woman that I had ever seen. Her skin was baby smooth and had a nice even tan. Her eyes were a deep dark chestnut brown. Her nose was sleek and slender. It fit her face perfectly. Her hair was light and flowed shoulder length, but it was when she smiled that I fell in love. That smile was the rainbow at the end of a storm, food to a starving man, an oasis in the desert. It was green grass and a warm summer breeze. It was pretty flowers and birds in flight.

When I first saw that smile and how it simply put a radiant flow through me, I knew right there that this woman had to be mine. I always felt that love at first sight was something you read about in books or see in the movies, but it happened to me. I knew right then and there that the good Lord put her on earth for me, and there wasn't anything that anybody could do to stop me from having her short of killing me.

We danced for a while, then went outside and walked the beach. I never dreamed or even thought about finding a girl before. I was notorious for being a first-class gigolo, but now I didn't even want to look at another. We talked the whole night away while sitting on the beach, watching the waves roll in. She had everything that could make me happy. First off, she was Italian; that was the most important. I had vowed to marry an Italian, and here she was. She loved baseball, and I hadn't even told her about my career yet.

When I did, she smiled and said, "That'll be fine with me." She was very family-oriented and a very independent woman, and that was something I admired. I never was one to boss or order anybody around and always felt that if you could do that to a woman, then she had no backbone. I wouldn't stand for anybody bossing me around, and I couldn't respect anyone who let me do it to them. Although I do feel that a man should have the right to make the important decisions in a relationship simply because he's a man and used to making big decisions. She agreed with me completely.

She was a nurse and was very intelligent. I was never as smart as Tommy, but I always did well, kept up on current events, and was generally on the ball about things. We'd communicate very well, in that respect. It's funny how I traveled five thousand miles to meet somebody who only lived twenty minutes from me. You could take every adjective in the English language that describes beautiful, multiply it a million times, and you'd still come up short for how I felt about Marie.

Needless to say, the rest of my vacation was pure pleasure. I was in love, and Marie felt the same way. Johnny and Frankie were happy for me and kidded me a lot about it. As close as I had come to dying only a month before, perhaps this was God's way of paying me back.

When we came home, I laid the law down with Johnny. "I'll work for you, but one night a week is for Marie, and when the weekend comes, I'll work the phones and take books, but then the rest is my time. I also don't want Marie to know anything we do here, okay?"

"Vinny, the fewer people that know what we do, the better off we are. I just want to be the best man when the wedding comes."

I couldn't wait to take Marie out and show her off. The first Saturday back, we went to New York for a show and dinner. I was all decked out in a suit, and she was beautiful in an evening dress. We made a very attractive couple. It was a beautiful evening, and although I desired her like no other woman before or since I didn't want to force myself on her, nature would take its course.

I had Marie over for Sunday dinner, and she fit in with my family like a foot in a shoe. My sisters took a quick liking to her, and my mother simply loved it when she got up, cleaned off the dishes, took them into the kitchen, and started washing.

For five months, I was walking on a cloud. I mean I had it all going for me. Marie and I were in love, sex had entered the relationship, and it was beautiful. I was making good money and not working for it, and I had received notice that I was skipping Class C ball and was to report to the Class B team at the end of February. If things went right, and there was no reason to believe that they wouldn't, I'd be in the big leagues very soon.

Then the blackest day of my life came, and my life hasn't been the same since. It happened about a week before I was to go out for spring training. It was a Sunday night. Marie had come over and spent the day and had gone, and I was getting ready to go to bed when I got a call. It was Marie's sister telling me that Marie had gotten into a very bad accident, and it didn't look very good.

I rushed across the hall and got Frankie to drive me to the hospital. All I kept saying on the way down was for God to please keep her alive.

She had had emergency surgery, but it didn't look good at all. Her insides were all busted up, internal bleeding couldn't be stopped, and she suffered from shock and trauma. When I got to the hospital, the whole family was there, and they were all teary-eyed. I hugged her mother and started to cry myself. I asked if I could see Marie. I was shaking like a leaf in the wind.

I walked into her room, and she had tubes and needles sticking all over her body. My beautiful angel was dying, and we all knew it. She was semiconscious but forced a smile. I'd given my life right there for hers if I could. She was so good, so sweet, so angelic. I was the one who played with the devil. It should've been me in that bed, not her.

She reached for my hand and spoke very softly. I don't talk about this much, but I went this far in the story so I should tell it all. She whispered to me that she had seen God, and he was beautiful, and that she wasn't afraid to die. She said he kept her alive so we could be together one more time. She said she'd always watch over me and that we'd be together again when it was my time. I looked at her, she smiled back, then she died. I held her hand and said a silent prayer. I swore then that I'll love her until the day I die, and I haven't doubted myself on that at all since that day.

I've been with hundreds of women since, and I've had a lot of good times, but I'll always love Marie. In a sense, I've been married to her for all these years. Not a single day goes by when I don't think about her or talk to her. I love her as much this day as the day she died. I've had a lot of relationships since, after all, I'm only human, but every woman knew from the very beginning that my love was for someone else. I'll die a bachelor by my own choice, and if there's any justice in this world, I'll have my Marie in another time and another place.

We didn't get home until the next morning. It was a long ride back. Frankie did his best to console me, but there wasn't much he could say. Facing it would have to come from within. I was bitter with God for taking her yet thankful He let her live long enough so we could be together one more time. I knew she was with him and was thankful for that too. I just wondered why it all happened.

The house was chaotic. My mother and older sisters ran off to church to pray. Lucy cried like a baby in my arms. I was all cried out. I turned and faced my father, even though he had tears in his eyes. He came over and embraced me, and I found more tears to let go. I never felt close to my father until that day. If anything good came from this, I knew how much my family and friends loved me. My family was very supportive, and my friends never left my side.

I didn't cry anymore after that day, not even at the funeral. I had a long talk with Father Virgilio, and he assured me that we shouldn't feel sorry for Marie. That in her death, she was reborn with the Lord. She had told me so. The people to pray for were her family and friends who would have to live the rest of their lives without her. Father Virgilio always made sense. I felt better after that and a lot closer to God. I had lost my bitterness and dedicated the upcoming spring training to Marie. With her help from heaven and my ability, I was going to make the big club that spring, at least I'd give it all I had.

The Big Leagues

I went to camp that spring as confident and positive as I've ever been in anything I've ever done in my life. It's very rare when any player can jump three levels of minor league ball and go right to the big leagues, but that was my goal if anybody had the determination I did, and if anybody was going to do it, I was.

From my very first swing on the first day of camp, I had it. In all my seventeen years of playing ball, I never had a sweeter swing than I did that spring. My first time in the cage that spring I had twelve swings and made solid contact twelve times. Think about that. I hadn't seen a pitch in six months, and yet I hit every ball on the nose. I didn't miss a pitch or even a foul one-off. From the first day, the reporters were all talking about Vince Donato.

I played like a player possessed. In all our drills, I was always first. In batting practice, I always stayed for more. When the intra-squad games began, I played as if each pitch were the last pitch in the last inning of the seventh game of the World Series. I didn't even go out. I stayed in my room and practiced my swing, or I talked baseball with the veterans in camp.

I was placed on the class B team whose hometown was right there in Sarasota. Paul and Jerry were also elevated to that team. Even then I could see that the three of us were just as good—if not, better—than any player on that roster, and I felt that it was just a matter of time before we'd all be with the A team and then with the White Sox. It was just a matter of time.

For the first week, we all practiced together, the White Sox, class A and B teams, and the more I saw of the White Sox, the more I started to realize that I really could make that big jump, their players were shit. Their starters were all-seasoned veterans well into their thirties and losing their skills, and their reserves were nothing more than journeymen ballplayers. Management said that they were looking for new faces to rebuild with a youth movement. Well, you don't rebuild with journeymen outfielders! I truly believed I had a good shot at it.

The week before the exhibition season started we had four intrasquad games. I got to hit against class-A pitching twice and major-league pitching twice. I tore it up. Like I said before, I had the best swing that I ever had, but I wasn't the only one in camp making a name for himself. Jerry was doing it all by natural ability; where I was pooped at the end of the day from concentrating and giving my all, Jerry was ready to go again. He was the greatest natural athlete on this side of Red that I ever met. I figured if they did take a player from our club to go to the big club, it very well could've been Jerry. I didn't hold it against him, he was my friend, and I would've been happy for him, but they weren't going to take him before giving me a long hard look. I'd make sure of that.

The night before the first exhibition game Byron Martin, who was the manager of the White Sox at the time, came into our room. We were scheduled to play against Boston's B team the next day while the big club traveled to Vero Beach to play the Dodgers. Martin talked in a high-pitched voice like his pants were on too tight. He surprised the shit out of Jerry and me. "I want you two to come with the big club tomorrow. You're showing me a lot of good stuff here. It's either for real, or you'll level off in a week or so, either way, it's worth it to me to see if you can make the club. If it's real, you'll get your shot." Jerry and I were ecstatic. Paul, although a little upset, was just as happy for us. We all knew that a pitcher takes more time to develop and that Paul would soon get his chance, but we were a little sad for him. After all, we all had the same goal.

I had a very good night's sleep. I wasn't nervous at all about facing big league pitching, that's how confident I was, besides, I knew that Marie was up there, looking after me, and she'd see to it that I'd do just fine. Jerry was quite different. He was so nervous that he got up and shit about six times before he finally went to sleep.

The game was just an exhibition game, but I was never into a game more. Jerry and I sat at the end of the bench and watched every play with the knowledge that we could be in there for the next pitch. When I was called I was going to be ready, I was going to have the feel of the game in me. An exhibition game or a real game still has to be played. There still are twenty-seven outs that have to be made, and there still has to be a winner and a loser, and I wanted that game pumping in my veins when Martin would summon me to go in.

My time came in the bottom of the eighth. Jerry and I were put in the field, he in center and me in left. It was a one, two, three inning with Jerry catching the last out on a routine pop. Jerry led off the top of the ninth by striking out. He came back to the dugout with a long face. He sat down and turned to me, saying, "Fuckin' ball broke two feet. Did I come close to it?" He missed it by about six inches. That's a lot to miss a ball by. If Jerry missed it by that much, how much would I miss it by? That pitcher was only a class-A pitcher, how good was a major league curve? I started to get some doubts, but I still was full of confidence. When my turn came, I'd still be ready, doubts or no doubts.

The score was tied so we came up again in the top of the tenth. I was scheduled to hit third in the inning. The first two batters made out, and I came up for the first time in a big league game. I remember looking in the dugout and seeing Jerry clenching his fist as if to say you can do it. The first pitch was a fastball on the inside part of the plate, and with a groove-like swing, I let loose and lined it down the leftfield line for a double. I ran so fast that I went into second base standing, way ahead of the throw. We lost the game, but I had my victory. I was off and running, and nobody was going to catch me.

The next day was a carbon copy of the first game. Jerry and I went in, in the late innings, and we each got one at bat. Jerry hit the ball this time; it was a confidence builder for him. All night long, he talked about how much that ball broke down and away from him, and he wondered if he shouldn't think about a year in B-ball for a little more seasoning. He flew out, but he had a real good swing in doing it, and he did hit the ball hard. My at bat was easy. After the previous game's hit, I felt I could've hit Sandy Koufax. The pitcher was a major leaguer, not a class A player.

Petie Mailot was a six-year veteran righthander with the Minnesota Twins and was coming off a very good year. He started me off with a fastball that was a little inside. That pitch set up the curve ball that was to follow. It came in high and hard, but I hung in there. I didn't bail out when I saw it coming toward my head. I swung as the ball broke down and away and made perfect contact. It almost took Mailot's cap off as it whizzed by his head and out into centerfield for a single. I was two for two.

The third game went the same way with the same results. Jerry hit the ball hard, a line drive right to the third baseman. He was swinging the bat better each day, and it was only a matter of time before he'd break out and go on a rampage. I singled sharply between short and third, my third straight hit. That night, Martin came to our room again. He told us that he liked what he saw of us, that in all probability, both backup positions for outfield spots would be open, and that we were two of six players who would be tried for those spots. I knew that Jerry and I were better than the two guys they had the year before and the two class A players hadn't shown anything yet. The jobs were there for Jerry and me, and all we had to do was take them.

The next day, Jerry and I got our first start. Jerry didn't waste any time making things happen as he lined a single to left field, stole second, then third, and then came home on an infield out. If Jerry wasn't as fast as he was, he'd be half the player, but with that speed of his, he was the most exciting player in camp. I was up twice before Martin took me out, but I did my damage too. I singled and then hit my first homer, a long drive well over four hundred feet to the power alley in left center. I was now five for five and showed no signs of slowing down.

After the game, a few of the beat writers came around to introduce the spring phenom to the Chicago fans. They each asked the obvious questions, are you ready for big league pitching, did you expect to be playing with the big club, are you awed by the majors, and so on. I answered each one as straight as I knew how. I told them that I felt both Jerry and I were ready for the big leagues and neither one of us was reluctant to take our cuts at a major league fastball. If the ball is over the plate then it's a hittable pitch, and it doesn't matter who put it over the plate, a minor or major leaguer. I even closed by telling them that I fully expected to see them in Chicago on opening day.

I won't bore you with details of every game, even though I can tell you almost to a pitch what happened. I believe the good players, the real hard-nosed players that love the game, can do that; I can remember back seventeen years ago to a certain pitch in a certain ball game and so can a lot of others. We're the true ballplayers. But to make it short, going into the last week of camp it certainly appeared that I had it made. I was the star of the camp, no doubt about it. I batted an even five hundred after forty-four at bats and led the team in hits, homers, runs batted in, doubles, and slugging. It was my camp, I owned it.

Jerry was a glimmering star. He'd do well for two games, then he'd botch up for a game or two. Still, that last reserve spot came down to him, and one of the guys who had played there the year before. It seemed like it was Jerry's potential against the other guy's experience, and if that was the case, then Jerry had it won hands down. Then came the day that Jerry will never forget, and we'll never know who Martin would've taken because while running after a routine flyball Jerry fell in a drainage hole and broke his ankle in two places.

It was a very depressing day for all of us. Paul and I reached Jerry in the hospital as soon as we could, and he was full of tears. The doctor told him he might never again walk right due to the severity of the breaks. It was a telling blow. He wanted to take an overdose of pills and kill himself. If he couldn't even walk right how, could he run and play baseball?

Jerry Alexander could've walked into the Hall of Fame. He had all the tools that the great ones have, but that broken ankle did indeed ruin his career. He made it back a few years later, through sheer determination, and he was very thankful that Paul and I didn't let him take an overdose of sleeping pills, but he no longer was the gazelle that everyone remembered. His speed was more like that of a lumbering catcher. He was taken out of center field and moved to other outfield positions, and first base, where his lack of speed wasn't a liability to the ballclub. Because he favored his ankle so much while running, he eventually hurt his knee and later on his ankle and knee; both became arthritic way before their time. His batting eye was still as keen as an owl's, but he had no power generated from his legs. He hurt every time he strode into a pitch. He's played throughout his career as a shell of what he could've been, and that was one of the greatest of all time.

I hit Chicago by storm. I had made it. I had done what I set out to do and what I swore to Marie that I would do. I was as proud as a peacock. I was the fourth outfielder, not a starter, but I knew sooner or later that my time would come. I hoped it was sooner than later.

Orange was just as proud. The mayor sent me a telegram, and the grammar school I went to sent me one signed by all the students. The guys called and said they'd fly out for opening day, and even my father, who knew nothing about baseball, said he'd fly out with them. It was a happy time in my life. I was a big-league ballplayer, and I loved every second of it.

I was awed by the size of the crowd on opening day. Comiskey Park is a great big ballpark, and when it's filled with forty-four thousand people, it can tend to excite a young ballplayer on his initial opening day.

I had gotten a lot of ink by the press all during spring training, mainly for two reasons. The first was because I deserved it. After all, I was the star of that camp. The second was because I always had something to say to them. Whether I had a good day or a bad one, I always answered their questions as directly and honestly as I could. Too many players get angry with the press and curse at them and shoo them aside like some fly that's bothering them, not me. The press is a powerful thing to have in your corner; it can make you or break you. I found that the more honest you are with them and cooperative, the better off for all involved. That's a creed I've lived with, and maybe that's one of the reasons for my popularity.

So because of all the favorable press I received, I just wasn't another name when I was introduced to the crowd on opening day. I was a player that a lot of the fans had read about and had come to recognize. I was the future of the Chicago White Sox, and they liked what they saw. I was surprised at the hand I received. Forever the showman, I tipped my cap and bowed to the crowd.

I didn't play that day or the next. As a matter of fact, I didn't play at all the first two weeks of the season. I didn't know what to make of it. I left Florida the hottest hitter on the club, so why was I sitting on the bench while we were losing eight of our first ten games? What was Martin up to? Where was the youth movement he was talking about? When was I going to get my chance?

After twelve games, I finally got my first start. We were playing in Cleveland, and it had to be one of the coldest nights I could ever recall. When the wind comes in off Lake Erie, it drops the temperature way down, and that night, it was about thirty-five, but I didn't even feel it. I had my first start, and I was positive I was going to do something to help the club get on the winning track.

I started in left field for "Hungry" Janks, who said his feet were too cold to play. This was the toughest guy in the league? I couldn't believe it. My first time up in the major leagues, I struck out. When I came back to the dugout, they all consoled me, except one guy, Hungry. "The least you could've done is fouled one off."

I didn't need that from him, not at that time. I felt dejected and hurt that I didn't even make contact in three swings, and I didn't need his needling. I told him to shove it, that if he wasn't such a baby and had cold feet, he'd be in there playing instead of sitting in the warm dugout.

He took it with a big laugh, then got serious. "If you ever talk to me that way again, I'll gobble up your ears."

A lot of guys were afraid of Hungry due mainly to his reputation, but I wasn't one of them. How could a thirty-seven-year-old timer handle a young guy like me? I started to approach him, but it was quickly broken up before it really amounted to anything, and then it was time to take the field again. When I returned after the half-inning, I sat at one end of the dugout, and Hungry sat at the other. Our paths never crossed again that night.

I did get my first hit, a sharp single to the left, but for the night, I was one for four, and come the next day, I found myself on the bench again as Hungry's feet warmed up.

Two more weeks, eleven games, went by, and I didn't get in any of them. For the whole month of April, I had played in just that one game. I was going crazy. I had to play. I was like a wild mustang that suddenly finds himself fenced in and can't do anything to free himself. I couldn't stand the inactivity, and I decided to go see Martin.

He had had a one-hundred-degree change from the man he was in camp. In camp, he was always smiling, always ready to give a helping hand or a word of advice to a younger player. He was sincere. A very kind man. He was the kind of man I would want to have as my first manager. He seemed to have the paternal instincts that Art Mannigan had, and I liked that. But now during the season, all he did was pal around with the other coaches and lock himself in his office. He played all his veterans every day, and he rarely talked to the younger players. He was moody and at times would yell at the writers, then turn around and be as humble as a priest. Bryon Martin was one hell of a strange man.

I asked him if I could talk to him privately, man to man. He agreed, and we went into his office. I told him how I felt, how I was going crazy from the inactivity. I told him I realized my role in the club was a utility player, but even utility players play once or twice a week. He told me he wanted to get off to a fast start and that was why he was playing the players he knew he could rely on. He told me that sitting on the bench was part of my education, to see how big leaguers play the game, and it would make me want it more and play better when my chance came, and my chance would come soon if I was just patient and waited. I thought it was a line of shit, but I didn't tell him so. I didn't want to make waves, so I thanked him and walked out, not feeling any better about the situation than when I walked in.

And then there was Hungry. Ever since spring training, he didn't take a liking to me. I couldn't figure out why. He never talked to me.

In our outfield drills, he always had a negative statement to say about me. The thing in Cleveland didn't help matters any either. It was better to have Hungry with you than against you because when he was on you, it made things tough. He'd always have something to say about people on the bench not earning their pay. He constantly got on the three rookies on the club, me more so than the other two. Martin was making it tough, and Hungry was making it tougher.

Then one day, it all came to a head as I knew it would sooner or later. An article came out in the *Sun-Times* by Brian Corcoran, who happened to become a good friend of mine, titled "Where's the Spring Phenom?" The article severely criticized Martin's policy of playing his *archaic* outfield while letting the phenom of spring training rot away on the bench. The club's fast start was down to a backward run, being in last place, and what harm could it do to play some new faces? The article closed by saying, "Donato should play for Hungry at least three times a week to rest the aging veteran before the hot summer days come along."

When Martin read the story, he immediately called me into his office. He asked me if I put Brian up to it. I saw he was mad and he was looking for an argument. I told him I knew nothing about it, that I had read the article, but I had suggested nothing to Brian. Martin then leaned back in his chair and put on a shit-eatin' grin, "It's all part of the game, son, that's why I love it so much. Your time will come. Now get the hell out of here." The guy changed from night to day. I swear that guy was ready for the looney tunes.

When I walked back into the clubhouse, I walked into a confrontation between Hungry and Brian. Hungry had Brian pinned to a wall with one hand wrapped around his neck, and he was flexing his bicep with his other arm in Brian's face. It was a classic case of a bigger guy picking on a smaller guy. "Archaic, are these the arms of an archaic player?"

Then he went eye to eye with Brian and growled at him, "I haven't had an ear in a long time and yours looks pretty good to me. If I read any more shit about archaic outfielders, I'll rip one off, spread it with butter, and have it with my morning coffee, do I make myself clear?"

I was surprised nobody interceded. They were probably all afraid to, but I had more than I could stand. I spoke up and told Hungry to leave Brian alone. "Why don't you pick on somebody more your size, who's not afraid to fight back?"

"Like you?" he growled.

I spread my arms open and motioned him to come and get it. Like a saloon when the gunslinger comes in to meet the sheriff, the clubhouse parted and left Hungry and me for centerstage. They all knew this was bound to happen, and now they were going to see it firsthand. I picked up a wet towel and whipped it at him, calling him an archaic outfielder with every lash. He rushed me, and I wrapped the towel around his head and dragged him down to the floor. I got one good punch in before it was broken up, and I saw the white towel turn red from blood. Hungry came out of it with a bloody nose, and we were quickly ushered in to see Martin.

Martin reinforced my opinion of him even more. He balled out Hungry for picking on a rookie then he balled me out for fighting back. What was I supposed to do, stand there and let him hit me? He screamed at us for about ten minutes then threw us out of his office. He never asked for an explanation or never gave either one of us a chance to talk. I don't know how he ever became a manager.

When we left Martin's office, Hungry immediately made threats to the effect that he'd get even for his bloody nose and that he'd see to it that I'd get mine. I told him I couldn't wait, and the next time we went at it, I'd make sure he didn't get away with just a bloody nose. The fight split the team. The older players quite naturally sided with Hungry, calling me a young and restless troublemaker. The younger players rallied around me, seeing me as one who stood up and wouldn't back down from all the bullshit that some of the older players threw around.

It didn't take me more than a month to make the headlines. What happened in the clubhouse was as big a scoop as Brian had ever gotten in his journalistic career. A big brawl between two popular players, and he was right in the middle of it. It was a dream come true for him. I thought he wrote a very fair and accurate account of what happened. He not only labeled Hungry old and archaic but also went as far as to say he was an old and archaic beaten bully, who was put in his place by a rookie who had the courage to stand up for what was right and what was an injustice being done to a reporter who was only doing his job.

The next day, a huge crowd turned out for our game. Before the game, I did my first live TV interview, and it was very exciting for me. I was myself, that is to say, I gave direct answers to the questions that they asked. I told the reporter that Hungry was embarrassing a man he obviously knew wasn't going to fight back, and I did the fighting for Brian. I told him that Hungry and I weren't talking, never did, and if Hungry wanted to even the score, I'd be available anytime. Of course, I'd rather be friends, but Hungry wasn't the type to forgive and forget, so it would have to be the way he wanted it. My interview was a hit. From it, the fans recognized me as a no-nonsense guy, a man of action, one who stood up for what he believed in and acted rather than relying on threats. I got warm ovations from the fans whenever I was on the field; however, I wasn't on the field to play that day either.

Late that night, I got a call from Johnny. He wanted to know why my name wasn't in the boxscores and why I hadn't been playing. He also asked if I gave Hungry a good beating. Apparently, news of the fight reached back home. I told him that I couldn't understand Martin, that he was a weird guy. I told Johnny about my talk with him and that I was going crazy sitting on the bench. Hungry didn't scare me. I told Johnny I could take him with no problems, but the fact that he was playing and off to a terrible start while I was just rotting away on the bench bothered me.

Johnny was sympathetic. "You want me to take care of things?" I didn't know exactly what he meant. I knew he had become very influential, but could he persuade Martin to sit Hungry and play me instead? I questioned him on it. "Look, I'll get rid of Janks so you can play and show Martin what you're made of."

I asked him if he intended to kill Hungry, not forgetting what he did to Sasso. "No, what do you think we go around killing every guy that bothers one of our people? I'll give him the same treatment that Sasso gave you in El Paso by the same crew. It'll lay him up for a few months and give you an opportunity to play. You just give me the word, and it'll be done." I knew it was wrong, but sitting on the bench was making me go out of my mind. I had to play.

Besides, Hungry deserved it, if anybody needed that kind of going over he did. I gave Johnny the go-ahead.

About a week later, we were in Oakland. I hadn't played at all in that time span, and I kept on wondering when Johnny would strike. It happened late on a Friday night in the hotel lounge. It seemed that a blond had accused Hungry of pinching her ass. Her husband, the short stocky guy who had given me the beating of my life, proceeded to hit Hungry in his kneecap with a beer bottle, then broke the bottle against Hungry's jaw. The results were astounding. Hungry Janks suffered a broken kneecap and a jaw that was broken in two places while requiring oral surgery as well. He'd be out of action for at least three months and maybe longer. It was finally my time.

I started in left field the next day and got two hits. On Sunday, I got two more. We then traveled to Anaheim to play the Angels, and I hit my first homer. It was a shot to the left that just about cleared the fence. I was feeling more at ease and getting into it. Major league ball was the ultimate high, and I was fixed on it.

We finished that road trip on the upswing and had finally started to play some good ball. We won every series, taking two of three in Oakland, Anaheim, and Kansas City and sweeping three in Milwaukee. We were coming home a hot club, but we were still in last place.

Brian wrote a nice article about how our winning streak just happened to occur when I was inserted in the lineup after Hungry's barroom mishap. I wasn't setting the league on fire, but for a rookie, I was holding my own.

When the Eastern clubs came into Chicago, we showed them we weren't the last place club that they thought we were. We continued our hot ways by winning the series against Boston, New York, and Baltimore, taking two out of three against all of them. We left Chicago to go East, the hottest team in baseball, winning fifteen of our last twenty-one. The Eastern swing would tell if we would stay that hot or be cooled off. I couldn't wait to get back home and play in front of my people.

I had had a real good homestand. A couple of homers, a game-winning hit in the ninth to beat the Red Sox, and a game-saving catch in the ninth to beat the Orioles, but I picked the wrong time to go into a slump. I've always said that I'm one of the best streak hitters to have ever played this game. When I'm going good, I can carry a team for weeks, but when I'm bad, I'm pure shit and couldn't carry a little league team for a night. I hit my first major league slump in Washington. I had two hits in the two games and wasn't swinging the bat real good at all. As a matter of fact, both those hits were bloop flies that landed in the back of the infielders and in front of the outfielders. I hadn't hit a ball solid in four or five games, and it was starting to worry me. We went to Baltimore, and it continued. I didn't have a hit in three games there, going, oh for eleven, making my slump two for eighteen. Going to New York, I had hoped I'd be a hot hitter, but it didn't work out that way.

Yankee Stadium was all I thought it would be. It could gobble up a young rookie the first time he plays there. Standing on the dugout steps and looking into that outfield, I could just see DiMaggio, Ruth, and Gehrig running around out there.

I thought to myself, *Am I that good to play on the same field that those guys played on?* I thought I could be, at least I had enough confidence in myself to think I could, and after looking around one more time, I ran out to the outfield to shag some flies.

That whole weekend series was played with the intensity that baseball was meant to be played. It had everything in it and in all my years, I've never played in a more emotional or exciting series than that one.

It started on a Friday night in front of forty-five thousand. That weekend was a giveaway weekend, meaning every day the Yankee organization was giving away something to the fans. They always had these giveaway games. When the poorer teams came in to entice the fans to come out to the ballpark, you never had to give the fans anything to watch the better teams. I had about fifty people in the stands that night, and if ever I wanted to break out of a slump, that was the night.

The Yankees were a determined ballclub. I could sense that determination as soon as they took the field for batting practice. We had done a number on them the weekend before in Chicago, winning two of three easily, and that had to leave a bad taste in their mouths. I'm sure it didn't hurt their cause any when a few statements were made as to how much we enjoyed beating them sort of paying them back for all the times, they feasted on the White Sox in their glory years. So when batting practice came, a time to kid around and pass the bull with the other players, the Yankees were silent, giving cold looks instead of friendly hellos. It'd be a lot different that weekend, that much I could tell then.

Just how different it would be was shown on the game's first pitch. Our lead-off man was Frank Quinn, a nice guy and a good little second baseman. Frank was decked by a high hard one that went right under his chin. Martin jumped off the bench and ran up to the edge of the dugout and yelled out to the Yankee pitcher that he'd get one in the ear for that pitch. The rest of our bench was up too, all shouting at George Lee, the Yankee pitcher. Lee was himself a nice guy and wasn't known as a pitcher who threw at anybody, but that one was at Frank's head, no doubt about it. We got the message, the Yankees came to play.

When Lee came up to bat in the third, these were the days before the designated hitter, our pitcher returned the compliment. This time it was the Yankee bench that was up and yelling the threats. The pot had just started to simmer, in the fifth, it started to boil. Iola Blue, the Yankee third baseman, was on first. A ball was hit to Quinn at second, and he turned to start the double play. Blue slid, if you want to call it that. It was more like a body block, five feet away from second to take out our shortstop, and I mean he took him out. Quinn ran over and said a few words to Blue who justified his slide by saying he was just trying to break up the double play.

Martin came running out from the dugout with fire in his eyes. He wanted Blue thrown out of the game for purposely running down our shortstop. Sam Weber, the Yankee manager, came running out because the umpire had ruled that Blue had indeed gone out of his way to break up the double play and had awarded an automatic double play to us. Weber and Martin got into it, jawing face to face in front of forty-five thousand screaming fans who cherished every moment.

When we returned to the dugout at the half-inning Martin was still hot. He said he'd give a hundred dollars to anybody who would take Blue out of the ballgame. God, it was intense in that dugout. Unfortunately, we couldn't get to Blue or Lee. They beat us three to one, but after the game, insults were flying everywhere, in both clubhouses.

Martin told the press that his team wouldn't be intimidated by those "damn Yankees," and he'd do the things a manager must do to protect his players. When quizzed further as to what those things were, Martin would only say that if Weber kept playing ball like that the New York fans would see soon enough how the White Sox players could protect each other. Sam Weber, in the Yankee clubhouse, was just about saying the same things, insinuating we were crying spilled milk because we hadn't won as easy as the week before and backing up George Lee's opening pitch by saying that "George Lee is as wholesome as apple pie and it's against his principles to throw a baseball toward a man's head." We all knew that Martin was throwing more bullshit than any politician ever did at campaign time.

Lee had me in his back pocket. I didn't get the ball out of the infield in four at bats and my slump is now two far twenty-two. After the game, my family and friends went out to eat, but I wasn't very good company. I was too worried about my slump to have any fun, so I went back to the hotel early.

Saturday was cap day, and a crowd of fifty-five thousand showed up. A fight almost started before the game between Blue and Martin over Blue's slide. If Chico Torres, our catcher, wasn't around to yank Martin away, I think he might've picked up a bat and clubbed Blue. We lost our starting shortstop for about two weeks with a twisted knee because of that slide, and Martin upped the bounty on Blue to two-fifty.

The game was another close one. It was free of any controversial plays until the sixth. Torres was on first. Chico was a big, strong, burly catcher, but he could run pretty well for his size. The score was tied at two, and Chico figured he'd start some action of his own, so he took off and tried to steal second. The throw was there in plenty of time, but when Chico slid, he kicked the ball out of the shortstop's glove. Weber came running out from the dugout, wanting Chico declared out for offensive interference. He put on a good show, kicking dirt, throwing his cap, and then going face-to-face with the umpire before getting thumbed out of the game.

Two innings later, Tommy Lakes of the Yankees went sliding into second, and he did the same thing Chico did, Kicking the ball out of Quinn's glove, only his was very obvious where Chico's was a more professional kick if you know what I mean. The umpire called Lakes safe, and it was Martin's turn to put on a show. He ranted and raved just like Weber did, and he even picked up second base and threw it into the outfield, and just like Weber Martin got the thumb too. So both managers were thrown out of the game, but they continued managing from inside the clubhouses.

Chico was up again in the ninth and was decked by one right under his chin. He got up and started to go toward the mound but was restrained by the umpire, who had his hands filled. Both benches were at the top of the dugouts ready to run out to do battle, and at that point, the pot was boiling. You'd have to figure that I'd be the first one out there, throwing punches and taking on anybody, but I was very worried about my slump, that was utmost on my mind. I was hitless in three trips, and I was then two for twenty-five, fighting was the last thing in my mind.

We eventually lost the game in extra innings, three-two. Martin closed the doors to the press and had a hard meeting with us. He said he didn't like getting pushed around by those "damn Yankees," and if the umpires weren't going to do anything about the beanballs and dirty play, then we'd have to do it ourselves. He ordered Joe Perch, Sunday's pitcher, to throw at the first Yankee that came up, and if Joe didn't, he'd find himself right back in the minors. He also put a price tag on George Lee of two-fifty. It seemed that George didn't like the accusations that Martin had put on him and called Martin a manager "who is sailing a sinking ship," saying "he wouldn't last the year at his position." Martin knew fully well that his orders would start the brawl that had been brewing for two days, but I got to give him his credit. He backed us up to the hilt and wouldn't let us take anymore. If we were going down at least, we'd be going down fighting.

Sunday's bat day crowd was well over sixty thousand, and every one of them knew that the pot was just about ready to boil over. That's all that was in the papers. Before the game, the umpires came into our clubhouse and warned us, the players, and Martin in particular, to cut out the shit, play good clean baseball, or suffer the consequences. Martin's response was for the umpires to tell that to "prickface Weber," then when they left he once again told Perch to throw at the first batter. After he told Joe to do that, that's when I got my mind in the right frame of mind for what was to come.

Perch's first pitch was right at Tommy Lakes' head. Lakes went down, the Yankees came running out, we came running out, and I was in my first baseball brawl. It was crazy. Some guys were going crazy. Chico must've wanted that two-fifty because he was tearing up Iola Blue. Martin and Weber were also pounding each other as were Tommy Lakes and Joe Perch.

As far as baseball brawls go, this one was one of the worst I, and even some of the old timers, had ever seen. I found myself arm and arm with George Lee. I wanted a piece of Blue because of that slide, and I would've even taken a piece of Lakes, but George Lee looked to me to have the face of a baby. I didn't want him. I figured I'd wait around until somebody hit me, or Blue or Lakes were free. But then George kept pushing and grabbing me and telling me to keep out of it. That was my intention, but I didn't need him to keep on yanking at me and shoving me away from the action. He had pushed me clear away from the whole scene. We stood out from the crowd, then I remembered the $250 bonus for taking on Lee.

I told him to keep his hands off me and stop shoving me around. He didn't, so I hit him, in clear view of sixty-five thousand fans. We weren't in that wild brawl, where you couldn't tell who was who; we were away from it all, and it made my punch more dramatic.

George dropped to one knee, holding a bloody nose. I went a little crazy and ran back into the crowd. The main fights between Chico and Blue, Martin and Weber, and Lakes and Perch had all just about been broken up when I came running in like a madman, leaped over two players, and wrestled Iola Blue down to the ground. It started everything up all over again. It took about a half hour for some kind of peaceful semblance to settle in over Yankee Stadium, when it did it seemed like the quiet after a storm.

As I came back to the dugout I spotted Johnny and the guys. They rose and gave me an ovation. Johnny yelled, "We were almost ready to join you. It would've been like old times!"

I had no doubt that they almost were ready to hop over the fence and run out and hit somebody. I'd put nothing past them.

We played a lousy game. Billy Daniels, who had replaced Perch, who was thrown out, only lasted two innings. They got four runs off him and four more off our relief pitchers. Their pitcher, Steve Palzak, was in total control. Palzak was pitching a three-hit shutout going into the ninth. He hadn't even come close to walking a man and he had seven strikeouts, and yes, my slump had continued.

I was up in the ninth, and the game was all over by then, but I was still looking for that one hit to get me back on track. Palzak quickly got two strikes on me then all hell broke loose one more time.

I should tell you about what ballplayers call the brushback pitch. When you want to deliver a message to a player or another team, a message saying don't mess with me because I'll take you any time, you throw one up and in, under a man's chin. Lee did it to Frank Quinn and Joe Perch did it to Lakes. You give the batter a fair chance to back off and get down. You don't throw to hit him. You throw to brush him back, get him dirty. The brushback pitch has been a part of baseball since the game was invented and we all know and recognize it.

Now when a team wants a guy, really wants to hit him, they throw behind him. A batter's natural reaction when a ball is coming toward his head is to fall back, if the ball is behind him chances are he'll fall right into it. It's a killer pitch. You might as well take a tire iron and bash a guy's head in with it because if a fastball ever lands flush on a batter's head it's all over, there's very little difference between the two.

Palzak's next pitch was thrown right behind my head, a high hard one true to form. I fell right into it, going with my natural reactions to fall back when I saw a ball come toward my head. Fortunately, it missed my head by a mouse's ear. You can't tell me that had perfect control for nine innings and all of a sudden missed the plate by six feet. No, he wanted me. It was probably because of my punching out his buddy George Lee. I took Palzak's pitch as a personal offense and immediately went after him.

We had our second brawl of the game. I went crazy trying to get to Palzak. I was held back by the home plate umpire and two teammates who had to pick me up and carry me back to the dugout. For my own good, Martin took me out of the game, came with me in the clubhouse, and helped cool me off.

The reporters in both clubhouses were having a field day, everybody had something to say. Perch was saying that he didn't want to throw at Lakes, but he had to back up his teammates. Chico was giving fair warning to Blue to not even look at him the wrong way or Chico would give it to him again. Martin was cursing every Yankee on their roster and had some special words for Weber. He praised his club for standing up to the bullying tactics and talked about his "tough rookie," meaning me.

When the reporters came to me I was still hot about Palzak's pitch. I didn't wait for any questions, I just stood there and told them what I thought of Steve Palzak. I called Palzak a gutless asshole and told them they could print it and I called George Lee the same thing because he probably told Palzak to get me for me hitting him. One reporter said that he had just come from the Yankee clubhouse and Palzak was saying that the pitch slipped and that I was just overreacting to a tight situation.

I exploded like a ton of TNT The nerve of that asshole to throw the ball at my head, almost kill me, and then deny it. Dressed in just my game pants and with no shoes or shirt on I ran out of our clubhouse and down the hallway to where the Yankees were. Of course, all the reporters followed, eagerly awaiting to see what the tough rookie would do.

The Yankee clubhouse was as crowded as ours was. Without my shirt on and wearing my gray pants, I wasn't as noticeable as you'd think I'd be. I was in enemy territory and hadn't been spotted. I paused for a quick moment to look for Palzak. I wanted him to tell me face-to-face that he didn't throw at me. If he did, I'd give him the beating of his life. I found him not more than three feet away from me. He was dressed in his civies and was standing while talking to a reporter. I rushed him, grabbed him by his jacket lapels, and shoved him into his locker.

"Tell me face-to-face you didn't throw at me, and I'll kill you." I've never seen a man so scared in all my life. He backed into a stall and kept on saying, "No, no." I was pulled off him by a few players, but I kept on yelling all the way, "I'll kill you! I'll kill you!" To this day, I can't understand why they didn't gang up on me. Lord knows there were enough of them.

When Martin and the rest of the club got word of where I was, they came charging to my rescue like the seventh cavalry. Once again, a big brawl almost erupted; this time it had to take the New York Police Department to calm things down. It was one hell of a mess.

I made the front page of all the Chicago papers the next day. The *Sun-Times* ran a picture of me being carried off the field by two teammates after I went after Palzak with the headline, "DONATO BATTLES YANKS: TAKES ON WHOLE YANKEE TEAM IN CLUBHOUSE" *The Chicago Herald* also had me on their front page. In three separate photos, they showed me hitting George Lee, running out to the mound after Palzak, and in the arms of an unidentified Yankee in their clubhouse. Their headline read, "SOX LOSE, DONATO K.O.'S YANKS" The New York papers were fair in their reporting of the fights, calling my actions on the field defensive for what they thought was an obvious ball thrown at my head. However, a few writers took sides. One called Martin the "hitman of baseball" and me "Martin's new buffer." He called my going into the Yankee clubhouse after Palzak, "as unprofessional a thing" in sports as he had seen in forty years of reporting. That same writer also called the umpires, "Four men who have no meaning or understanding of what their job entails." I guess he meant that the umpires had let it get way out of hand.

In all my years, I'll never forget that series. I think playing in front of packed houses every day had a lot to do with it. When you're playing before forty or fifty thousand people, every game excites you and drives you to play to the absolute best of your ability. When there's a sparse crowd, it's hard to do, that drive has to come from within, but in front of a big crowd, it makes it that much easier.

We traveled to Boston the next day, and I was mobbed by reporters. They all wanted a piece of the brash rookie who took on the Yankees singlehanded, and as always, I gave them as honest an interview as I knew how. The reputation had arrived.

I finally came out of my slump in Boston, and I went on to have a very good rookie year. Hungry never returned, his leg never healed correctly, so I finished playing the rest of the season. I finished that year with sixteen homers and over seventy runs batted in. Those aren't bad stats for anybody to have let alone a rookie. I made the all-rookie team and earned a few other postseason honors. But most important to me was the respect I earned from my peers as a hard-nosed tough baseball player who wouldn't take any quarter and gave none in return. To me, that's what the games are all about. It's okay to be friendly off the field, but once I'm playing, it's all business, and that, too, has stuck with me throughout my career.

Off the field, I had a pretty good time of it too. I had an apartment down near Rush St., where most of Chicago's nightlife is, and soon I became known as the "Duke" of Rush St. Never one to shy away from women, I quickly took advantage of my celebrity status. I was in the gossip columns almost daily, some of it true, some of it not. I'd be seen with some of the most beautiful women in Chicago on one night and some of the most beautiful women in say New York the next. The reputation was now complete. I was the hard-nosed ballplayer who not only liked to play with a baseball but also liked to play with the women.

When the season was over, I went back home and worked again with Johnny. He was getting bigger and bigger in his operation, and just as long as he kept me away from the hard goings on in his line of work, I had no second thoughts about working for him. Besides, the money he paid was almost as much as my baseball salary.

I won't dwell on my career year by year. It'll take too long, but I'll go over the things I think you should know, the interesting points that have made me what I am today. My second year was just about the same as my first, statistic-wise, but my reputation had made me a very controversial player wherever I went. In every town in the American League, I was the first one that the reporters flocked to. Whenever trouble arose on the field, I was the first one that the opposing players came after. I was either booed or cheered; nobody was neutral about me. The Yankees left me alone. I guess they didn't want any more of that crazy stuff in their clubhouse, but the Orioles picked up where the Yankees left off. It culminated in a big brawl in their park, and I got the shirt ripped right off my back.

That fight in Baltimore made headlines but not as big as the headlines I made in Chicago with Ali Shabazz, the heavyweight champ. Shabazz was training in Chicago for an upcoming title fight that was going to be held in Comiskey Park. I had always been a boxing fan and went to his workouts almost every day to watch him train. It seemed I got as much attention from being at his workouts as Shabazz did. Just as many reporters would flock around me as would the champ. I knew that sooner or later, the inevitable question would come up, and one day in Brian's column, it did.

He wrote of how good a fighter he thought I would've made, judging from my incidents on the ballfield. He might've been right too. I'm over six feet and go a solid one-ninety and could always hit. It's just that I never had the opportunity to get involved in the fight game, or otherwise I think I might've given it a shot. Brian's article went on to say that a fight between Shabazz and me would draw better than his upcoming title fight and would probably be a more competitive fight as well. He was writing it with tongue in cheek, but a lot of people took it quite seriously.

The next day, another Chicago paper ran the tale of the tape between Shabazz and me, and the differences were not that drastic. They listed my opponents as George Lee, winner by knock-out, Steve Palzak, winner by technical knock-out, New York Yankees, winner by technical knockout, and John Thomas of the Baltimore Orioles, winner by knock-out. It was quite impressive and very cute, but anybody in their right mind knows that an amateur wouldn't stand too much of a chance against the heavyweight champ of the world. It was a joke, and that's all I took it for, but Shabazz didn't see it quite that way.

The day the second article appeared, I attended Shabazz's work-out, and it created a real big stir in his camp. I was asked by reporters if I could take him, if I wanted to spar with him, and if I feared him. I was honest and told them that it would be a good fight, but his experience would win it for him, and then I busted out laughing. I was pulling their legs as much as their articles had pulled mine. Shabazz was pissed off though, he didn't like the tone of the article. It wasn't right for an amateur, not even a boxing amateur, to be compared with him and he very vocally told me so from the ring.

I hammed it up a little bit for the reporters, making a fist at him and cocking my right arm getting ready to throw one, thinking Shabazz was onto what I was doing, but he wasn't. He started getting abusive and the names became a little too serious for playing around, and finally, I had to tell him to shut up, or I'd quit playing and give him a beating. He threw a pair of gloves at me and told me if I could get the shit stains out of my pants why didn't I try on the gloves and give it a go? It was obvious to all that what had started in a jesting manner had become very serious.

The reporters told him to let it lay and so did his corner, but he would have none of it, "You come to my camp and take over like you're somebody here. Well, you're nobody in my camp, but another guy who pays his dollar to see the Champ. Now put the gloves on or beat a path to the door punk." The last guy who called me a punk got a ham sandwich stuffed in his face. I didn't have one handy then, but I ran into that locker and changed as quickly as I could. I had quickly become very pissed off and had every intention of taking it out on that loudmouth champion. I didn't like him too much anyway.

I figured to even get a good shot at him I'd have to get inside. He was so quick with his feet, if you remember, that it would be almost impossible for me to keep up with him. I'd have to stalk him and wait for the opening that would come, then throw the right and hope it connected. I figured after he peppered me with a few jabs, he'd prove his point then tire of me and quit, but I had no such notion. I wanted him.

Somebody had called a TV crew, and in the fifteen minutes, it took me to change it seemed like the gym had swelled to four times its size. The place was wall-to-wall people and the cameras turned me on. I came out of that locker all pumped and ready to do battle.

The first round was all his as he danced circles around me while throwing his jab, laughing, and talking to the crowd. "No baseball player can lick me," rat, tat, tat, with his jab. "I'm the champ of the world. You'll find out when I knock you out sucker," Rat, tat, tat. I admit his hand speed was something I never saw. I got hit with four punches when I only saw him throwing two. It was fantastic, but those jabs hardly hurt at all. He had no power behind them.

The second round was a duplicate of the first. He was putting on a show at my expense. The punches were getting harder, and the frequency of them was becoming dangerous. He kept on telling me, soon I'd be in Never Never Land, and I had no doubt he was gearing up for the knock-out when I saw my opening and let it fly. He fell to one leg and held on to the bottom rope. He was kneeling, and it was he who was in never never land. His handlers rushed in before I could land another punch, and I would've too and laid him down on the canvas. I walked over to him and told him I was content playing the thing out, but when he called me a punk in front of everybody, then that did it. He said he'd get me, and I told him he'd have to stand in line and take a number for that.

I was the lead in a story on all the evening news programs all over the country. My phone was ringing off the hook. I was about as hot an item in Chicago as the great Chicago fire itself. That night I received a standing ovation, and to top it all off, I hit a homer to win the game. I was having an affair with a city, and I loved every day of the relationship.

In my fourth year, I received my first and only serious injury. I was out trying to stretch a double into a triple, and while sliding, I caught my leg in the leg of the third baseman and tore ligaments. I had an operation, and that's when I became very active in the affairs of Chicago's hospitals. Ever since then, I figured I'd raised over four or five million dollars for the hospitals of Chicago through various functions that I ran like a fall invitational golf tournament for ballplayers only when the season's over, celebrity telethons. I've run parties and affairs with the affluent circles of Chicago and all its athletes. It was something I never got into until I had a stay in a hospital. They need all the money that they can get, and a man in my position can see to it that they get it, and that's what I did.

The player they brought up from the minors to replace me was none other than my old buddy Jerry Alexander. Jerry had overcome a severe handicap to make it back all the way. His being called up made it complete. The three stars of the El Paso club had now made the big leagues with the addition of Jerry. Paul had been rookie of the year the previous year. I should also add that another member of the Texas League came to the big leagues that year and that was Jack Ronan, the umpire who had given me so much trouble in Amarillo.

The trouble never stopped when he hit the big leagues either. He just doesn't like me; that's all there is to it. In all my years, I've been thrown out of eleven games in organized ball, and Jack Ronan has done the ejecting in every single one. I've just about given up trying to figure out why. It's natural in baseball to argue a close play and, in the process, blow off some steam at the umpire, but Ronan is the only umpire I've ever come across that'll have none of it, at least from me. But now I've learned to adjust to it, and I don't even argue the case anymore. I'd hate to have him do a big game though when the chips were down and have him call one against me, then you'd see trouble. But my clubs have never had big games, at least not the big games of a September pennant race, except this past year, and eight or nine years ago, we were fortunate that Ronan had no say in the outcome.

A few years after my knee injury, I started a hot and torrid affair with Patricia Best, who was Chicago's premier anchorwoman on the evening news.

I had met Patty at a benefit dinner that I ran for one of the hospitals and immediately took a liking to her. What guy wouldn't? She was tall and lean with beautiful blond hair and a natural look about her. She looked like she belonged in an Ivory soap commercial; she was extremely attractive.

But she didn't seem too receptive toward my advances. She said I was certainly handsome enough for her, and she was attracted to me, but she didn't want to become another notch on my gun. She had heard all the stories about me and would rather have had a more serious-minded man. I understood where she was coming from, but it didn't stop me. She would be a hard egg to crack, but I loved the challenge of doing it.

I finally talked her into a date after four or five refusals. I took her to a cozy little Italian restaurant on the North Side and then out dancing. She was good company, and we had a hell of a good time. When I took her home, she was very surprised that I didn't come on to her. Some girls you do, some you don't. Patty was one you left alone; otherwise, you'd never get it.

I asked to see her again, and she accepted. Right there, I knew I had her. She said yes in a second. In a month, we were the hottest couple in Chicago. We appeared in the gossip columns almost daily, and she was a frequent visitor to the ballpark. It took me a while to get in bed with her, but when I did, it was well worth it. Patricia Best, newscaster, was one hot story in the sack. She could do it all!

After a few months, she kept telling me she was in love with me. I was very fond of Pat and told her so many times, but I also told her how I felt about Marie, and she'd have to accept that, or we couldn't have a relationship. I had given up other women for her, even on the road when you don't have that steady sex, and it's so easy to come by, but I could never stop loving Marie. She accepted it, but it still bothered me that she said she loved me so much.

I figured I'd stay with her that off-season, to see if it could possibly work. I enjoyed her and looked forward to being with her. I could love Marie and still feel strongly about another woman. Patty was great; she understood perfectly. She got me a job at a local station doing sports. I loved it. I was a natural in front of a camera and had a good time doing the Bears' games.

FIFTY-SIX

I had heard a lot about the Chicago winters but never expected it to be as bad as it was. That was the only off-season I ever stayed in Chicago, and the weather had as much a part to do with me never staying again as anything. I have experienced some cold winters. I mean New Jersey isn't exactly Florida in the winter, but that winter in Chicago was the worst thing I've ever experienced. For a stretch of eighteen days, there was below-zero weather. There was cumulation of over one hundred inches of snow, and to top it all off, I caught a mild case of pneumonia. I couldn't have been happier to head South for spring training.

Going into my sixth year in the big leagues, I had been very consistent, always around the fifteen-home run range and always close to seventy or eighty runs batted in. My average was just as consistent, always in the two-seventy range. I wasn't a superstar but a good, steady, everyday player. Maybe because Patty had settled me down, or maybe because I had matured, but from the opening game that year, I had it all going for me. I had the swing that I had in my first major league spring training camp, and it lasted the whole year.

In my nine years there, the White Sox were never in a Championship series or even close to it, except that year. We were in it up until the final weekend until we lost three straight to Minnesota to finish one game out of first place.

Every player wants to be in the World Series. What are you playing for in the first place? When you play one hundred and sixty-two games, play for seven months, and lose out by only one fuckin' game, it hurts. I didn't get over that last game loss to the Twins for weeks. We had Paul on the mound, who was on his way to winning the Cy Young award, and some hot bats in the lineup, but we lost four to three on a three-run homer in the ninth. It was devastating.

Individually we had some real good years. Paul won twenty-five games, and Jerry batted three hundred with twenty homers, but I carried the club that year. I had my greatest year before or since. I hit twenty-eight homers and drove in one hundred and twelve runs. For the only time in my career, I hit over three-hundred, three-o-five. I played in the All-Star game and finished second in the Most Valuable Player balloting. It was certainly a year to remember.

After that year, I wanted to return home. Patty didn't want me to leave her. We had been together for over a year and a half, and she loved me very much. She wanted to get married in the spring. It was out of the question. I did think about staying another winter, but I had been away from my family and friends too long and missed them very much. I decided to return home. Patty said if I left her, it was over. Patty Best was close to me, but my family and friends were blood. There was nothing closer. I returned home fully knowing a good woman would leave my life because of it. It was something I had to do. I don't look back on what could've been, but Patty was and still is a special person to me. She called me the first night home and asked me to reconsider her proposal. I did and gave her the same answer. She met another guy that winter, and in the fall, she had her wedding. I sent her a wedding gift and wished her well; it was the least I could've done.

After the year, I had I returned home a hero. I never had a reception like that. All my family and friends got together and crowned me their MVP. It made the loss of Patty a little easier to bear.

Johnny had a different job for me that year. He had branched out into the exporting business and had opened up a clothing store featuring the latest in the European fashion scene. He wanted me to be an advisor to his help. "Sort of throw your influence on the customers. Tell them the suit looks good on them, and that it's the latest style. Nobody can bullshit like you." The job was a natural for me. I have always been clothes-conscious, and when Johnny's store did fashion shows at local malls and clubs, I naturally did my best to look my sharpest in the best clothes that money could buy.

That job opened the door for my modeling career. We were doing a show in a mall in Long Island when a fashion executive happened to catch me and approached me after the show. He said with my national appeal and good looks, and with his agency, he could make the right deals for me, and we could take off. We not only took off, but also we soared like a rocket ship. Before I knew it, I was in the best fashion magazines and doing professional shows all over the country for the latest designers. The money was fabulous, and the women I met were from another world. I quickly forgot about

Patty Best for the time being. Ever since then, that has been my job in the off-season. Of course, I still work in Johnny's store, but only on a limited schedule. He advertises when I'm going to be there and draws people by the hundreds every time the advertisement goes in the paper.

But keep in mind that although Johnny had gone legitimate in one respect, he still had his organization, and that year he put me to the test. One time, he flew out to Chicago and stayed with me for a while. He was always welcome. He asked me if a ballgame could be fixed and if I could do it. I was shocked to think that he thought that I'd actually do something as low as throw a game. I let him have a verbal beating. I was never afraid to tell him off, and that night was no exception. He told me to calm down. He was very happy to see that I was beyond approach but wanted to know if there was anybody in the club who could be approached. I told him he'd have to find out himself, and if I found out that anybody on my club was throwing a game, I'd kick that player's head in from home to centerfield.

He would never give up. He was always like that. Once he had his mind set on something, he'd never quit until it was clear to him. We argued, then yelled at each other and almost came to fists, then argued some more. Finally, we sat down and sensibly figured it all out. I would never throw a game. That much was perfectly clear, nor would I finger a teammate to be singled out. That was just as clear, but I did arrange to tell Johnny the inside scoop on our club. Things like who was pitching with a sore arm, what pitcher had a jinx on us, what team our pitcher could always beat, who was playing hurt, and things like that. There were things that any true devout follower of our team would know if he dug a little, but things that the average fan would never read in the paper. I'd tell Johnny my opinion on a game, either I thought we could win or I didn't based on this information, and he could do with it what he wanted. By no means was it guaranteed as a sure thing, and I made it clear that Johnny understood that. Too many things can change the outcome of a ballgame to say it's in the bag, but my opinion was as close to it as he was going to get.

In the first month, I gave him ten games I thought we should win. We won only six of them. Those four losses cost Johnny plenty of money because based on my information, he was fixing the Vegas odds in his favor. He was big in the Vegas betting parlors and the money he threw around, and his inside information, fixed the odds many times.

The next month, I gave him thirteen games, and I was right on nine of them. We kept it up the whole year, and I proved to be close to seventy percent. After the season, I told Johnny that I just didn't feel right doing it and that he'd have to find somebody else for the next year. He found a player in the National League who gave him the same information. He didn't pick them as good as I did, but Johnny has had him on the payroll for a long time and has made tons of money off him. To this day, he won't tell me who he is, and I'd like to know.

I went back to being the just average ballplayer after my super year. I guess the good Lord let me have my one good spot in center stage just to let me see what it would be like. I was a pretty good boy for the next couple of years. I got thrown out of three games, all by Ronan, of course, and put on a good show for the fans in doing it after one of them. We were in Baltimore when I argued a third strike that I thought was at least ten inches too high. I ran into the dugout and started throwing out everything. I started with the bats, then gloves, the trainer's bag, and even our portable watercooler. It got me great headlines and also a five hundred dollar fine from the commissioner.

I also got in one more big brawl while I was in a Chicago uniform and it was with my old friend Steve Palzak. I never did give him the beating he deserved so many years before, but when the opportunity arose I jumped at it.

A fight had broken out around second base after a tough slide had knocked over their second baseman. I was in the dugout and like everybody else I came running out looking to see what I could do. I was trying to break up two guys if you could believe that when I saw Palzak standing right there next to me. I hadn't been that close to him since that day in the Yankee clubhouse. I mean, we never traveled in the same circles. I turned and hit him a good shot, then jumped on him, and we wrestled down to the ground. All the time, I kept screaming at him that I was getting even for the pitch at my head. He gave me a good go at it, but he wasn't anything I couldn't handle.

Yes, I had some exciting years in Chicago. A lot of ups and a lot of downs. A lot of cheers and a lot of boos. But my ninth and final year, there was the most controversial of all.

It started with a woman, what else? I had met her in a club, and she totally lit my fire. I mean she had so much sex appeal she made my knees buckle just by looking at me. She was the most sensuous woman I had ever met in my life. A little weak on the personality side, but she more than made up for it with the things she could do for a man. She was great.

Iris happened to be a Puerto Rican, and a very dark one at that. Jim Wagner, who was our manager at the time, called me into his office and told me point-blank that he didn't like me going out with a nigger, to dump her. I told Jim to shove it, that I'd go out with whoever I wanted to, and if he didn't like it, he could do something about it. I never liked him anyway, from the first day they hired him. He had a lot of nerve overthinking in terms of white-black in the position that he was in. If people ever found out about that he'd be out of baseball quicker than Jerry Alexander could steal second base.

The fact that Iris and I kept a lot of company together started to take its toll. I heard some remarks from a few of my teammates and almost came to blows over it more than once. I was surprised that they'd act like that. Once the incidents hit the press it became an issue with Chicago's fans. I never heard more racial shit coming from the stands than I did at that time. I've never been a prejudiced person and the things I was hearing made my stomach turn. Those people were sick and needed help. It's a shame, really.

The gossip columns had a field day. They had me getting married, getting Iris pregnant, and even had us flying down to Rio during the All-Star break. The stories that come out in times like that are amazing. One of the papers said they even interviewed the travel agent who booked our flight! It was all bullshit of course.

The pressure was getting to Iris more than me. I had just as many, if not more, supporters than there were people who cursed me for going out with Iris, remember, I was still Vince Donato, their crowned *Duke* of Rush St. Pressure and the headlines were a way of life to me, but Iris was bothered very much by it all. I tried to console her the best I could, but it was affecting her very much, even her performance in bed had gone downhill, and that's when it started to bother me.

It finally came to a head one night in a club on the North Side. I was out with Jerry and Paul, and their wives and Nick Scarpa, a friend who I met through my association with Johnny, Nick's wife, and Nick's bodyguard. Yes, Nick Scarpa was with Johnny's organization. It was a Saturday night, and we were all having a good time dancing and enjoying the floor show. The booze was flowing, and the laughs were plenty.

At the next table was another large party. They were having just as good a time as we were, the booze and laughs were flowing from their table too! Suddenly one of the guys recognized Paul and then the rest of us, and the insults about the White Sox started flying. That we could take. We were ballplayers and had been exposed to that sort of stuff hundreds of times before, but the personal insults started getting way out of line, especially about me and Iris. Like I said, we were all pretty much into the booze, and it didn't take me long to get one going. I jumped the guy with the loudest mouth, and Jerry quickly followed in. Nick, his bodyguard, and Paul followed up. It was like a fight in Dodge City. Tables and chairs were flying everywhere. I never saw a guy handle himself as well as Nick's bodyguard. Man, that guy could fight. Before we knew it, four or five other guys had jumped in, and the police had to be summoned to break up the whole thing. They found a gun on Nick's man, but fortunately, he had a carrier's permit.

This had to be the scoop of all scoops for the Chicago papers. Here was Vince Donato, the darling of Chicago for so many years, mixed up in a nightclub fight with a black girl at my side and known racketeers carrying guns. The papers wouldn't let up for days. Poor Iris, she just couldn't take it all. All she wanted was a little fun and a little lovin', and she had never expected all the publicity. It broke her, and three days later, she committed suicide.

I thought I'd never feel as low as the day when Marie died, but I came close to it then. I got a hold of Brian and lashed out back at the press. In an exclusive interview, I blamed the Chicago media, its papers and local news shows, and all the gossip columnists for Iris' death. It was the media who killed Iris. They weren't ready for their *Duke* to get involved with a black Latin girl. I charged them with murder.

Jimmy Wagner went on a rampage after my article hit the press. He said I had brass balls to blame the media that built me up throughout the years with the suicide of Iris. We got into a big shouting match in the clubhouse, and I wound up giving him a good beating. If Jerry hadn't pulled me off him, I think I might've killed him. Once again, I was in headline city, and the whole affair just wouldn't rest.

I was suspended from the club indefinitely pending an investigation. Wagner said he wouldn't manage anymore unless I was off the club. I retaliated by saying that I wouldn't play for a racist manager. It had the city of Chicago bubbling like a glass of champagne.

A couple of days after my fight with Wagner, I got a message that the commissioner wanted to see me in New York. I figured it was about this whole incident, and frankly, I was glad that the commissioner was getting involved. I didn't like the way the White Sox management was handling the whole thing. It seemed that they were sitting on it, waiting for the headlines to die, before doing anything about it.

When I got to New York, I was very surprised to find out that he didn't want to talk about it at all. He wanted to know what my association with Johnny was all about. He wanted to know from me what Johnny did, how he made his living, and what I did in the off-season with him. I got very snippy. I told him if he wanted to know all those things about Johnny, why didn't he ask Johnny himself? He got just as snippy as he threatened me with permanent suspension for association with a known racketeer if I didn't answer his questions. Now the shit was really hitting the fan.

There were just the two of us in his office, which made it nice. I didn't like being threatened and told him so. I got up from my seat and walked around his desk and got right down in his face, eyeball to eyeball. I told him I thought he was a pig-nosed prick face that was squealing in the wind. Johnny Mezzanotte had never been arrested for a crime in his life. What was alleged and what was fact were two different things. I told him that if he suspended me for my association with a lifelong friend, I'd sue baseball for millions for violating my constitutional right to make a living as I saw fit, and if he didn't believe me, I'd have my lawyer in his office that afternoon to get the proceedings started.

He was scared, and I knew it. He half-heartedly came back with some shit about Johnny's reputation and that I shouldn't be involved with a man of his standing. It wasn't good for the image of baseball. He said he'd think about it, and I should come back the next day.

I came back the next day all right and had Tommy and Johnny with me. The commissioner seemed to go in shock when he saw the three of us walk in. I kind've thought he got the impression that we'd pull out some guns and let him have it.

Johnny was very polite. He told him that for a living, he ran an importing business of custom-made Italian men's clothes, and he had never been arrested for as much as a parking ticket. If the police ever asked him questions about friends of his he cooperated with them to the best of his knowledge. He laid on the bullshit. He got a little tough when he told the commissioner that if I ever got suspended for being his friend he'd personally back the suit against baseball with not only his money but with all his sources, including his long list of influential friends in high places. He then ended by telling the Commissioner he wouldn't have a chance.

Tommy took the floor next and ran off a lot of legal mumbo jumbo. In essence, the commissioner had no legal grounds for suspending me, I did nothing wrong, and if I was suspended, baseball would have a black mark against it for suspending one of its most popular players. Tommy also made good our threat to sue and told the commissioner to talk it over with his lawyers, and he'd soon find out that we were right.

The next move was the commissioners. He paused for a moment, then came out with it. He said that he was under a lot of pressure, that there were a lot of rumors involving professional gamblers and players, and he was led to believe that I had something to do with it all. He told us to forget it, that nothing would come of it, that he should've known a player that plays the game as hard as I did would have nothing to do with gambling and baseball, and that as far as he was concerned, the case was closed. But let's face it, when he saw Johnny and Tommy come walking in, he shit blue; the guy fell under the pressure they presented. Anyway, he has never bothered me since, and to my credit, I've never given him a reason to.

With that off my back, I flew back to Chicago on the first flight I could get only to find the biggest surprise of my life waiting for me. I had been traded! I couldn't believe it. I had been one of the most popular players ever to play in the Windy City, and yet I guess the Iris affair, the big fight that resulted, the punching out of Wagner, and the call to the commissioner's office over alleged gambling all pushed management too far. It was time to let go of the *Duke* of Rush Street before I caused any more negative damage. In fairness to the management, I'd have to say that in my nine years there, they treated me extremely good, and I had no qualms when I left. I was sad to leave some good friends, but in a positive sense, I was playing closer to home and going to a contender, something the White Sox had never been.

My mind was very foggy at that time. I had gone through the most hectic week of my life. On Saturday night, I got in a big fight that saw me spend the night in jail. On Monday, a woman who had been very dear to me committed suicide. I punched out my manager and was suspended from the club indefinitely on Tuesday, the commissioner threatened me with a lifelong suspension on Thursday, and on Friday, I learned that I had been traded. Other men would have broken under all that pressure, the press was everywhere, and everywhere I went, there was a microphone in my face, but I took it. I was a man. What was I going to do? Run and hide? That's simply not in my makeup. So I packed my things and headed for Beantown.

I was concerned about how the Boston fans would receive me. The incidents of the previous week were not only in the Chicago papers but also all over the country. Would they be for me or against me? Would they boo or cheer? We'd soon find out.

I arrived too late for Saturday's afternoon game, but I was penciled in to start Sunday's game. It was a packed house. Fenway always seemed packed, even when it wasn't, but on that day, they had their thirty-five thousand, and every one of them wanted to see me.

In my seven years in Boston, I've never had a complaint about how the papers handled me. Both the Globe, the Herald, and the smaller papers have always been very fair and honest in their reporting, and that Sunday was no exception. They all ran feature stories on me outlining my baseball career on and off the field. They all seemed to sum it up in the same way, Judge Vince Donato by what he does on the field as a ballplayer, a solid one who could help the Red Sox to a pennant, and not by what kind of trouble he gets into away from the ballpark. His private affairs were his own and the fans should stay out of them. I appreciated the stories very much. The *Boston Press* and I would get along just fine.

I took the field in the top half of the first to mixed emotions, although I have to admit I heard more boos than cheers. I left the field in the bottom of that inning to a standing ovation for fifteen minutes that cemented me in only one inning as one of the most popular players ever in Boston. Now let me tell you what happened in that inning that turned Boston on to me.

Just as I took up more space in the sports pages of America's papers that week than any other player or sport, so did America's relations with the Middle East take up the front page stories. I have never been too political and I can't recall which countries were involved, they all seem the same to me, but some of our ambassadors and embassy personnel were getting harrassed over there. They were getting assaulted, verbally abused everywhere they went, eggs thrown at them, and everything short of being shot. The image of America, the home of the brave, was being challenged over there and at home as well. It was very common to see students burning the American flag, shouting anti-American slogans, and defacing pictures of Presidents all over American campuses and cities. It reminded me a lot of the anti-war movement during the Vietnam era.

So here I am in left field getting ready to play the Orioles when all of a sudden this guy jumps out from the stands and runs into the field carrying an American flag. He was tall, very dark, and wore a turban. If I had to bet I'd have bet that he was a student from the Middle East in one of Boston's many colleges. So he stops about five feet from me and starts pouring lighting fluid all over the flag. He took a match out and started to light a fire on the flag. I acted in a flash. I ran over to him, pushed him out of the way, and rubbed the flag in the grass. He didn't soak the flag enough because it hardly caught fire and was very easy to extinguish. He came back to me, and I dropped him with a right. He went out cold.

I heard the fans cheering as if I had hit a homer to win the World Series. I hammed it up. What else could I do? I picked up the flag and ran it all around the ballpark. The place went nuts, absolutely out of this world. They started singing God Bless America and wouldn't stop. It was the most exciting moment in baseball that I've ever had. I'll never forget how proud I was to run that flag around the park. I kept thinking of my uncle who died at Pearl Harbor and how my father always used to say he died defending his country. It was a proud moment for everyone there.

Once again, I was the headline story for the nation's press, only this time it was for a positive thing I had done. I received letters from thousands of people all over the country, even the president called me into the clubhouse after the game when he found out about it. I was on the national news shows, and I even made the cover of *Time* magazine! I had taken an opportunity and made the most of it and turned a city of mixed emotions into one of joy and happiness for their new ballplayer. I had become so popular in Boston after that that they even made a comic strip character after me.

I was riding the wave of popularity when I almost fell in love for the second time in my life, and it was very hard not to. So hard that I wonder now if I had made the right decision. Maybe things will change, but as of now, true love never happened between the two of us. Let me explain.

We were out on the coast about two weeks after the flag incident when I was asked to do one of the talk shows. They were always after me whenever I was on the coast to do those shows. I always had a good story about a fight from the old days or a past lover that would be good for their ratings. I always liked to go on them, and it gave the folks a kick to see me on TV.

Luellen Lee, the famous movie, star was also on that night. Now there's a woman. She has got to be one of the most beautiful women of our time. She's got it all going for her, looks beyond compare. A body that never quits, personality personified, and she has never been affected by all that Hollywood bullshit. She has remained her own woman.

So we finished taping the show, and I was ready to go back to the hotel. We had an off day and I was looking forward to a little rest to hit the hay early. Luellen came up to me and asked me if I'd take her for a bite to eat. Shit, I was like every other guy. I was in awe of the woman, and she asked me to take her to eat! I had never felt uneasy with any other woman before, and God knows there have been hundreds, but here was one of the most desirable women in the world, a woman who could have kings, statesmen, and movie stars, and she picked me, a kid who used to rob chickens from Spinelli's chicken yard to take her out to dinner. My heart skipped, but the man in me would never let an opportunity like that slip away.

I said, "Of course, only if we go Italian."

She knew of a good Italian restaurant outside of LA, and that's where we headed. I can't remember when I had a more enjoyable time. She was so easy to talk to. In no time, I lost that sense of inferiority I had and quickly became myself. The hell with kings, statesmen, and movie stars, she was with me, and those others could take a hike.

After she heard my stories about the old days in Orange with the guys, about El Paso and Jerry and Paul, and about my family and Aunt Petronelia and countless other stories, she drove me back to my hotel, and we stopped in the lounge for a nightcap. I tell you, if I still didn't love Marie, I would've fallen in love that first night. What I didn't know at that time was that Luellen already had.

We took a dark booth away from the crowd and continued our conversations. The talk ran smoothly the whole night. I hadn't met somebody since Marie who could bring out things in me like I knew Luellen could. Then it got serious. She told me she had to be honest, that honesty was her only policy and she liked it that way, she told me that since the first time she saw me on the cover of *Time*, she felt attracted to me. When she read the story, she felt compelled to call me on the spot but instead settled to wait for when I came to the coast. She had set the show up that night to have me on when she appeared, and she had the whole evening planned.

She didn't like to pull punches and she had to say how she felt. fter spending five hours with me, she knew right there that there could be nobody else in her life. Shit! Imagine how I must've felt. Here, was the most beautiful woman in the world, guys would cut off their right arm just to sniff the seat she sat on, and here she was telling me there could never be another. I jumped at the opportunity. I asked her to take it to my room.

She shook her head with a little smile. "I don't jump in the sack at the snap of a finger when every good-looking guy asks. I could've slept with some of the most famous men in the world, but I left them all playing with their dongs. If you want me, you have to show me that you deserve me, and so far, there have only been three men who have deserved me. You show me that, and you'll be the fourth."

Wow! My mind was blown. Luellen Lee, the glamorous movie star, was an old-fashioned girl at heart. She'd make my mother proud. Underneath all that glitter, she was down to earth, a girl who wouldn't give in without a fight. I loved it. I asked her how can I prove to her that I deserved it when she lived in LA, and I lived in Boston.

"You'll find a way."

I did. I saw her the next afternoon for lunch, and that night, she came to our game. I happened to hit one out that night, and when I crossed the plate, I tipped my cap and bowed in the direction where she was sitting.

She couldn't make the next two games, but she did manage to fly down to Oakland, and we spent some time together there. Our relationship was definitely growing.

We flew back to Boston, and the first thing I did when we landed was to call her. We arranged to meet in New York in ten days, she'd be doing some promotional work there for a new movie, and we'd be playing the Yankees. We spent three days with each other, and it turned on the gossip columnists there. Our pictures were all over the papers. I was on the verge of falling in love. Luellen Lee was the closest thing to Marie that I had ever met. It was heaven in one sense, and I was afraid in another.

Before we left New York, I drove to Marie's grave. I kneeled and had a long talk with her. I wanted to love Luellen, to give her what she deserved. I was ready to settle down, to be serious with one woman, and I couldn't find a better one this side of Marie than Luellen, but being so close to Marie just reenforced my love for her. I could never love another.

Luellen and I spent three years together, and we still see each other from time to time. Our relationship has been great. At times, I'd spend the off-season with her in California, and then during the season, we'd make plans to meet throughout the country. Luellen was perfect, she would've even given up her career for me, but she wasn't Marie. Luellen understands how I feel about Marie, but she can't understand how I could love someone who has been dead for such a long time. She has even been to Marie's grave and has prayed to her to let me love someone who could give it back to me. It has been a touchy situation throughout the years.

I have told her a thousand times that I could love her physically and emotionally, but I could never love her with the strength that I love Marie. She has asked me to marry her. She said if I refused she would understand but we were both in our early thirties and we couldn't go on like we were, that we'd either have to shit or get off the pot. She wanted me to say yes but I had to say no.

I told her I cared for her too much. It wouldn't be fair to her to marry her while I loved Marie the way I did. I told her that I was probably wrong, that if I went to a psychiatrist, he'd probably find something wrong with me for loving a dead woman, but that's the way it was. I told her that she was as close to me as any woman had ever been, but the answer was still no.

That was four years ago, and she was very upset about it. I feel for her, but what could I do? That's how I feel. In the four years since we've still seen plenty of each other and she's asked me again to marry her and again, I had to say no. Then last year, right before opening day, she shocked the shit out of me. She told me that I was her Marie, that I was stuck with her for life, that she could never love another, and she could live with me under the situation, and that if I didn't want to marry her, then I could have her the way we had it. So that's how it stands. We see each other the way we always have, in cities throughout the country and during the off-season. I see other women. I can only give my love to one, and she knows it and accepts it. I feel sorry for her that she has chosen to live her life that way, but that's how it goes.

The Gang's All Here

1

It was a beautiful day for a ballgame. The sun was shining a bright-yellow gold, and the sky was a beautiful robin's egg blue. The grass was real as the Jersey Riders were ready to open the American League season in front of fifty-six thousand fans in their new ballpark, Jersey Stadium. Tex saw to it that each fan was given free of charge a souvenir program to remember the occasion. It was one of the many promotions he had planned for the season.

Vince had received over fifty complimentary tickets. His family and friends would be there along with a few of Johnny "Midnight's" friends. They were all seated together in the section that Vince had asked for, behind the home-team dugout.

Naturally, Tex and his wife were there, and seated with them, by personal invitation from Tex, was the Commissioner of baseball, who before the game went up to Johnny and Tommy to renew old acquaintances, and the Governor of New Jersey.

This opening day was a happening. Tex arranged for the first ball to be thrown out by the oldest living ex-major leaguer on record. He was Emil Lomax, an ex-Philadelphia A's who played in the early twenties. Emil was ninety-nine and barely made the throw from his seat to the catcher. Tex also hired the country's hottest group to sing the national anthem. He left no stone unturned. When the first pitch in the game was thrown, the scoreboard exploded with an array of fireworks that spelled out, "We're on our way."

But they were far from on their way in playing the game. The Baltimore Orioles gave the Riders a pasting, fourteen to two, and the game wasn't even that close. The Orioles pounded four pitchers for twenty hits and four home runs while the home team could only manage five hits and none after the fourth inning.

Tex knew his team wouldn't be a serious contender right away, but he did hope that they'd be competitive. He assembled the best team he could, and they even went five hundred in spring training, but this was the regular season now and the games were for real. Tex's twinkling hope for an opening-day win quickly died after the fourth and was buried by a five-run Oriole sixth.

The Jersey Riders were a mixture of young players and aging veterans. Tex had hoped that he could get a good mixture of the two. At first base was Kent Huff, a tall, lanky, twenty-year-old who was in his third year of professional baseball. Huff probably should've been left in the minors for more seasoning, but he was the best first baseman in the organization so he won the job.

The second baseman was Isoruko Ishito, the first Japanese player to play steadily in an American Big League ballclub. Ishito or Shit, as he was nicknamed, was another of Tex's promotions. Tex reasoned that if he could make his team different in some way from other teams, it would be to his advantage at the gate. Who wouldn't pay to see the first Japanese player in America? It did make sense. He was the star of the Japanese league and took a lot of Tex's money to come to America. It seemed he spent it all on blue suits, for everywhere he went Ishito was dressed in a blue suit and red tie, always bowing and saying in broken English, "So nice to meet you." Ishito was the perfect gentleman on and off the field.

The shortstop was the best player that Tex could put on the field. Hector Cedeno was the prize of the minor leagues when Tex selected him in the draft, and he soon proved all the experts right when he started his first game in the big leagues at only nineteen years old. Speaking no English, like Ishito, Cedeno was the key man in the only non-English speaking double play combo in the major leagues.

Around the hot corner was Clem Stallings, a veteran of ten years who was getting his first starting assignment in the big leagues. Clem sat on the Yankee bench for his first three years then was traded to the Baltimore Orioles where he sat for five more years before they traded him to Cincinnati. In ten years in the major leagues, he only started in a little over three hundred games, a little more than thirty a year.

Tex saw Stallings as a man ready to break out of a career slump that labeled him a *utility* player and nothing more.

Vince was in left field, and in the center was Marty Millar, a Canadian-born ex-Detroit Tiger who had been a star in the league seven years previously. Millar was now in the twilight of a fifteen-year career. It was Marty Millar who homered in the seventh inning of the seventh World Series game to give Detroit the World Championship and it was Marty Millar who for eight straight years never batted below three hundred while winning five gold gloves for his defensive play in the outfield. At thirty-five, Millar still had some good ball left in him, but aching knees had caused a problem in recent years. Tex counted on him for at least one hundred and thirty games.

The right fielder was none other than Vince's closest friend in baseball, Jerry Alexander. After hearing Vince rave about Jerry that night on Tex's ranch, Tex went out and got him from the White Sox the very next day. He had planned a retirement, but Tex's offer and the opportunity to play with Vince again prolonged it until next year. Even though his knees and ankles were full of arthritis, and he only had one good throw-a-game left in his arm, his hand-eye coordination was every bit as good as it ever was. Tex counted on Jerry for one hundred games and to be the catalyst for Vince.

Behind the plate was Darnell Taylor, an All-American fullback at SMU that Tex had helped to recruit for his alma mater. Taylor wasn't half the baseball player that he was a football player, but Tex saw enough potential in him to offer him a very lucrative contract that the NFL couldn't touch. In convincing Taylor that baseball was the more promising of the two sports, Tex's organization had won their first battle in a long line of victories that Tex was sure would come.

The pitching staff consisted of four starters whose combined professional record was twenty-seven wins and eighty-nine losses, but the fifth starter was Kelly Dailey, an ex-Atlanta Brave that Tex purchased on the free agent market for more money than even Tex would care to talk about. Dailey was coming off a twenty-win season and was in the prime of his career, and Tex figured that Dailey would be the solid pitcher who could give him seven or eight good innings every fourth day. Tex announced to all owners that whatever the price for Dailey was he'd top it, and he did. The bullpen was made up of three pitchers in their midthirties with sore arms and two kids who could certainly throw hard enough yet lacked the experience to be good major league pitchers.

The manager that Tex kept such a secret from the press until he was *unveiled* at a gala dinner in New York was none other than the famous Walter "Hippity" Hop, making his last stop on the road that was sure to lead to the Hall of Fame.

Hippity, so named because in the first game he ever played in he was hit on the foot with a pitched ball and "hippity-hopped" around the batter's box until the pain subsided, was the perfect man for Tex's team.

He came up in the late forties after spending eight years in the minor leagues, so he knew the frustration of trying to make it, something a manager of a new team would have to have. He started for three years with the Phillies before going off to the Korean War, losing two years of playing time. Those two years were in his late twenties when a ballplayer was right in his prime, and when he returned, he found his skills were no longer there. He bounced around for another five years, going to the Dodgers, then the Braves, and finally playing his last years for Cleveland. He started managing immediately after his last playing year and after only four years of minor league managing got hired by the Detroit Tigers. He managed for over twenty years in the big leagues with five different clubs before announcing his retirement. There were many good times, his clubs won four World Championships and lost two, and many bad times, he also had six last and next-to-last clubs. It was a long and exciting career and he finally called it quits after his last team finished thirty-five games out of first place. It was time to pack it in until Tex called and made him such an offer that he had to come out of retirement.

Hop never shined on the ballfield, nowhere near as good as the shortstops of his day, and as a manager, he was only as good as his players, but where he was head and heels above all his peers was in the press room. No player or manager in the game could ever be better than "Hippity" Hop when it came to handling the press. He was a reporter's strawberry shortcake after a filling dinner. They just couldn't get enough of his wit and wisdom. He had a language and a way about him all his own.

Of all the great quotes in the history of the game, "Hippity" Hop could easily be credited with half of them. When asked why he always rode in the rear of a plane rather than upfront with the rest of the coaches, he replied, "Did you ever hear of a plane backing into a mountain?" On a catch by the great Willie Mays, Hop told the *New York Press*, "That was possibly the most impossible catch I possibly have ever seen."

In one spring training with the Tigers, he told his team, "I want everybody to line up by numbers, according to height." It had reporters rolling in laughter and his players full of confusion.

While touring on the banquet circuit one year after a World Series championship, he announced to the audience, "I've had so many chicken dinners I feel like a rooster in a hen house." One reporter asked why he kept an old beat-up radio in his office when he could easily afford a new one, "Because it plays all the old songs," was the answer.

Commenting on some of his current players, Hop had the press in stitches when he described Vince as the "current heavyweight champ of the major leagues," Isoruko Ishito, his second baseman, as a "polite man, but I wonder how polite he'll be when somebody knocks him down on his kazooki while sliding into second." His pitching staff brought out this gem. "I've got five fathers and five kids that still think the stork brought them."

If ever there was a manager who could take the pressure off a losing ball club it was Hop. He'd make the Riders the darlings of the press even if they didn't win a game all year.

After the game, Vince invited Tex and Roxanne to Domenic's for what Vince described as "the best Italian cooked meal you'll ever have, hostesses by the prettiest hostess in any restaurant, my sister Lucy." It was an invitation that the Texan could hardly refuse, while Vince longed to get back in the old neighborhood and see a few old friends.

Vince spotted a few of them immediately. He stopped at the bar and introduced Tex to Frankie and Red, who left the one-sided game early, then to Lucy. Vince was all smiles. Coming home to play was his appetizer, being with his family and friends like this for an entire season was the main meal.

Lucy took some time off to sit and have a bite with her brother and his boss. Tex let Vince order for them, and Lucy made sure that it was just right. When the first course came, mozzarella carozza, an appetizer of cheese and bread deep fried, Tex and Roxanne couldn't have enough. They gobbled it down like piranha feasting on an unlucky calf that fell in their stream.

When the first course was through, Tex's mood seemed to change. His smile was gone, and his face was sour. Vince asked if it was the food. "No. The food was great. It was the way we lost today. We got blown right out of our park."

Vince was a little surprised that Tex would take a loss, especially an opening day loss, so hard. "Tex, you better get used to losing because this club is far from good. Don't say that Gilroy, and I didn't warn you. It's not easy putting a successful ballclub on the field."

Lucy, as attractive as she ever was in a brown dress with gold earrings standing out against her olive skin, looked at her brother. "It looks like it's going to be a long year."

"Well, we can win our share of games if everybody plays up to their potential," quickly answered Tex, "we do have major league potential on our club."

Vince wondered if his boss was going to be like this all year. If so, there was going to be trouble. A man of Tex Hardin's drive doesn't take losing lightly and the Jersey Riders were a losing team. Vince hoped his fear wouldn't involve him, but somehow he knew that he'd be in the center of the storm.

A main course of veal piccata turned Tex's frowns back to smiles and the conversation from baseball to Vince and Luellen. Roxanne, with an ulterior motive in mind, asked if he had heard from the star lately.

"She called last night. She always calls before opening day to wish me luck for the coming season. She signed to do a new picture that will be shot on location here in New York. She'll be here from about mid-May to September. Sounds like a long production to be shooting on location for four months."

"What's the movie about?" asked Lucy. Then turning to her guests, she said, "I just love movies, and ever since Vince met Luellen, she's told me so much about the movie business. It's an exciting business, but the hours are more than you'd think. She told me she puts in a thirteen-hour day when she's on a movie. That's too much work for me."

"Hell," responded the cowboy, not giving Vince a chance to talk out the subject of the movie, "back on the ranch a thirteen-hour day ain't even a full day's work. I sometimes put in seventeen hours a day."

"And I think you've had too much wine," said Roxanne as she laughed and fluffed off her husband. "Tell me, Vince, is your situation with Luellen the same?" Her body ached for him. She could never forget their afternoon together.

Vince immediately picked up the direction of her question. He wanted her too, but only in a physical sense, yet he perceived that she wanted more from him than just his body. "Yes. The situation is still the same, although I must admit there are plenty of times when I feel like giving in and getting married. I mean can I find better than Luellen? I keep telling myself no. So why don't I do it? Because I always think of Marie and then I know I can't give all my love to Luellen and that's not fair to her, it's the same old story."

"My brother told you about Marie? She was a gem. Pretty as a picture and such a pleasing personality. They would've made such a great couple. It was a shame. I tell him all the time to get married. He's the only one who hasn't given my parents any grandchildren. There's no logical reason why he shouldn't marry Luellen, and I tell him that constantly. He can still love Marie, but where Marie is now is doing him no good. But my brother is a *capodost*, a hardhead, he'll never listen to me." Lucy quickly put a small piece of bread in her mouth and then excused herself from the table. "If I sat and ate all night, I'd get fat, and the work around here would never get done.

You two come any time you want, and, Vince, I'll see you soon." She bent and kissed her brother on the cheek and ran off to the kitchen.

"She's a doll," said Roxanne.

"Yes, sir, that woman is a real lady," added Tex as Vince noticed more than politeness in his tone. If Tex thought that he'd put his brand on that Italian mare, Vince would see to it that he'd have more trouble with her than with a wild herd of mustangs.

After some small talk, Tex excused himself to go to the restroom, leaving Vince and Roxanne alone. Her question was to the point, without any subtleties. "So when can we get together again?"

Vince sipped some wine. He knew that he held the upper hand. "So what is it that you want from me? Then I'll tell you when we can get together."

Her answer was just as quick and to the point as her question only a moment before. "I want you to make love to me as much as you possibly can whenever you can. I want to be with you at any opportunity. I want the body and the man."

"You better put things in perspective. You're a married woman, and because of who you're married to, I have to be a very careful man. I'll never turn down the chance to bed down with you, and I'll never forget our afternoon together, but if I ever give myself to any woman, it'd be to Luellen. You and I can have a physical relationship whenever possible, but I want to set the law right now, and that is that Luellen comes first with me, and all you'll ever be, as long as you're married, is somebody on the side. As long as we both understand that, everything will be okay."

She had predicted the answer. A dead girl didn't bother her. A dead girl couldn't give him love, couldn't make him feel the pleasures of being a man, and couldn't compliment him wherever he went. It was Luellen Lee, the glamorous movie queen, that worried Roxanne the most. She had to know where Vince and Luellen stood so she could organize a plan to come between them, now she knew.

"That's fine with me. Tex is staying for tomorrow's game, then flying back to Dallas. I told him I'd like to stay an extra day or two to do some shopping in New York. We've got a suite in the Hilton across from the Stadium. I'll be expecting you when he's gone."

Tex returned with a smile on his face. "A real nice crowd of people here. Your friends wouldn't let me pass them without having a drink with them. They were surprised that I knew so much about them. Told them all you told me. I even told Red I would've liked to see him run with a football the way you said he used to before he got hurt."

"That must've started him with some stories".

"I believe he would've had me there all night if Domenic hadn't come out from the kitchen to meet me. Nice little crowd of people you got here, Vince." Lucy passed by with two dinner guests. "Yes, sir, a real nice crowd."

2

"It looks like a long season, uh, Hip?" asked a reporter.

"Well, it'll be over when it's finished." It was a classic example of how Hippity Hop could twist the English language. "Any thoughts on today's game?'

The old man with the limp and crew cut stared at the reporter. "I thought about the Gettysburg Address in the fourth inning when Alex hit that three-run homer."

"Come again?"

"Mrs. Alex was my fourth-grade teacher, and it was in the fourth grade when I learned about the Gettysburg Address."

When the laughter subsided, another reporter asked, "You've given up twenty runs in two games and scored only two. Is the pitching that bad?"

"Shit no. When you score only two runs in two games, I'd say the pitching is pretty damn good, wouldn't you? Of course, on the other hand, we did have a good crowd today, and we hit a lot of fair ball outs. The Jap made two pretty good plays in the second. I gave him a good pep talk before the game. Told him I had a lot of confidence in him and to ignore the shitty nicknames."

"What did he say?"

"I don't speak Japanese. I couldn't understand him."

"Then how did he understand you?"

"He must've. He made the plays I told him to make."

It was as if Hippity was in his glory days with the Tigers. Surrounded by seven or eight reporters, his quick answers and one-liners, along with his mastery of the English language, made everyone forget that the Riders were once again trounced by the Orioles.

FIFTY-SIX

If Hop was the king of the interview, then Vince was surely the prince. When they were through with the old man, the reporters went to Vince, who was dressing and a little hurried.

"What kept you guys? I waited so long that I had to start getting dressed, and now I'm in a rush to leave. Make it quick."

"What's the story with this club?"

Vince was as direct with a question as his manager was elusive. "We've got some talent here but not enough to do well. Cedeno will be a star, and Dailey is a top-notch pitcher, even though he didn't show it yesterday. The rest of us are either too old or too young to matter. Hippity is the star of this team. Stick with us, don't take us too seriously, put down everything Hip says, and it'll be a lot of laughs. That's it, fellas. I got to run."

Vince made plans to meet Roxanne at the hotel lounge later in the night after Tex had left, but first, a dinner at Domenic's awaited him with two of his closest friends, Johnny "Midnight" and their lawyer, Tommy Dara.

The three ate a very hearty meal. Every meal that the round little balding Italian cooked for his brother-in-law was made with a little extra of the chef's pride in his profession. He owed Vince a lot, and he saw to it that it was carte blanche treatment for his party whenever they came in. The important talk occurred during coffee and after dinner drinks.

"So how's the Vegas thing?" asked Vince.

"It's going real good," answered Johnny while sipping anisette. "We've got four betting parlors that are strictly our operation and partnership in two others. We're looking to open in Tahoe and Reno by football season. Locally, our books do a lot of business. The lotteries hurt us some with the numbers game but this past football season was a record high for us. As long as we set the line from our Vegas operations, it's like playing on our home field with our own rules."

"Sounds impressive."

"We hold our own. I still keep my hands in the drug business because the money is too good to pass up. As long as I'm careful, which I always am, the Feds will never get me. We do a little strong arm and some fencing, but our main business is gambling and clothes. As long as there's a jerk out there, that'll put money on a team to cover a spread. I'll have no complaints. What about you? You going to marry Luellen or what?"

"A lot of people have been asking me that lately."

"It's still not Marie, is it?" asked the lawyer.

"Yeah, I guess it is. Anyway, it's my problem. I've been doing a lot of thinking about it. I'll get married someday."

"What about your career? Is this it?"

"Probably. It's too bad I never played this close to home before. It's a shame these people have to see me as I am as opposed to the player I used to be. I could've turned this town on, but I've mellowed out the older I've gotten. Shit, I haven't got in a good fight since I don't know when."

"For you to say that you must've mellowed. But it's good to have you back with us. I mean we don't see you like we used to. You go with Luellen in the off-season and only come here for holidays. We're still family, even if we don't see you as much. It's real good to have you here."

"Here here," added Tommy.

"It's good to be home, thanks. You at peace with everybody?"

"We have to kick ass once in a while, but on the whole things have been pretty quiet. We're the strongest out of the five families, but we're no match for any two against us. I don't think any of that will happen. The last war was about twelve years ago, and we all learned our lesson from it. By the way, Nick Scarpa gives his regards. Says you still owe him that bail money from that fight he got in with you over that Puerto Rican girl."

Vince smiled. "That was a hell of a brawl. You know I never told you, but you should look into getting that guy that was with Scarpa that night to come to work for you. I never saw a guy kick ass like him in my life. He was an animal."

"You don't know who that was?"

"No, should I."

"Tell him, Tom."

"I know you'll never forget the guy in El Paso, but did you ever see the other guy who held back your two buddies?" asked Tommy.

"No."

"Well, you were sitting with him that night."

"No shit. Get your ass kicked one time and sit and drink with the guy the next."

"It's really strange."

"That's the business."

Vince took a quick look at his watch. It was time to leave to meet Roxanne. "Look, it was real nice sitting here with you two. You're my brothers, and you know that. We're home through the week then on the road for a week. I guess I'll be here every night by eleven unless we have a long game. There's always a box for you guys at the stadium, just let me know."

"Who you whackin' tonight?" asked Johnny.

"Johnny, if I told you, you'd never believe it."

"Try me."

"Tex's wife."

"Are you on shit or what? The boss's wife?"

"I got to run. Let me say goodbye to Lucy." The tall ballplayer, impeccably dressed in a rose-colored jacket and gray slacks, all from Johnny's store, went into the kitchen looking for his sister. He found her filling a pot with water to boil for pasta. When Domenic took a break, which wasn't too often, Lucy filled in as chef.

"Lucy I got to run," he said while leaning over and kissing his sister's cheek. "I'll be in tomorrow at about the same time."

She gave a kiss to the air and then said something that didn't please her brother, although he didn't show it. "You know Tex called today." Vince didn't seem too surprised. He had been around too long, and he recognized too well the looks that Tex had for his sister. After all, when it came to women, Vince and the Texan were cut from the same cloth. His suspicions of the previous night, it seemed, had turned out to be true. "Oh, what did he want?"

"He said he'd like us to cater the postgame meals twice a week when you're home. He said he couldn't get over how good our food was, and he was sure the players and press would love it too."

Vince was silent for a moment. *That sly fox*, he thought, getting at her through the restaurant. It's as good a move as any. In fact, it's the only way. His thought was interrupted by her asking if should she do it. "Sure, why not? A little veal and peppers, baked ziti, some sausage, and potatoes, but don't go overboard. Most of the guys eat out later anyway. How much did he say he'd give you?"

"He didn't. He said if he could make it he'd be in once a week to eat here himself, then he'd settle up."

"So it looks like you have a new customer."

"Yep, and he'll give us a lot of business too."

Vince looked at her and felt a deep warm love. If it made his sister happy to take on the Jersey Riders as a steady customer, then it was alright with him. She was old and experienced enough to take care of herself with Tex and if there ever was any trouble he was always right there. "I love you. I'll see you tomorrow."

The lounge was small and dark while only a few people sat at the bar. Vince entered and stood tall, looking for Roxanne. He found her sitting alone in the back corner at a table for two. The two role-played a scene that Vince had used a hundred times before.

"You sitting alone by choice, or did your boyfriend leave to do tinkle?"

"By choice." The smile was genuine.

"Mind if I join you?"

"No."

"Can I buy you a drink?"

"No thanks, I have one."

There was a pause for a second then an introduction. "Oh, by the way, my name is Waldo Lippinclit."

The pretty Texas burst out in laughter and grabbed his arm, still trying to be serious. "That's a hell of a name, Waldo. What do you do?"

"I blow the bugle at the racetrack. I've got a great set of lips you know."

"Oh, I didn't know that."

"Want to find out?" With that one line, Vince had changed the scene from one of humor to passion. Their eyes met above the table while their legs met under it. "I'll leave first. Give me five minutes, then come up. I'm on the fifth floor, suite 5A. I'll leave the door open."

After she left, Vince sat by himself and finished his drink, then had one with the bartender, who had recognized him. The two drinks took close to twenty minutes. After a third, he finally thought it was safe to go to his pleasure without arousing any suspicion. He took the elevator to the eighth floor and walked down three flights.

The door was open, and he walked into a beautifully spacious suite consisting of fine French provincial furniture throughout the rooms. He walked through the living room down a long hallway until he finally found the master bedroom. The light was dim, and his pleasure was seductively sprawled on the bed in a blue negligee with a garter belt and matching stockings. She turned down the bed to reveal pink satin sheets. "I bought them after he left today." She walked to him and kissed him long and hard, her tongue going deep in his mouth.

"I've waited seven long fuckin' months to have this is me again," she said while caressing his crotch, "you've got a hold on me that I don't ever want to break."

Vince was very aroused. His hands quickly undressed her, and he picked her up and took her to the bed.

That night rivaled the torrid afternoon in the servant's house, but rather than having to worry if Tex was coming or not Vince stayed the night. After a full morning of more joy with each other, Vince finally dressed to go to the ballpark. An afternoon game was scheduled and reporting time was eleven o'clock. It was very convenient for Vince that the hotel was but ten minutes away from the park, and it gave him more time to romp.

"I hope it's an easy game today, no running," said Vince, while putting on his uniform.

"Why," asked Jerry, dressing in the next stall.

"I got blue balls. They're killing me."

"Been fuckin' all night again, uh?"

"And morning too."

"When you gonna' settle down and marry Luellen? You can't live this kind of life forever, you know."

"I've been thinking about Luellen a lot. Maybe you and my sister and Johnny are right." Then a broad smile broke out on his face. "But if I ever get married, then who'll be around to satisfy all those other women?"

Jerry laughed with him. "You got a point there."

The Riders lost their third game, again by a wide margin, and followed that with two more losses. They took to the road as the only team in the majors not to have won a game.

An eight-day six-game road trip was no help to them. They lost three in Boston, to which their manager said, "I feel like the whole league is a tuxedo, and we're a pair of penny loafers." Three more losses in Baltimore proved that Hip would be the only bright spot on this road trip.

In a game that they lost in the ninth inning because of a collision in the outfield, Hip told the press, "In all my years, it's the darndest thing I ever saw. You got Millar, a French-Canadian calling for the ball in English, Cedenō, a kid who can't speak any English except hamburger, calling for the ball in Spanish, and the Jap calling for it in his mumbo jumbo, and they say it's an American game! I don't need coaches. I need the Berlitz school of language."

It was very fortunate that the press had seemed to take Vince's advice and not to take the team too seriously as yet. The headlines and stories seemed to focus more on the postgame interviews of the manager rather than the game. Besides, the Yankees were off to a good start defending their championship, and the Mets were off to an equally good start. If the average fan in the metropolitan area wanted good baseball he had his choice of both the New York teams.

The Riders returned home and saw no hope in their losing streak being halted because they had to play three games with the Yankees. Tex flew in with Roxanne hoping to add a little incentive for his team and hoping that Vince would explode in front of what was sure to be packed houses and do his *thing'* as the cowboy put it. It didn't happen.

In a three-game series, the Riders were outclassed, and Vince Donato was as passive as the rest of his teammates. The three losses extended the losing streak to twelve. It wasn't funny anymore. It was starting to get pathetic. The hitters weren't hitting the ball hard, and the pitchers weren't getting anybody out, and worst of all, from Tex's viewpoint, the fans had stopped coming to the ballpark already. The opening three-game series drew in excess of over one hundred thousand and the first game with the Yankees drew close to forty, but the remaining two barely drew ten thousand each as it wasn't a question of who would win but by how much would the Yankees win by.

After the third loss to the Yankees, Tex was furious. He had never experienced such loss in his life, and it was burning him hotter than fire. He closed the clubhouse to all reporters and lambasted his team. "You guys are the sorriest bunch of ballplayers in the major leagues. Where's your professional pride? Everybody is laughing at you. It's killing me, but I can't do a thing about it. You can suck it up and start trying a little harder. Don't you want it? Don't you want to come into a winning clubhouse? What's missing? I wish somebody would tell me. I didn't expect a pennant the first year but shit, I sure as hell didn't expect my team to be as noncompetitive as this. Hell, the fans aren't even coming. They've given up on you already."

He walked in circles in the center of the room while making eye contact with as many of his players as he could. "It has to come from within. Hell, you're all supposed to be major league players. I could've got minor league players to lose twelve in a row and I'd pay them a lot cheaper than I'm paying some of you. A tradition has to start here, right now. A tradition that says I'm a Jersey Rider, and I'll bust my ass to do what I have to do to win me a ballgame. Let's start putting things together and believing in ourselves. The losing has to stop. The giving away of ballgames has to stop or as sure as my name is Texas Sam Houston Hardin I'll fire every last one of you and get me twenty-five new ballplayers." His voice had slowly reached a controlled rage.

He stopped, and once again looked at his players' faces, then finding the manager, he said, "Hip, I want to see you and Vince in your office."

The two veterans looked at each other. They had been around too many owners in their day not to know what was about to happen. It was time for the real heart-to-heart talk between the manager, his captain, and the owner.

"Alright, so what the fuck is it with this team. Are we going to play like little leaguers all year?" continued to rage Tex in the private of the manager's office.

"Hippity" was calm. "You've assembled one of the most half-assed ballclubs I've ever been associated with. You want me to go over each player?" He knew he was right. His years of experience were no match for what Tex thought he knew.

"Yeah."

"you got a first baseman that is two years away from being in the big leagues under normal situations. The second baseman doesn't understand what we say and we don't understand what he says. We got a communication clap "Hop had to throw that in. "He might've been the best in Japan, but don't forget we kicked their ass good in the big war. Cedenō is a diamond in the rough, he's your hope for the future. The guy at third never started in his life, and he played for some pretty shitty teams, but here he starts, what does that tell you. I would've liked to have my outfield ten years ago but now they're all looking to find something to do when they retire. They're all too old to play this game the way it should be played. My catcher should be in the NFL tackling runners not chasing after passed balls, and with the exception of Dailey, I ain't got a pitcher on my team that's worth a pig's shit. I can't get filet out of chop meat Tex, and I got more chop meat on this club than any butcher shop in town."

Tex stood silent. He knew what his manager had just told him was the truth, but it wasn't in his make-up to accept failure. His failure to lure Frank Gilroy from the Red Sox to run his club from the front office forced Tex to take some ill advice and hire what he called a first, not a general manager but a "general committee" of supposedly bright baseball men who put together his team. So far the committee wasn't working.

"Did you see the figures from the gate? Thirty-nine thousand for the first Yankee game, and then we don't draw over twenty for the next two combined? Are these people tired of us so soon? If we can't draw with the fuckin' Yankees in here, then we're in deep water. And what the fuck's the matter with you?" Tex yelled as he directed his conversation Vince's way.

If it wasn't Tex talking, Vince would've jumped at him, but with the boss, Vince decided to remain cool. "What do you mean?"

"I mean I've seen no fireworks from you yet. Hell, these are your people. When are you going to turn them on?"

"Hey, look!" He pointed with his finger. "I told you when we talked in October that if things happen, they happen. I'm not starting any fights just for your enjoyment. I thought we had that straight."

"We did." He paused to wipe some sweat from his brow. He always started to sweat when he was nervous. "But, Vince, we're a roped calf before we're even out of the gate. I want to see this stadium packed like it was opening day, don't you?"

"Sure I do."

"Then fuckin' do something about it, mister!" With that, Tex quickly left and slammed the door behind him leaving two very confused people.

"He's lucky I don't break his neck. That'll put people in here. What's he want from me?"

"Relax. He's a kook. I wish I could figure him out, but I can't. What's he want from me? I can't win with this ballclub. Ride it out. Next year, it'll be somebody else's problem."

"But it's our problem now Hip, and it'll be our problem all year."

3

"Any ball hit that far should have a flight number on it." The reporters laughed, while Hop recalled how Jerry Alexander's first home run of the year gave the Riders their first win, a six-to-five thriller in extra innings.

The team celebrated the ending of a fourteen-game losing streak, the longest in the history of the major leagues for the start of a season, by throwing Ishito in the shower just after he had donned his blue suit and red tie. Hop was next to be thrown in, and then Dailey, who had pitched all ten innings to win his first game after some good performances came up short. It was all good-hearted baseball fun, the kind little leaguers do after a big win, and to the Riders, this was the win that got a very big monkey off their back.

Tex had made a public comment in Baltimore, just before the Riders arrived, that he soon might make major league history by calling in twenty-five new players and getting rid of his present team if things didn't turn around soon. His comments made headlines all over the country and forced his manager to say, "I hope he wears a catcher's mask when he tells Donato he's fired."

Even though they won their first game it failed to start a fire, and the losing continued. Going into the middle of May and coming home from a two-week twelve-game road trip, the team had won only five of thirty games and was so deep in last place that the next-to-last club was eight games ahead of them. Tex had made two more public statements about how bad his team was but managed to stay away from them, only visiting them once when they played in Texas, to which Hop said, "Going to Texas knowing he's there is like going to the principal's office after you've gotten caught playing hooky, you know something bad is going to happen."

FIFTY-SIX

The rich Texan was indeed as hot as a branding iron when he met with his manager in Arlington. Once again he threatened to get rid of all his players if things didn't turn around. He stormed Hop's office in Arlington Stadium and almost became violent to the point where he had lifted a chair high over his head and was ready to throw it against the wall when Riley French, the ace man in his organization, stopped him from the violent act.

Tex slammed it down, saying, "We've got to turn it around. French tells me we're deep in the red already. I've never been involved in a losing investment in my life, and I'm not starting now. When we come home, I want people in my park, and there are two things that'll put them there, a winning team or a Vince Donato show. See to it that one of them gets started."

Tex and French left the gray-haired manager speechless for one of the few times in his life. He thought about quitting right there, telling Tex to shove his team up his Sam Houston ass, but thought differently of it. Hop was from the old school and its creed said once you sign a contract that's it until you're fired. He knew the team wasn't going to turn around, and he also knew that Vince wasn't going to dance to Tex's tune.

That night after the game, Hip told Vince what Tex said. "He's going crazy, Hip. I think he's starting to lose some marbles. This whole scene is a blow to his ego."

"Well, are you a company man?"

"You ought to know better than to ask me that. I get paid to play ball, not start fights for Tex Hardin. If there's ever going to be a fight, it looks like it'll be between me and him."

"Don't go hero on me now. Play it by ear."

"I will, for now."

The long silver-colored Cadillac slowly pulled up in front of the hotel, and Vince ran out to get in. He had been waiting close to an hour and was just about to walk away when she finally arrived.

"You're late. It's not like you to be late with me," he said sternly.

Roxanne looked worried. She was biting her bottom lip, and her eyes were darting around from one end of the road to the other as if she wasn't even thinking of where to go. "He's going nuts. He's out there at the ranch, banging things and throwing things around. He's cracking up over this team, Vince. I'm starting to get a little scared. All he talks about lately is how bad the team is and how much money he's losing. He doesn't even have time for me."

"What does he say about me?" asked Vince, not caring about Tex's temper tantrums, having heard about the scene in Hop's office at the stadium. Tex's temper was old news.

"You're second on his list. He says he'll make you turn on, but he doesn't know what it'll take. He called you chickenshit the other day." Vince laughed as she continued. "Frank Gilroy is first on his list."

"Gilroy?"

"Tex says that if Gilroy had any hair on his balls, he would've taken his offer and built a real team, not the bunch of little leaguers he has now. I'll tell you, he's obsessed. He could be a strange and dangerous man when he's like this. I've seen it before."

Vince wasn't listening. "So he called me chickenshit. He wants me to turn on. He wants headlines."

"Yeah. He said the only time people read about you is when you make an out with a runner in scoring position and that'll never draw the fans."

The ballplayer inched closer to her and gently stroked her breast. He started a slow wet nibble on her earlobe. "Headlines like Vince Donato found in bed with owner's wife?"

"That's exactly what he's talking about only that one is out of the question.

"What about Luellen?"

"What about her?"

"Isn't she coming into New York soon to start shooting that picture?"

"Yeah. She'll be in next week."

"What if you have a big break-up with her? Real dirty. Won't it get all over the New York papers? That's the kind of stuff Tex wants. You'll make him happy, and the fans will have so much interest in your love affairs, they'll flock to the stadium. I think it's a great idea."

Vince was playing her on. He saw through the plan immediately. "It is a great idea. The papers wouldn't leave us alone. There'd be gossip columnists at every game. They'll be everywhere, but there's only one thing wrong with your plan."

"What's that?"

"I'll never get Luellen involved with the press like that. She's too decent a person to drag over hot coals. She doesn't deserve something like that. Besides, I love her. Your idea is more suited to a woman like you in your situation with me, but as you said, that's out of the question."

Vince's last sentence hurt in a way she felt she could never feel. It upset her to the point that for the first time in their many interludes together she failed to reach her ultimate high. She felt she was making progress in her quest for Vince's love but it appeared now that she had underestimated the lure that the glamor queen had on him. She'd have to find a way to split the two for good if there was ever a hope of her having him.

The Riders came home from Texas determined to start playing better. In a closed meeting with the players, Vince stood up and said what was on his mind, what had been bothering him for the last three or four weeks.

"I'm a proud man," he said. "I can take losing, but I can't take being embarrassed night after night. It's getting to me. I don't want to go around kicking ass on this team, but if that's what I have to do to get some guys motivated to play, then shit. I'll do it. I'm thirty-seven fuckin' years old and one of the oldest players in this game, and I break my ass every night. There's no reason why we all can't. Maybe the cowboy is right. Maybe we don't want to win. Maybe we've gotten so used to losing that it has become a way of life. Well, I'll never get used to losing, and none of you should either." When he was through, he sat down and looked straight at the floor. That speech was something that wanted to come out for a long time, but the time and place weren't right. The last loss in Texas, giving up four runs in the bottom of the ninth to lose it, made that night and that clubhouse the right time and place.

Jerry was the moderator of the meeting and asked if anybody else had anything else to add. Darnell Taylor stood up and directed his question across the clubhouse toward Vince. "Just who do you think isn't motivated on this team, and who do you think isn't breaking his ass on this club to win?" The question was put in a way that seemed to knock on trouble's door. Taylor thought Vince's statement was directed to him.

Jerry sensed a black cloud coming over the meeting and inched closer to his friend. He'd seen Vince throw punches at lesser statements, and he wanted to be close if anything started so he'd be in a good position to break things up. Vince stood and looked across to the well-built ex-football All-American. *You for one*, Jerry thought. Oh, Christ, he went and did it now.

Taylor wasn't expecting such a direct answer back, and very quickly, the fearless linebacker on the football field had quickly become intimidated. He had just found out that Vince Donato wasn't an easy person to bluff just by using tough words and a rough manner of speech.

Vince continued, "You have a lot of talent Darnell, but all your talk around the clubhouse is negative. I never hear you say, 'I'm gonna hit one out tonight,' or 'Tonight I'm gonna call the best game of my life.' The other day when Shit got tumbled at second on that double play, you came back to the dugout and laughed at it. That's your teammate, and he just got taken out on a double play trying to win a game, and you laughed at him. That's fuckin' bush. Did they laugh at you when you missed a tackle? Sometimes you play like a coming star, and other times I wonder where your heart is." Vince was being as direct as he knew how. Feelings never mattered when Vince was making his point; it was his way.

Taylor felt embarrassed. Everything Vince said was true, and he knew it. He looked over to the tiny Japanese player, welts on his chest and arm, and realized that he had been going through the motions thus far. If that tiny little Jap can give him all then I could too he reasoned.

He looked up at Vince and said, "I'll put some numbers on the board, and at the next meeting, the only thing you'll say about me is that I'm playing the hardest ball you;ve seen in a long time."

"I hope so, Darnell. I hope we can all turn it around, and I can say that about everybody in this club."

The first game for the pumped-up Riders was against the Boston Red Sox. It was Vince's first appearance against his former team, and he was anxious to do well. He wanted to show Gilroy that he had some sting left in his bat by possibly belting a few out.

Before batting practice for the first game, Frank Gilroy came over to talk to his ex-outfielder and friend. He was a little heavier since Vince last saw him in Dallas on Tex's ranch, but the smile and sincerity were still there. "So how's things being at home?"

"You should know. This team can't play ball. I had to give a clubhouse speech yesterday to try to shake a few guys up. I hope it worked."

"That's out of character for you isn't it."

"Well, sometimes you got to do some out-of-character things to get a few things accomplished. Anyway, the kids are pumped up. They want to kick your ass in this series. The older guys, there's not much you can tell them that they don't know."

"I understand this Cedeno is a hell of a player, and the Jap isn't as bad as people thought."

"Cedenō is great. The kid was born to be a shortstop. The Jap has a lot of heart but not that much talent. Still, he gives 100 percent every game, and that's all we can ask."

"How's things with the cowboy?"

"Frank, the guy's a fuckin' nut. You mark my words that before the year is out, there'll be a lot of trouble around this park, and most of it will be started by the cowboy."

"Oh?"

"Shit, this guy wants to win the pennant. He doesn't realize we'll finish in last place."

"What about Hip?"

"He told him. I was there. Tex wants people in the park. He wants that green that good attendance figures can bring. We haven't drawn since the opening series and the first time the Yankees were in here. It's killing him not to win, and it's absolutely murdering him to be in the red so soon. Then to top it all off, he's been on my back a few times."

"About what?"

"He seems to think that I should go out and start a fight every night, bang every girl I see, and get in a nightclub fight, you know, the reputation."

"Didn't we tell him that if it happens it happens?"

"Yeah, but he wants it to happen. I'm trying to be good, but if he keeps on my back, I'll give him headlines that'll make his head spin."

The fat Beantowner laughed. "Vince, you and I both know that he's baiting you. If you explode because of it, it's exactly what he wants you to do. You'll be playing right in his hands."

Vince took a few swings in the batting cage as Gilroy spoke, "I know it. You think I'm a fool? When I do explode, it'll be much more than he bargained for, and you can take that to the bank."

The Friday night game drew only five thousand as they witnessed a decent try by the pumped-up Riders, which still netted the same result, a six to five loss in ten innings. Taylor lived up to his promise by hitting a home run and throwing out two would-be base stealers, but it was the relief pitching that allowed the Red Sox to score two in the ninth to tie the game and one in the tenth to win it.

Tex flew in with his wife for Saturday's helmet day promotion. It was the first big promotional day on the schedule, and Tex was sure that he'd have his stadium packed for the free helmet given to all children under fourteen. The owner was very disappointed. Detroit was in Yankee Stadium, and at the time, they were the hottest team in the American League and led the Yankees by two games in the standings. The crowd in Yankee Stadium was in excess of fifty-six thousand to see the first and second-place clubs go at it.

The Meadowlands Racetrack instituted day racing that weekend and that not only drew over forty thousand to the track but tied up all the access roads to the Rider's side of the complex as well. Then to top off Tex's day it happened to be a beautiful Saturday afternoon and that meant that thousands of fans were on their way to the Jersey shore for some beach and sun. The final blow that killed Tex's helmet day was a rock festival that was held in New York's Central Park that drew in excess of another forty thousand. It seemed that everybody had someplace else to go because only seventeen thousand turned out for their free helmet. The results were the same as on any other day, a Rider loss.

At dinner that night, Tex was furious. He was beaten, but by his admission, he wasn't defeated. Not by a long shot. The tall Texan had a lot of tricks up his sleeve, and it was time to use a few. His guests that night at Domenic's were his manager, Frank Gilroy, Vince, and of course, his wife.

"Frank, I'll give you a blank check to come on over and straighten out my club."

The beantowner shook his head. "I told you once before, Tex, I'm a Boston man my whole life. I wouldn't leave for all the gold in Fort Knox. It would be like asking you to leave Texas and live here. It's unnatural."

"I guess you're right there. I can understand that. Then give us a few suggestions. An avenue to take. I'm tired of getting beat every night to an empty house."

Frank looked directly across into Tex's face. It was crying out for help. The general manager felt sorry for him but after all, he did warn him that it would take more than a lot of money to compete in the area with an expansion team. "There's nothing I can tell you about the game that Hip hasn't already told you. Let's face it. Your team is one of the worst that's come along since the '62 Mets, and they were the pits. You can lose as many as one hundred thirty games, and nobody around here gives a shit. I guess you just have to ride it out. You have some good players, but you need a whole lot more. My suggestion to you is to get rid of that committee you have and hire yourself a good experienced baseball man who knows how to run a club from top to bottom."

"Like you," answered Tex.

"Like me. Only I'm not in a position to make a move, but there are a few I'd recommend."

The Texan seemed impatient. "Hell, that's next year. I want to salvage something out of this year."

"This year's lost, Tex, face it. You're not drawing. People would rather go see the Yanks or the Mets, they both have good years. Nobody wants to see a team flub games day after day when they can see quality baseball some place else." Gilroy's statement was straight as a line. It hit home.

Tex pointed his finger as if to make his point clear to all. "I can draw here. I know it. There are enough people in this area to support three teams. They did it for years when the Dodgers, Yankees, and Giants were here, and they can do it now. I've got a trick or two that I've yet to play. I'll draw here before the year is out. Just as sure as the sun sets in the West, I'll put people in my park. You can take book on it."

Roxanne seemed bored by the whole discussion. Baseball was all she had been hearing for months and she was tired of it. "I hope so. Now can we change the subject?" There was only one thing on her mind, "when is Luellen coming in to start the movie?"

Vince answered quickly, "She'll be in on Monday." He had only one thing on his mind too. "How long will you be staying?"

Tex sprung one of his previously mentioned tricks to his dinner guests. "We're staying, and I'm traveling with the club. From now on, I'll be around for every game. I'll save this team all by myself if I have to."

Vince immediately looked at his manager who had almost choked when he heard Tex's surprise. Having Tex around for the rest of the season would not only put pressure on Hop but would almost assuredly mean that a confrontation between Tex and somebody on the club, in all probability Vince, was a sure thing. Vince wasn't too happy for Hop because of the pressure he knew he'd have to take, but he relished the thought of finally having it out with the cowboy and getting him off his back. Vince's thoughts turned to Roxanne as she never took her eyes off him, waiting for him to look her way. "You'll be here all season too?"

She smiled a smile that only a lover could recognize. "Of course."

It was a smile that swelled his loins with lust. Throughout all the years and all the women, he had never had anybody as sexually satisfying to him as Roxanne. Just the thought of her never failed to excite him. Luellen coming into town at the same time that Roxanne would be staying would pose a slight problem, but it was a problem that a man of Vince's experience could handle. At that time, he was sure of it.

After dinner, the group partied out to a local nightspot for some dancing. Tex thought that a little music and fun would sort of take the pressures off all of them for a while. He also suggested to Lucy that she take off early and go with them. Vince saw Tex's move but went along with the suggestion. Peak dinner time was over and the captain would be able to handle things and besides, his sister deserved a night out once in a while. It wasn't that Domenic was a stick in the mud. After Vince straightened him out years ago, he became very attentive to Lucy's every need and took her out quite often, it was just that Lucy was always a party girl and loved to dance, something Domenic never did. As long as he was there, Vince knew that his sister was safe from the Texan's charm. So they all left Domenic's to dance the night away, or at least until one-thirty, Vince's curfew.

Very quietly and without fanfare they entered the club in pairs. Being celebrities as they were, they thought it better if they went in pairs rather than together. Vince and Lucy went first, followed five minutes later by the Hardins, then Hip and Gilroy. Vince was recognized immediately, and after a few handshakes and hello, how are yous things settled to normal until Tex walked in. The outspoken Texan drew more attention with his Western wear than his public notoriety. They were in the city, and the fashion was city fashion. Perhaps in Dallas Tex would look as normal as a bird on a tree but in this nightclub in a tough section of Newark, he stood out like a yellow suit at a banker's convention. Nevertheless, after the catcallers and jokers stopped having fun at Tex's expense, things settled down.

Tex met Vince and Lucy on the edge of the dance floor. They had been contemplating stepping out, but neither one of them knew the latest dance that everybody seemed to be doing. "I saw this out on the coast, but I never learned it," Vince said to her.

She pointed to a couple near them. "Watch them. They're good." They watched until the song had changed, then they looked at each other and nodded in unison. "Got it?"

"Let's go." Within seconds the brother and sister team showed that you needn't know all the dances to be successful on the floor. Having a little natural rhythm, the ability to catch on quickly, and a flair for your own style was all it took. The two looked like they were dancing together for years.

Tex was amazed. "Will you look at that? That rascal can sure cut a rug," he said to his wife, "and she's not bad either." He couldn't take his eyes off Lucy. He was fascinated by her charms and her natural beauty. This was a prize worthy of any great hunter, he reasoned, so how does a bald, fat, Italian cook wind up with her? Tex just couldn't figure it out. Surely if she was shown some of the finer things in life she'd possibly consider spending some time with him. Tex was extremely confident in his abilities as a man that he could win her over and force her into making a decision. He'd done it many times before and he was confident he could do it again.

He took his wife out on the floor next to Vince and Lucy. Waving his hands and arms wildly about he said, "Is this how you do it?" It brought a laugh from everybody near them. His natural athletic ability started to show, and within a few minutes, he was no longer embarrassing himself. He and Roxanne were matching Vince and Lucy step for step.

The music was slowed down with a ballad, and that's when Tex grabbed for Lucy, leaving Roxanne for Vince.

"We're going to have a good summer," Roxanne whispered into Vince's ear, "but we've got to be careful. Tex is as cunning as a fox. He may even know now…we'll never know. Sometimes he scares me with the things he knows. He finds things out and uses them to his advantage."

"Relax," answered Vince, forever calm, "If he knew, he'd have it all over the papers, hoping it'd put people in the park. He's smart all right, but he's got to get up early in the morning to outsmart me!"

She felt him grow in her loins, and if it was at all possible, she'd do it to him right then and there. "Oh, Vince, I've got to have you, when?"

"It's going to be tough with him around all the time. It's got to be your time and place. I'm always free."

"Even with Luellen coming?" She wanted him to make a commitment.

He didn't. "There'll be plenty of time for both of you."

"Ever been to Texas?" asked Tex, turning on the country charm.

"A long time ago when my brother played in El Paso."

"Ah," he spoke as if she uttered a foul word, "El Paso, the dirty border town in the middle of nowhere. You should spend some time out on the open range. Rise early and see the sun come up like a big gold five-dollar piece just sitting in the sky. Take a deep breath and smell that clean fresh prairie air. Pick up a yellow rose, smell all its fragrances, and admire its pure natural color, it's almost like a ray of sunshine growing right there on the stem. Yes, ma'am, my ranch is indeed a work of nature, almost as if the good Lord himself went out to create the perfect picture and put it in my backyard. You know I've got a stream where the water is so clear you'd swear you were looking in a mirror, and every morning whenever I'm there, I have to share that water with two cute little jackrabbits. After they take their morning drink, they stand up on their hind legs, take a look at me, wiggle their noses, and then go off as quick as a spark. Darndest thing I ever saw."

"It does sound like God's own work of art. Maybe some day I'll take a ride on your ranch, and then I could see it all with my own eyes."

"Hell, make it now. Pick a date, and I'll fly you out."

"You're kidding!"

"Hell no. The range is made of beautiful things, and having you out there would make it a little prettier."

"I appreciate the offer, believe me, but can you take us all?"

"All? Oh, that's right. I forgot, Domenic and the kids."

"Can't forget them."

"No, we can't. You know dancing here real close with a beautiful woman kind of gives me goosebumps, and I forget what I'm saying. Excuse me."

"Besides, what would we do with Roxanne? She'd only be in the way." Lucy was joking, but Tex didn't see it that way.

"Hell. I'd find a way to get rid of her if you ever came out, that'd be easy."

Suddenly Lucy became a bit nervous. Only then did she realize that Tex's pleasant politeness and courteous charm were more than what they appeared to be. She had handled many a shark before, in her single days when she had to ward them off like ants on a fallen crum, but this one was different. He was an attractive man with a definite sense of personality about him. You could call it hot or cold but you had to call it something. All the plusses added up until she came up with the minuses. Minus number one was her husband and minus two was his wife. She admitted that she was tempted. What woman wouldn't be? To have a man as good-looking, and as wealthy as Tex Hardin after her was a feather in any woman's hat, but she was in love with Domenic and her family. Tex could have his good looks and all his millions, Lucy would be happy being Domenic's wife and mother to their children. She would admire Tex from afar, but when it came close, she'd have to remember her priorities.

It finally happened on the following day. The explosion from Vince that Tex had waited so long for finally came and how the fans loved it, what little of them there were.

Vince was having a terrible day both in the field and at the plate, and the Riders, as usual, were getting beaten by the Red Sox. Before they even came up in the bottom of the first, the Red Sox had taken a five-run lead. Vince fouled out in the second and dropped a fly ball in the third. He had a throwing error in the fourth, and with a runner in scoring position in the fifth, he fouled out again, throwing his bat in disgust. By the time he came up in the seventh, the Red Sox owned a nine-to-nothing lead. He struck out on three swings and didn't even touch the ball once. That strikeout was the light that lit his fuse.

FIFTY-SIX

He threw his bat and kicked his helmet halfway up the first base line, and immediately the home plate umpire, Vince's professional nemesis Jack Ronan, yelled, "You're out of the game for that tantrum!"

Vince was shocked. Frozen in his tracks, he turned and looked at Ronan. Throughout the years, he had seen hundreds of temper tantrums far worse than the one he just put on and never had a player been ejected for it. An umpire has to have an understanding about a ballplayer that they have to let off some steam once in a while and throwing a bat is one way to do it. As long as nobody gets hurt in the process an umpire should never eject a player for it. But Jack Ronan was no ordinary umpire when it came to Vince Donato.

Vince walked back to him with fire in his eyes. "Are you fuckin' kidding or what?"

"I warned you once not to throw that bat. I won't stand for any of your fits in my game."

Vince was dumbfounded. "You have to be the most fucked up umpire to ever put on a blue suit. Are you throwing me out for throwing a bat? It's done every day in every park in the big leagues."

"Well, not this day in this park."

By now, Hip had run out to protect his player from doing something bad. Everybody in the park knew of the feud between the two and Hip just didn't want anything rash to happen.

Tossing his hat high in the air, Hip yelled at Ronan, "Here, throw me out for that! You ain't got the balls to. You can't throw out my guy for throwing a bat. It ain't baseball."

"Yes, I can because I just did, and if you don't get out of here soon, you'll go too."

At that, Vince exploded into Ronan and met him face-to-face, eye to eye, while the crowd roared with envy to hear the words their ballplayer was yelling in Ronan's face. "You no good asshole. I should've kicked your ass in El Paso years ago. Well, remember this, before I retire, I'm going to wipe home plate with your face."

Before he could say anymore, Hip backed him out and took his place in Ronan's face. "Let's face it, Jack. You never liked my guy in the first place, and furthermore, he never liked you either."

"He can't talk to me like that Hip. Keep his mouth shut, or I'll hand him into the commissioner."

Vince shouted back, "I'll kick his heartless ass too!" By now Jerry and Darnell Taylor had to come out to restrain their teammate. Otherwise, he just might've cleaned home plate with Ronan's face. Hip kept up the argument, "Just because we're a last-place ballclub doesn't mean you have to make a call like that."

"I did. Now get out of here before you're gone too. I don't want to hear any more from anybody on your team, or I'll forfeit the game."

Hip calmed down immediately, held up his index finger, and asked to be heard from one more time. It was a sneak attack in the best tradition. Ronan gave him permission to speak once more.

"I hope next time you shit, there ain't no toilet paper 'cause you remind me of an unwiped ass. YOU'RE SHIT, ALWAYS WERE AND ALWAYS WILL BE!" Hop yelled out his last statement so all the fans in the empty ballpark could hear it. The laughs were as if they were at a Broadway comedy.

Ronan gave the thumb and said, "Hop, you're out with Donato."

Before he left, the little manager kicked dirt on Ronan's shins and then ran into the dugout with Vince, arm in arm. The fans gave them a standing ovation.

Tex loved every second. He stood with excitement with the rest of the fans. "Look at them Roxanne," he said while watching the sparse crowd, "they're turned on to him. They're excited. See what he can do to them? It's electricity when he gets going. They're his for the asking. Wait till tomorrow's game when they read about this in the papers. It'll draw an extra five thousand just to see if they'll go at it again."

But the fans didn't come the next day. The argument had been well publicized in the paper, but it was also well publicized that Ronan's crew was moving on to Baltimore and wouldn't be doing a Rider's game for quite some time.

But Monday happened to be a big day for Vince. Still upset over what had happened, he was extremely happy that Luellen was arriving. He felt more at ease with her than with any other woman.

A little tender loving care was just what he needed at the time. Still upset over yesterday's game, he couldn't have been more happy than to see Monday come, knowing that Luellen would soon be there to listen and console.

Her plane didn't land until three. Vince took Lucy with him to meet her at the airport. After posing for a few pictures with the press, they quickly went to Luellen's hotel to unpack and then out to the ballpark.

"It's only been four months, but I'm really glad to see you hon," Vince said as he reached across the front seat of the car and held her hand while driving to the park. Part of what he said was genuinely true, and some of it was a little exaggerated. He always made her feel wanted though, even if it meant stretching the truth. She was such a good and kind person toward him and loved him so much that he'd tell her anything she wanted to hear just to make her happy.

"You having a tough time?" she asked.

"Ronan threw him out of the game yesterday," said Lucy.

"I swear to God I'll get that guy before I quit." He clenched his teeth and held up a huge clenched fist. "I'll smear his brains like scrambled eggs with just one punch."

"Now don't talk like that," answered Luellen in a calm, motherly way. "It's only a game, Vince, nothing to get upset about. Little boys play it every day, and they never rant and rave and go around scrambling up people's brains. What do little boys have that keeps them cool, and why don't you have it?" She held his hand with both of hers.

Vince was silent as he continued to drive. *She's right*, he thought to himself, *here I get all upset over some jerk who's not even worth the shit on my shoe, and he's got me committing murder. It's only a game. Two days from now, nobody will even remember it.* He turned and said to her, "You're a sweetheart, and I love you for it."

She smiled her beautiful smile that had millions of men captivated and said, "Maybe I should manage your team. You might do a little better with a change of personnel."

"It's not the manager's fault. He can't hit the ball or pitch it. I blame Tex. He went out and hired a committee of guys who thought they knew baseball and told him what players to get. Tex went out and got them, and the results are that we stink. It's embarrassing, and worst yet is that the people aren't even coming to the games. If somebody sneezes on the third base side, somebody on the first base side yells, "God bless you. The stadium is empty every night, and it's killing Tex where it hurts him most—in the wallet. When the Mets started, they were shit too, but at least people came to see them."

"Tex must be taking it hard. I understand he's a man who doesn't take losing lightly."

"He's so pissed off he doesn't know where to turn next. He seems to think that I can cure his attendance problem with some of the things that I've been known to do…"

"Like fighting with umpires," added Luellen.

"Yeah, like fighting with umpires. He was all smiles last night after the game, even though we got our asses kicked. He came up to me in the clubhouse and shook my hand, saying, 'It was about time' to wait until today, that my argument will mean at least five thousand more people for today's game to see if we go at it again. But, honey, I can't go out and purposely start trouble."

"It usually finds you," added Lucy.

"Yeah, it usually does. The cowboy just doesn't understand. He just doesn't understand."

The Riders lost again that Monday night and Luellen saw firsthand what Vince had been talking about. The home team had a four-run lead going into the eighth inning, but two errors helped the Indians score three runs, and Cleveland added a five-run ninth to win the game nine to five.

For the first time, the little gray-haired manager started to show a strain on his face from the continuous loss. His postgame statements were out of line for him, short and to the point.

He became a normal interview until a reporter asked what type of pitch it was that the Cleveland first baseman hit for a ninth-inning grand slam. The wit seemed to come back as quickly as it had left. "It was a fastball. It got out of the park faster than any ball I've seen all year."

Luellen sat with Tex and his wife in Tex's private box. It was the first opportunity that Roxanne had to view the enemy close up. The pretty Texan quickly realized that she was no match for Luellen when it came to looks, but her edge was that she knew how to please Vince, and if she was to win the war, it would have to be with her womanly talents, along with an arsenal of tricks that she had been thinking of.

After the game, the four went to dinner at Domenic's. For the first time, Vince started to get more than angry with Tex when Tex suggested that the more trouble Vince got in the better for attendance it would be.

Very quietly and with a professional killer's calm, Vince said, "What if I pick up this plate and throw it right in your face and then go run to the papers to tell them what I did? That'd be the controversy you want, wouldn't it? That'd be the trouble you're looking for, wouldn't it?"

Tex answered with a smile. "Let's be serious, Vince."

"I'm dead serious." His eyes were menacing, and for the first time, Tex realized that it was no joke, that Vince was close to the edge. It was exactly what he wanted but not there and then. "Calm down now. Let's keep it peaceful."

"Then get off my back about this trouble shit." His voice was still calm, but Tex knew that one more word, and he'd find his face full of food.

At that moment, Lucy came over to see if everything was going smoothly with dinner. Tex jumped at the opportunity to get out of his situation by using Lucy as his shield. "Lucy, did you hear the way we lost tonight? A grand slam in the last inning. It's a dying shame. Tell Domenic to come on out and have a bite and why don't you sit down with us too." His voice was almost pleading, fully knowing if his sister and brother-in-law sat down, Vince wouldn't cause any unnecessary trouble.

Thinking along those same lines, Luellen suggested it was indeed a good idea, and Lucy called into the kitchen for her husband. The short balding chef came out smelling of garlic and oil, kindly declined the invitation, but told Lucy it was okay for her to sit and eat. Peace was restored for the moment, but Tex knew that he had finally gotten on Vince's back and an explosion was due very soon.

Once in the confines of his bedroom, Vince opened up to Luellen. There were a few things on his mind that were bothering him and Luellen was the only person he felt comfortable telling. It was hard for him in some ways. A man, he felt, should be able to handle his problems, but she loved him, and in a weird sort of way, that made it possible for him to confide in her his deep thoughts and feelings.

"This whole scene bothers me. He's going to push me too far and some bad things are going to come out of it. He almost had me tonight. The funny thing about it is that I know that's what he's trying to do. He's been baiting me about this all year. When it explodes, and it will, he's not going to get the best of me much longer, some dirty things are going to come out. I just want you to know that what you'll read about is nothing serious."

Her look was puzzled. "I don't understand?"

"Now you don't, but when it breaks, you'll know exactly what I'm talking about."

"You're strange tonight."

Vince ignored her conclusion and pointed to three letters on his dresser. "See those letters? Go get one and open it."

She rolled over and went to the dresser. She picked up a letter and read it. Her face turned white, and her mouth opened. It looked like she had just witnessed a horrible scene, and the camera was zooming in for a close-up.

Vince continued, "The second one came about a week after the first and the third one came three days ago, all postmarked from Texas. Now who do I know in Texas that wants to kill me and why is he bothering me here all the way in Jersey?"

Luellen asked, "Did you take these letters to the police?"

Vince smiled. "Don't you see? He's behind these too. He knows that sooner or later the press will find out about these letters, and when they do, it'll be front page stuff, and then the stadium will be packed to see the player being stalked by the mysterious assassin. It's his ace in the hole. If he doesn't get me to explode one way, he'll try another."

"What if it's not him."

"It's got to be him. Who do I know in Texas that would do something like this to me? I haven't lived there in eighteen years since my days in El Paso. The only other time I've been there, aside from playing, was for a few days last October on Tex's ranch. I've got no enemies in Texas, at least nobody that'll take time out to write death letters to me. It's got to be him."

She hugged up to him, shaking from fright. "I'm scared for you. I don't want anything to happen in any way. I'd feel a lot safer if you told the police."

"They'd only have to make it public. It would be their way. They'd have to. Besides, that's just what he'd want me to do. If it'll make it easier, I'll tell Johnny. If it turns out that it's not Tex and somebody does want me out of the way, I'd rather have Johnny behind me than the FBI."

She kissed him and rested her head on his chest. There was a silence, and then she spoke, "There's a few things on my mind that I'd like to air out."

"Such as?"

"Such as how are we going to play it while I'm here. I suppose you're seeing somebody."

Luellen was one person Vince never hid the truth from. "I'm seeing somebody, but it's a physical relationship and nothing more. It's not important to you to know who she is or when I see her. While you're here, you'll come first. There's no question about it."

Vince could tell she was hurt; she started shaking again. He wished he could give her what she wanted, but they had been through it many times before, and it always ended up the same way. He sensed another discussion about the same subject was about to come.

"I can't take it anymore, Vince. I've done a lot of thinking. When the picture is over and I leave New York, you've got a decision to make. Either I hear wedding bells or I'm putting you out of my life. I can't live like this. I can share you with Marie, but I can't share you with other women, not anymore. I want to have children, and I want you to be their father, but if you won't, I'll find somebody else who'll father my children and love only me. Keep this in mind, I mean what I say, once I leave, I'm never coming back, no matter how much it hurts. You know how long I'll be here. It's plenty of time to make up your mind. It's the biggest decision you'll make in your life, and I hope you make the right one."

Her power play caught Vince a little off guard. He was expecting the same old argument about marriage, not the situation she had presented. He was quick to reply, "First of all, don't you ever dictate terms to me again. No man ever got away with it, and you, well, I'll let it go this time because I guess I understand how you feel and what you're going through, but don't ever do it again." He paused to let what he just said seep in. His upbringing always put him on the offensive side of things and he felt her ultimatum to him was like a quick punch to the face that was intended to make him weak and vunerable.

He didn't fall for it, but he became more sympathetic to her as he went on. "I've thought about marrying you. Lately, that's all everybody has been saying, 'Why don't you marry Luellen? She's so good for you,' and they're right. I think I'm coming to an understanding with myself in regards to Marie in so much as how much of a role she plays in my life. I've thought about raising children and settling down too. Maybe it's just as good that I have to make this decision now because if I don't make it now I doubt If I ever will. So I'll give you your answer, but at the end of the season. You can stay around a little longer, it won't hurt you."

"Fair enough, but I mean what I say."

"So will I."

4

Vince walked up to Tex's box before the game carrying a bat in his hand. For a brief second, the cowboy thought that Vince would use it on him and backed off, going up the aisle out of reach. "I want to talk to you after the game, Tex. Something's come up that I think we should talk about." True to his code, Vince was facing his problem eye to eye. After the game, he would confront Tex with the death letters and ask him if he was behind them. He would act according to the answer that he received.

Tex was happy to oblige, relieved that the anger from the previous night had left his left fielder. "Sure, Vince, I'm open to any of my players who want to talk things over."

Roxanne, sitting still in the box listening to Vince's request, thought differently from the other two. Vince and she had been keeping secret company now for over three weeks, and she was confident that she was making progress in her battle to lure Vince from Luellen. *Could it be he wants to tell him all about us?* she thought. *That'd be just his style too, walk right up to Tex and tell him.* She couldn't wait for the game to be over so she could find out.

The Riders beat the Indians six to one in one of the few easy games of the year. Dailey pitched a four-hitter and Ishito, reacting to the fans' chants of BANZI, had three hits and two stolen bases. The win gave the Riders two wins in a row, having won the previous day three to two on a Jerry Alexander single in the ninth inning. After the game, Hip held court for the reporters, who seemed excited at the prospect of the Riders starting a streak of good luck.

The old man was never better as he had them in stitches. "Dailey did his impression of last year when he won all those games in the other league. Today his fastball was not his slower pitch, but his change was as fast as it's ever been. Taylor's homer was gone as soon as it reached the stands, an automatic four bases. The kid's coming around ever since Texas, and he ain't even tackling guys up here. The Jap ate fish eyes and rice last night, that was his three-hit meal. He'll eat the rest of the fish tomorrow, and maybe that'll be his four-hit meal." Suddenly Tex walked into the clubhouse, and the laughter stopped. "Oh, oh. Here comes the cowboy. I got to be serious now."

Tex looked at the still-smiling faces of the reporters and yelled to his manager, "Tell them about our streak, Hip."

"That's right, fellas. Today we won our second in a row, and if we win tomorrow, it'll make three."

The laughter couldn't be subsided. Tex was angry. He didn't want this kind of attention, although, in part, that was one of the reasons why he hired Hop. He wanted some positive press for once. His team had won two games in a row for the first time, and he wanted them to get their just due. He began to walk toward the group to add his comments when Vince grabbed hold of his arm.

"Forget them. They're only having some fun." He held up one of the envelopes. "This is more important. Let's talk in Hip's office."

Vince closed the door behind them and came right to the point. "This is the fourth death threat I've received postmarked from Texas, and I want to know if you have anything to do with them."

He was genuinely stunned. "Me?"

"Yeah, you. This is something that you would plan up in that deceiving mind of yours. Sure, I could read the headlines now. "Death Threatens Donato's Every Move." There'd be thousands of people at every ballpark we go just to see if that day was the day that a shot would ring out from the stands, and I'd get it, and all those people would mean more money for you. So what's the story, Tex? No bullshit."

He put his hand over his heart. "Vince, I swear to you I know nothing about this at all. If you're in trouble, let me help you."

Vince paused to gather his thoughts, all the time keeping his eyes on Tex. "You don't know anything about these letters?"

"No."

His voice turned loud and showed his frustration. "Then who the fuck in Texas wants to kill me?"

"I don't know, but we'll find out. We'll call in the FBI and get to the bottom of it."

Vince wasn't convinced of Tex's innocent manner. "No. No FBI. That's just what you'd want. The FBI would mean a lot of press, and that would lead to higher attendance, and that would make you smile, wouldn't it?"

"Jesus, Vince, what kind of a guy do you think I am?"

"I won't answer that now because it doesn't matter here, but I'll tell you this, and you can bet your life on it. If I find out that you're lying to me and doing this for your own pleasure, you'll pay the price. Believe me, so help me, God, I'll make you pay."

The Texan turned white with fright and sweat started to break out on his forehead. His voice cracked when he spoke, "Believe me, I didn't do anything."

"In time, we'll see. If any of this leaks out, I'll blame you, and then I guess that'll prove my point, won't it?"

Tex regained some of his composure. Normally he would never allow anybody to talk to him in this tone, but in Vince Donato, he knew he met his match, and then some. Tex knew his day would come, and he also knew that he'd have the last laugh too. "I'll keep my mouth shut, but you be careful. If there is somebody out there crazy enough to send you these letters, then he's also crazy enough to pull the trigger."

"I'll take care of that if and when the time comes. Now there are reporters out there who'll want to know what we talked about here. You tell them that I asked for a loan for a new business venture, that's no news to them, and they'll leave right away."

Just as Vince predicted, there were five reporters standing outside the door, hoping to break a story first, but they were all disappointed when hearing the reason for the private conference.

Vince dressed quickly and went looking for the only man who could help him find the writer of the death letters, Johnny "Midnight."

Walking from the players' exit, he passed Roxanne, who was waiting for either Tex or Vince, whichever one came first, for information on their talk. She was quick to ask him what he told her husband. "It was personal between Tex and me." She was anxious. "Well, tell me, was it about us?"

Her eyes looked down, then back up toward him. The look on her face pleaded for him to be gentle. She said, "I thought that maybe I was beginning to grow on you, and maybe you'd force Tex into a decision so we wouldn't have to hide it anymore." She shuffled her feet and took a sigh. "But I guess I was just hoping for a small miracle."

He looked at his watch. It was a Piaget that Luellen gave him as a gift. "I guess you were. He'll be out soon. I have to go. Call me." He left her with watery eyes. Vince knew very well that she wanted more of him than his manly talents, and in some respects, he had begun to enjoy the danger associated with their rendezvous, but to him, she was nothing more than a good piece of ass. To get involved with her was totally out of the question. If she cheated once, she'd do it again, and Vince could never stand for a cheating woman, not when she was his.

5

There was no dinner at Domenic's that night. From the ballpark, Vince drove straight to Frankie's house to inquire about the whereabouts of Johnny "Midnight." Vince hadn't seen too much of his old friend since his arrival home. Frankie had been to opening day and one or two games after that, and Vince met him at Domenic's once or twice, but Frankie was a family man, and he gave his family as much of his time as he possibly could.

After working long hours at Port Newark, attending union meetings, and attending his Sons of Italy functions, Frankie's leftover time naturally went to his kids and wife. Vince understood it all, as did the rest of the old gang. Frankie had little time to run around with Johnny like when they were younger, but his loyalty remained without question to the man who had gotten him his job on the docks and saw to it that he kept it through many a layoff.

He was happy to have Vince in his home. "I thought you forgot where I lived."

Vince put a hand on his friend's shoulder. "I never forget where good friends live. The birthday gifts always come to this house for your kids, don't they? I don't forget Frankie. I have to find Johnny tonight. It's important."

"You in trouble?"

"No."

"Look, don't lie to me. If you're in trouble, then I'm in trouble. I may be a family man, but I can still go out and break a few heads if I have to."

Vince laughed. "Who you kidding? You always left the fighting to me and Johnny. But seriously, I have to find him. You know where he's hanging now?"

"You can probably find him in the Ironbound section of Newark. Lately, he's been going to a bar on Jackson Street called Ralph's Bar and Grill. He goes with Tommy and Red. They go there because there's an old Italian guy there who makes broccoli and cavatelli like you never had in your life."

"Better than Domenic?"

"I'd have to say so. They took me there one night and I couldn't believe it. They go there and play a few cards, then eat. If he's not there, you can call Donna. She might know where he is, but you know him, he could be anywhere."

"I know. I called Donna, and she said he doesn't come home till after two almost every night. He calls her at about twelve. I left her the message." After a cold beer, Vince left Frankie's looking for Ralph's Bar and Grill in the Ironbound section of Newark, hoping that Johnny could find the pieces to fit the puzzle that had developed.

Vince found the place, but Johnny wasn't there.

This guy just could be anywhere for the night, he thought to himself. He called his wife one more time. It was ten after twelve, and he was hoping that Johnny had made his midnight call. Donna gave him a New York number where Johnny said he could be reached.

A deep voice answered the phone, "Yeah."

"Johnny 'Midnight' there?"

"Who wants to know."

"Vince Donato."

"When you guys gonna' win a game?"

Vince didn't want to hear it. "Just put Johnny on."

There was a pause, and Johnny came on, "What's up?"

"We have to talk. I need your help."

"Where you at?"

"Ralph's Bar and Grill."

"Is the old man there tonight?"

"I don't know."

"If he is tell him I'm coming over, he'll know what to do. We'll be there in a half hour."

After he hung up, he went to the bar and asked if the old man was there saying that Johnny "Midnight" was on his way and requested him. The bartender yelled down to the bar that Johnny "Midnight" was on his way and a little old man with white hair wearing baggy pants and spectacles left his barstool and went 'into the kitchen behind the bar.

It was forty-five minutes before Johnny came walking in with Red. Unlike Frankie, who had ties with Johnny's organization but wasn't officially linked, Red had become Johnny's right-hand man, and a better one couldn't be found. They took a table in the back where Vince told Johnny his problem.

"And you think that Hardin's behind it all."

"I don't know," Vince answered, "it sounds like something he would do."

The old man came and brought them an antipasto of white onions, tomatoes, provolone, pepperoni, salami, black olives, and hot cherry peppers, along with bread and wine.

"If he's been here all this while, then how are the letters postmarked from Texas?"' asked Red, nibbling on a white onion and a piece of bread.

Red's right. If he's behind it then he's got somebody in Texas mailing those letters for him. Somebody he trusts very much. Have any ideas?"

Vince quickly came up with a name. "Riley French. He's a fag that takes care of all of Tex's finances. Tex trusts him with everything. If anybody mailed those letters for him, French did."

"Okay, we'll get right on it for you, but if it's not Hardin, you'll need protection. You going to the police?"

Johnny was interested in the way Vince answered his question. "I came to you, didn't I?"

"You did right. You're one of us, and we protect our own. But if it's not Hardin, I'll have Red shadow you until we nab this guy." At that moment, the little old Italian man came with a big bowl of broccoli and cavatelli. The smell of garlic cleared the smell of bar smoke. "Bravo, maestro." The old man nodded and smiled, showing brown front teeth.

Johnny looked at Vince. "Now eat, and don't worry about it. You're in good hands."

They stayed until well after three, drinking wine and reminiscing about old times. It was fortunate for Vince that the next day was an off day. He slept till one, and then he and Johnny went to watch Luellen, who was on location on Wall Street.

It was two days after the meeting with Johnny that Vince got the answer. While eating at Domenic's with Luellen, Johnny and Red joined them. As always, the serious talk came with coffee.

"It's not Hardin," said Johnny. His voice was calm, "We sent a guy to go feel out this French fag. If he knew anything about those letters, my man would've got it out of him."

A silence covered the table like a fog over a London Street. "So what's our next move?" asked Vince.

Red answered his question. "You're stuck with me, brother. I'm going to be your shadow for a while."

"You know we're going to Texas this week."

"So am I. I'll be with you all the time. Ain't nobody getting to you unless they get to me first."

Johnny leaned back and lit a cigarette. His manner was cool. He seemed to enjoy the challenge placed before him. "You have to give us some time. We think we know who the guy is but finding him will be hard, even for us. Why didn't you tell us you fought with a guy in Dallas."

Immediately Vince recalled the night in the sex club where he brawled with a much larger man and won hands down. He snapped his fingers, "That's right. That big guy. I gave him a beatin' and he'd swore he'd get me. I didn't take him seriously, you know how many guys say they'll get even but never do. The police must have his name, they were there."

"Tex whitewashed the whole thing. He had all the papers destroyed. We'll get him. Just hang with us, when Johnny 'Midnight' goes after a guy that guy gets caught. I promise you that."

The Long Hot Summer

1

That Monday, the Riders flew to Detroit for a two-game series. It was uneventful as the Tigers, in the midst of a great year, took both games with ease.

With Tex's cooperation and approval, Red accompanied Vince on the road trip. Vince told everyone who asked that Red was a dear and close friend, and all his life he wanted to be a ballplayer and live like one, so Tex gave him permission to travel with the club. Naturally, Red would pay his own expenses, but he was just happy being around professionals. Little did everyone else know that Red was a professional in his own right, and his game was played for keeps.

From Detroit, the Riders flew north into Milwaukee. When the team arrived at the hotel, a message was waiting for Vince at the front desk. It was in a long envelope and typed on it was Vince's name and the name of the team. Vince had no idea who could be leaving a message for him, but Red knew immediately. He took the envelope from Vince's hand and opened it.

"Look's like our man is here," he said while looking around the lobby. "Here, read it."

Vince took the paper from his hand. It simply said, "I'm here to see you play or see you die. I haven't made up my mind yet." Vince looked at Red and said, "Maybe we could trace the typewriter?"

Red laughed. "You think we're the FBI, or what? If he's around here, we'll get him."

That night's game was a thriller from the very first inning. Dailey was on the mound and continually worked himself out of numerous jams in almost every inning protecting a one-to-nothing lead.

In the top of the seventh, Vince came up and led off by hitting a towering homerun deep into the left field seats. While rounding the bases, he couldn't help but think that his assassin had his eyes glued to him every step of the way. He was right. As he approached third base, Vince looked up into the crowd, and there, sitting right behind third base about ten rows up, was the man that Vince had so badly beaten months before in Dallas. Their eyes met, and the man smiled at Vince as if to say I can kill you anytime I want. It was a smile that told the ballplayer that there was no bluff in his actions, that they were for real.

Vince stopped his homerun trot and took another look to make sure. It was a long time ago, but Vince had an uncanny knack for faces, and he was sure that that was the man. He confirmed it when he slowly got up and quickly started walking up the aisle, knowing then that Vince had indeed recognized him. He stood tall, just as he had done that night, and carried a cowboy hat.

Vince looked at the crowd seated over the third base dugout and tried to find Red. Red's eyes were anxious as he knew his friend wouldn't stop in the middle of a home run trot unless something had come up. He stood up and waved. Vince finally found him.

"The guy with the cowboy hat." He pointed to a man walking up the aisle. "That's him." Red quickly looked up the third baseline but picked him up too late. He was gone. Vince ran into the stands and up the aisle, but the man seemed to disappear into the air.

As to be expected, Vince's running into the stands seemed to cause quite a stir. His teammates, thinking someone possibly threw something at him, were led out of the dugout by Darnall Taylor, his chest bulging, to come to his aid. On the other side of the field, the Milwaukee club came running just to see what was going on. When Vince Donato was involved, it could be almost anything.

Reporters surrounded Vince after the game like sharks smell blood in the water. By no means did Vince want the truth to be let out, still believing it would play into Tex's hand, so he quickly and calmly made up one of the most incredible lies ever imagined. He had to come up with something, and a man with a gun was the quickest thing he could think of.

"Look, fellas, I'm not bullshittin'. I saw a guy with a pistol, and he was pointing it at the home plate area." He was careful to say the gun was not pointed at him for fear it might stir up ideas in the heads of the reporters. "I didn't know what to do, so I just went after the guy like any honest red-blooded American would do."

"Isn't it strange that nobody else saw the gun?" asked a small reporter with a day-old beard, standing on a stool in the back of the crowd around Vince's locker.

"I just hit one out. They all could've been looking at the ball, the pitcher, or me. Fans look on the field, not at each other. Enough saw him run out. He probably packed it away."

"Sure the gun wasn't pointed at you?" asked a man from the Milwaukee Star.

Vince forced a smile. "Other times yes, this time no. I've been a good boy this year. I'm telling you the guy had it pointed toward home plate or even the Milwaukee dugout or even the other side of the field for that matter but definitely not at me."

"You know this will make you out to be a hero all over again. Sort of like when you got the guy in Boston trying to burn the flag."

"Well, let's put it this way. I couldn't just stand there and let the guy shoot, could I? I did what I had to do."

After the press had left to meet their deadlines, the police entered. Vince told them the same story in the same convincing manner, and the police were as gullible as the press had been. When Vince Donato lied, he was as convincing as a man on the gallows declaring his innocence; no one doubted his word.

As to be expected the little white-haired manager couldn't keep fully silent on the incident. "I'd like to see the attendance figures on the game. I wonder if they counted Vince as part of the crowd or not."

Considering the circumstances, Vince wisely decided to stay in his hotel room that night. He was sitting, playing cards with Jerry and Red, when someone came knocking on the door.

"Think it's him?" he said to Red.

"We'll never know till you open the door," answered Red, fully knowing that a move like Vince had imagined was out of the question.

Vince opened the door, and Tex walked in full of smiles. "So our friend is here in Milwaukee. I do assume that that was him you ran after and not a mystery man with a gun."

Vince was slow to answer. "Yeah, it was him."

"Still think I have something to do with it?"

"You might."

Tex took a glance at Jerry. "I told him. I figured he could get hit with a stray bullet or something. He should know the dangers of rooming with me."

Tex shrugged him off. "Ah, it won't come to that. This guy's bluffing."

Jerry answered back. "Tex, if the guy is serious enough to fly from Texas to Milwaukee, then the guy is serious enough to pull a trigger."

Tex slowly nodded. "Maybe so. Are you doing anything else about it besides having Red as your bodyguard? Sure you don't want me to call in the police?"

Red spoke with a firm voice. He stood and with a solid grip held Tex's arm and ushered him to the door. "I can take care of everything, Tex, and I don't even wear a badge. Thanks for dropping by." He opened the door and led Tex out. "I don't trust that guy. I just don't trust that guy."

They sat down and continued to play cards.

They were still playing till close to one when the phone rang.

"Who's calling at this hour?" asked Vince.

"Maybe it's Johnny, and he's got a lead," suggested Red.

Vince picked up the receiver. "Hello."

The voice was recognizable to Vince. "Almost got me today. I bet you'll be looking into the stands at every game now. Getting a little nervous?"

Vince was stunned to think that the man would have the gall to call. He paused and then grouped himself. "You and I can handle this another way."

Red and Jerry looked up from their cards. They both knew who it was. Red came close and put an ear to the receiver.

"Oh?"

"If you want me that bad, you can meet me somewhere, and we can slug it out, man to man. Of course, it'll end up the same way as the last time."

There was a loud laugh on the other end of the phone. "You're a tough guy to the end, aren't you? I'm going to kill you, Vince. I'm going to fill your body with holes, and if your nigger friend wants any of it, I got a few with his name on them too. It may be in Texas this weekend, or it may be the last game of the year, but this is your last season, my man. Enjoy it while you can." He hung up, leaving Vince listening to a dial tone.

The ballplayer was shattered. His usual calm composure was shaken. His face turned white and began to sweat. His palms were moist as he wiped them against his trousers. Red noticed it immediately. Being in the business that he was in made him handle it with a professional skill not taught in any school. He put a hand on Vince's shoulder to steady him. "Relax, brother. The guy's bluffin' right now. He wants to make you sweat a little before he makes a move."

"Well, I'm sweating. Face-to-face, I'd fight King Kong, but this type of shit scares me. I'm a bullseye everywhere I go for that fuckin' nut."

Red looked away. He knew what Vince had said was true, that, in fact, he was a walking target, and he was powerless to do anything to help his friend until the assassin acted first. He tried to convince the two of them who seemed equally concerned. "I wouldn't worry about it too much now. Johnny has a few more men waiting for us in Texas, where the danger would be most obvious. We'll be safe there, but I just don't think this guy is going to do anything at this time. He's having too much fun at your expense."

Vince took a deep breath and exhaled. It always relieved the tension in him. "I hope you're right Red. I sure as hell would hate to get shot away from home. I was born in Orange, and I'd like to die in Orange, and anyway, I'd like to get a chance to get this guy before he gets me."

Jerry stood up from the card table and hopped on his bed. "All this shooting business scares the shit out of me. Let's put it away and get some sleep. Tomorrow's another day."

Vince and Red agreed. They all went to bed knowing that tomorrow or the day after tomorrow or any day after that could be Vince's last. Jerry silently said a prayer for his friend. "God, he may deserve a lot of things for some of the stuff he's done, but he doesn't deserve this. He's too much a man to be stalked and hunted like an animal. Look after him, God, and while you're at it, please don't let me get hit by a stray bullet."

Jerry wasn't the only one who had the Lord's attention. Red was also in conversation. "Lord, I don't know how we're going to get this guy. I swear I don't know. Please don't let him get Vince. He's been too good of a friend to die the way Johnny and I expect to go. If somebody has to get killed out of all this, then let it be me, but let it be me after I get him first."

On the other side of the room, in his bed, Vince was the third person in the room, praying to his Maker. "Good Lord, You and I have been close a long time. I've walked a thin line for years, but I've always done what I thought was right. When my time comes, I know I can face You with a clear conscious. I don't know if my time is near or not, but if it is, please just let me live long enough to get the guy. I don't mind going so much, we all have to go sometime but don't let anything happen to "Red" on account of me. This isn't his fight. It's mine, so please don't let him get hurt."

The Riders won the next two in Milwaukee, with no more word from the assassin, and then it was off to Texas for a weekend series with the Rangers.

It was well over one hundred degrees when they landed. It reminded Vince of his playing days in El Paso. *It's always hot here*, he thought, *then thinking that this was the home of his assassin he silently said to himself, and it may get hotter*.

They were met at the airport by two men who were sent by Johnny. One man was very tall and reminded Jerry of Paul Tannen. They both had the same country-looking features. The other man was short and well-built, with jet-black hair and deep menacing eyes.

The two worked for the Dallas organization, which worked hand in hand with Johnny. They had been informed of the problem and had spent a week investigating.

The short one spoke first and in a Latin accent. "We don't know too much about this guy. We know he drives a red pickup and likes my kind of woman. He used to go to that sex club all the time, but now he doesn't go anymore. They know him there but not by name, only by face."

The tall one added, "We named him 'Buffalo Bob.' If he's around, we'll get him. If he's not, we'll get him sooner or later. It's just a matter of time."

Vince still wasn't confident though. The two men knew their target and had spent time stalking him. He'd be safe with these two for now, but he still kept looking over his shoulder at all times, and he remained a bit apprehensive.

Vince tried to hide the fact that he was becoming nervous over the whole situation but it was starting to show in his play. He misplayed a fly ball in the Friday night game that cost the Riders the lead and subsequently the game. On Saturday, he jumped at home plate when a firecracker went off in the stands and took quite a while to regain his composure to get a bat in the box and hit.

He didn't leave the hotel the entire weekend, except to travel to and from the ballpark. He ate all his meals in his room. On Saturday night, he normally would've been on the prowl, but instead, he confided his hunting to the hotel lounge, and as usual, he found a companion for the night.

They lost all three games in Texas, and for Vince, it was a relief to get out of there, alive. The ride back home was extremely turbulent, but it didn't bother Vince as he passed the time with Red in the back of the plane talking and laughing about old times. Vince recalled a story about a fumble by Red in a big football game and how Johnny had made money on it. "We all felt sorry for you. We really did, but Johnny had a lot of money on West Orange in that game and your fumble lost the game for us. Why do you think Johnny took you out to eat that night? He felt guilty that he made so much money on your fumble."

Red laughed. "Yeah, I really did feel bad, and that dinner didn't make me feel any better, just fuller. When it comes to business, there's nobody better than Johnny. He'd put the whammy on his mother if it meant making money."

Tex filtered to the back of the plane where they were. He was becoming a target for a lot of snide backstabbing remarks from the players and knew when to keep his distance from them, but the talk up front with the press was beginning to bore him, and despite his presence to the players, he knew Vince was always good for some candid conversation, so he sat and made himself comfortable. "I understand the press at home made you out to be a hero for jumping into the stands after that man with the gun. Hell, that's the kind of stuff that'll bring people into the park, maybe now we can turn some profit. Now we're starting to roll. There's even a whole batch of fan mail waiting for you back at the stadium."

Vince smiled. It was an evil smile. "So now that you finally got what you want, you're going to get off my back, right?" Tex returned the smile. "Don't hit me with that shit-eatin' grin either Tex, I mean it. I have enough problems without you on my back."

Tex stood up from his seat and stretched. He was tall, and with his ten-gallon hat on, he almost touched the ceiling of the compartment. "For now, I'll keep away, but nothing has changed. I still need you and what you can do if I'm ever going to turn a profit."

Vince reminded him by pointing a finger, "See, you're starting again."

"Okay, okay. Enough for now. Let me go sit with my manager and have a few laughs. He then said in a voice loud enough for the players to hear, 'After having a series like we just had, I can use a few laughs." He walked down the aisle to where the coaches and press were all seated. Naturally Hip was holding court. The conversation was about the value of an experienced pitching staff during a pennant race.

Hip talked in a language and manner only he seemed to understand and comprehend and closed the conversation by saying, "And I never liked beans on a Friday in Amarillo because they ruined my Saturday steak."

Tex was perplexed. "Say that again?"

"Shit. Everybody knows a starting pitcher will never eat beans on a day before he pitches because it'll make him fart too much and give him too much gas which will tire him out for the next day's start. Now when you got gas you don't eat meat because it makes it hard to digest which in turn ruins your Saturday steak because now you can't eat one, but I was never a pitcher so that never affected me anyway, even in Amarillo, where they got great beans. Follow me now Tex?"

Tex turned his head toward the aisle to see all his coaches and the beat writers biting their tongues trying not to laugh. Then he realized he was being put on and laughed out loud, "Yeah, Hip, now I get it."

2

Once he was at home Vince felt a little more comfortable with his situation. Being only twenty minutes from Johnny and his powerful organization and having Red move in with him seemed to give him added confidence. He was sure that things would work out and the fright and apprehension that showed in Texas were now a thing of the past.

The club would be playing at home for ten days and the first thing Vince did was see Luellen to explain to her the Milwaukee incident. When photos appeared in the papers of Vince running into the stands Luellen quickly called him in Milwaukee to find out if everything was all right. At home, Vince told her at length what he didn't have time to tell her on the phone. He also told her, like he told Jerry, that if she was to be around him she'd face the danger of being hit by a stray bullet. Luellen cupped his face in her soft hands and kissed him. "If you're facing trouble, then I'm facing trouble. I want to be with you whatever the consequences may be."

He wasn't as honest with Roxanne as he was with Luellen and Jerry. If I tell her about "Buffalo Bob" she'd blab it all over, he thought. With her, I'll let her take her chances. Besides, she's a cheating wife and a cheating wife deserves anything she gets.

After seeing Luellen and stopping off at his mother's to say hello, he traveled to Tommy Dara's office for some legal business that he had been thinking of ever since the Buffalo Bob affair started.

"Tommy, I want to draw up a will."

The lawyer looked at Red, then back at Vince. "Considering the circumstances, I think it's a good idea."

"So how much am I worth, and where do we start?"

Tommy walked over to a file cabinet and pulled out a large folder. He sat down at his desk and started figuring. After studying and figuring for about twenty minutes, then calculating figures on a computer for ten more, he took off his glasses and leaned back in his chair. "Vince this is a very rough estimate. I'd have to study it at length to be more accurate, but I'd say you're worth roughly about three and a half million."

Red exclaimed, "Holy shit."

Vince was proud. He looked at Red and smiled.

"I've taken into account your contract, stock, bonds, funds, certificates, real estate, your money from modeling and other endorsements, your insurance and pension. I'll leave out, for now, your jewelry, cars, clothes, and other assets like that."

"Guess I did all right for a kid that used to steal fruit from the freight yard."

Tommy laughed. "We're real proud of you Vince, really we are. You're the only one of us that made it without pulling strings."

"Well, maybe just once. Don't forget Hungry Janks."

Tommy showed embarrassment. It was he who placed the call to the hit team to set up the former ballplayer in California. "Well, just one, but you would've made it anyway."

Vince started. "Let's make this clear cut. Give each one of my sisters five hundred thousand each. They'll probably die themselves when they find out what I'm worth. I know Marvin will. He never thought too much of my life as a ballplayer anyway. Set up a twenty-five thousand dollar trust fund for each one of their children to be collected when they turn twenty-five."

"Twenty-five?"

"I think by the time you turn twenty-five you should know the value of a dollar, I did. Besides, it'll help them more at twenty-five than at eighteen or twenty-one.

"The balance I want equally distributed to St. Mary's Hospital in Orange, Children's Hospital in Chicago, and the Boston Medical Center."

"What about Luellen?" Tommy asked.

Vince paused a second. "If I ever get through all this I think I'm going to marry her. That's all she wants. Anyway, what can I give a woman that has everything? You can give her my Saint Anthony's medal, that's the type of thing she'd want."

"Your parents?"

"My father wouldn't take a dime, you know that. They've lived their life. Let the money help my sisters and their kids."

Red asked, "What about your friends? Shit, I ain't that rich that I can't use a couple of dollars."

Vince laughed. He knew Red too well to think that he was serious. "Okay, Mr. Jones. Tommy, leave exactly two dollars to Mr. Therow Jones, John Mezzanotte, Frank Lupo, and yourself."

"You're kidding."

"No, man. Two dollars will give you all a bet at the track. Bet it wisely." They all laughed.

"Well, besides that it's certainly cut and dry, no loopholes, and I'm sure no one will ever contest it. I'll draw it up, and all you have to do is come by tomorrow and sign it." They shook hands, and Red and Vince were off to the ballpark for a game with the front-running Detroit Tigers.

That night's game saw history made as the Tigers unveiled a rookie sensation named Gelford Gordon, and what he accomplished that night in Jersey Stadium was far beyond anyone's expectations.

Gordon stood six feet three and weighed barely one-ninety. He had long sideburns and two big front teeth. His hair was a sandy blonde and was ragged under his cap. He looked more like a pipe cleaner than a pitcher. He was called up from the Tigers farm team in Evansville, where he had won seven and lost three, because of injuries to their pitching staff. There were small flashes of speed in his pitches in the minors but nothing to prepare his coaches for what was to come.

His first pitch to lead-off hitter Cedeno was a fastball strike. It wasn't just a fastball but an explosion. It went by Cedeno so fast that his eyes didn't make the adjustment from the mound to the plate quick enough to swing even if he wanted to. The next two pitches went by Cedeno quicker than light and the short-stop had struck out on three pitches without ever seeing the ball clearly to swing the bat.

Ishito was called back to the dugout from the on-deck circle. “Listen, ‘Shit’,” said Hip, “this guy looks like he’s got great stuff. Better swing hard in case you hit it.” Hip loved to play his word games with the tiny Nipon, who had trouble understanding modern English let alone the language his manager spoke.

Ishito struck out in the same manner that Cedeno had, on three pitches without ever swinging the bat. Milar came up next and he fouled the first one off. In the dugout, Hip said to his players, “See, the kid is out of gas after two batters. Marty will get a hold of one.” But Milar struck out on the next two pitches. Gordon had struck out the first three men on only nine pitches.

His miraculous streak continued in the third when he struck out the remaining three men in the batting order. In his first major league start, Gelford Gordon had struck out the first nine men he faced and used only thirty pitches to do it!

Cedeno struck out again to lead off the fourth and that tied a major league record for consecutive strikeouts at ten. The small crowd of six thousand seemed to come alive on every Gordon pitch. As Ishito came to bat the message board told the crowd of his record, and in unison, they started to chant, “Strike out! Strike out!” The hometown fans were rooting for the opposing pitcher.

Ishito didn’t have a chance as Gordon whiffed him on three fastballs and the pitcher was given a rousing standing ovation. Hop, true to his reputation as the royal clown of the game, walked out to the mound and motioned the home plate umpire to join him.

“Come on out there with me Bill,” he said to Bill McCauley, a longtime friend, “let’s see if the kid’s got a heart.”

When he finally came face-to-face with Gordon, the old man said, “Stand still, son, while I feel to see if you got a heart. Maybe they made you up, and you’re a robot or something.”

Hop felt his heart then reached down to grab his wrist and feel for his pulse. “He’s got a heartbeat and a pulsebeat so I know he’s alive. You on any drugs kid?”

Gordon smiled. He knew that Hop was playing his role. "No, sir."

"Then how in hell you throwin' that fuckin' ball so fast?"

"Catcher hasn't even called for a change-up yet Mr. Hop so all I been allowed to throw is fastballs."

Hop nodded. "Oh, is that so! Well, why don't you ease up a bit and let my guys hit the ball so we can at least run on down to first base?"

"Oh!" exclaimed Gordon as he put his arms out, "You want me to throw lefthanded."

Hop broke out in a wide grin. He had just met his equal with a one-liner. "You just keep it up, kid. You're doing fine."

Gordon did better than that. In his first major league start, Gelford Gordon tied a major league record with nineteen strikeouts and pitched a three-hit shutout.

All the Riders were full of praise for the young righthander, but naturally, it was their manager who had the one line to sum up the night's frustration. "That was very possibly the best pitching performance that I've ever seen so far this year in my life. He wasn't just fast, he was faster than a blink, and my guys had their eyes closed all night long."

Just then, Tex barged into the clubhouse in a fury and quickly changed the mood from one of quiet respect for a remarkable pitching performance to a funeral parlor silence. He was raging mad, and when he began to yell, all the players knew what was to come.

"I can't believe the mood in here. I really can't fuckin' believe it. A fuckin' rookie comes in here in his first start and blows you out like some little leaguers and you sit here like it was a common everyday thing. He belittled you in front of your fans. Doesn't any one of you have any heart for this club? I swear I don't know what else to do."

Hop quickly answered for the players. "What do you want us to do, go over there and kill the kid? A game like this happens now and then. When a guy is on, he's on. Let's face it, the kid had great stuff."

Tex's face turned red with anger. He pointed a finger at Hop. "Bullshit. Tell me a rookie should strike out nineteen guys in his first start, and I'll say you're full of shit."

The clubhouse had now turned into its funeral parlor silence. Tex looked around and tried to catch a player's eyes. They all evaded him. Tex didn't look at Vince. If he did his eyes would've met their equal, instead, he focused on a short balding scribe who was busy writing notes on his pad. Tex's veins were bulging in his neck as he ran over to him and pulled the pad from his hand. "So I'm acting like a chicken that lost its head, uh? You're right. It's because I'm madder than hell and I have a right to be." He put his arm around the reporter and faced his team, pointing to all of them. "Why am I madder than hell? Because these fuckin' guys refuse to play the way their supposed to play, the way I know they can play. I think they're fuckin' shit, every last one of them."

Throughout Tex's tirade, Vince had kept staring at the owner waiting for the right moment to defend his teammates. He knew that they were all intimidated by the rich Texans and were powerless to act to the verbal abuse they were taking. But with Vince it was different. He was intimidated by no man and it was about time he stood and defended his peers.

"You know for once you're right. We shouldn't have lost like this tonight and don't think that the ones that played in this game don't feel embarrassed in their own way because I know they do. But you have a lot of nerve to come here in a player's clubhouse and belittle us like we were some little boys that didn't know right from wrong." He took a few steps in Tex's direction. Immediately Jerry thought that Vince was going after Tex and stepped between Vince and his path toward the cowboy. "It's all right," assured Vince, "no trouble. Tex, I'm going into the trainer's room which is off-limits to you and the press. I'm going to sit there a while and try to get this game out of my mind. When I come back out to change I don't want to hear any more shit from you about how my teammates play this game. If anybody's doggin' it around here I'll be the one to set them straight, not you. I don't need any ich oil man with no baseball knowledge at all coming into my clubhouse and bad-mouthing my teammates. Now do I make myself clear?"

It became so quiet that the only noise heard was that of the ceiling fans as they spun in their circular motion above. All eyes were on the Texan, it was his move. He looked at Vince intently and saw there was no bluff in his eyes.

I've got him close to the edge, he thought, *the breaking point is almost here. This will do for now.*

He took one step forward, then turned and walked out, slamming the clubhouse door behind him. The press quickly followed, all rushing to meet their deadlines with the top story of the day. The players all rushed to congratulate Vince. Now they were sure they had a leader.

3

The press printed the confrontation in the clubhouse exactly as it happened and very quickly the fans and press took sides. The side that backed the owner reasoned that the players were all professionals and should indeed be playing a better brand of ball than they had been exhibiting. They felt that it was the owner's right to give them a little hell when things weren't going well just like any other employer has a right to come down on his employees when they're not performing up to their capabilities.

The argument for the players seemed just as logical. Articles appeared saying that Tex Hardin was in a game he knew nothing about. Tex was a football man, not a baseball man. Sentiment was also expressed that Tex had no patience. After all, his team was an expansion team, and expansion teams never did well in the beginning. If after five or six years, the normal time allotted for an expansion team to show progress, they didn't improve, then Tex could rant and rave all he wanted. But to do so in the middle of their first year was a little out of the ordinary.

For two days, Tex wasn't seen at the ballpark. He had become a mystery man. Lucy would tell Vince he'd show up for an early dinner, chat a little, then leave. He had become a mystery man to Roxanne as well. He would come in late at night and leave early in the morning, very rarely conversing with his wife at all. He had become the favorite subject of many of the reporter's columns, and it was bringing to his club the publicity he so much desired, but attendance was still a disaster. They were averaging a little over five thousand a game. Something would have to be done if they were ever going to turn a profit.

The two days that Tex played the ghost made it very convenient for Roxanne to be with Vince. The first day she spent at his townhouse for a lustful afternoon, while Red sat out front in a lounge chair reading a book.

On the second day, Red chauffeured them to an adult motel on the other side of the George Washington Bridge. Their Roxanne became electrically charged as she reached new heights in her lovemaking with help from pornographic movies and adult stimuli in their room.

Vince loved every minute of time spent with her. To him, the affair had stopped being one of total lust, although he still was as receptive as ever to it. Now he enjoyed it because he was playing with something that Tex owned, and he knew he could have her any time. He knew that to Roxanne he came before her husband and that would always be so, she had told him many times.

Luellen was working very hard on her movie. She was the actress of her day. Her work was considered by many to be as good as any that had ever appeared on the screen. It didn't come without hours and hours of steady work and study. She had become the consummate professional, and now she was at the height of her career.

After putting in eleven or twelve-hour days, she would seclude herself back at her hotel and wait for Vince to come. He would usually arrive after midnight, coming from Domenic's with some veal or other food for her. There they would talk about each other's days and share their ideas and thoughts until it was time to go to bed. She'd be so tired that sex would seem out of the question until she got in his arms. That's when her body seemed to come to life and the frolicking would begin. It would last well into the night. She would rise early, have a quick breakfast, and then be off to the set by seven, leaving Vince alone in the huge bed.

That routine went on for a week. Tex had remained a mystery man, only being seen in quick glimpses coming to and from his hotel. Vince would see Roxanne every day, play ball, and then stay with Luellen every night. There was no word from "Buffalo Bob." Things were looking good for Vince Donato.

FIFTY-SIX

On the eighth day of the homestand, the roof fell in on him with a loud clang. It was Monday and Roxanne started Vince's day by calling him and telling him that they'd have to cut their afternoon short because of some business she had to attend to in the city. All her womanly powers had failed to lure Vince away from the star so she decided to concentrate her efforts on making Luellen leave him. She had arranged to have lunch with her on the set and there she would tell her of the affair she was having with Vince. Naturally, she kept her appointment a secret from Vince, telling him that her business was something she had to do for Tex at a bank.

She arrived at Vince's an hour earlier than normal. If she had to leave early she fully intended to arrive early. She, like Vince, loved every second she spent in lust with him, and planned for every moment she could get.

Red took his familiar position on the lawn chair in front and after greeting her when she arrived sat down to continue reading his book. Reading was a new experience for him. He had normally read only the sports pages of the paper and the Racing Form, but at Johnny's wife's insistence, he thought it would be a good idea to broaden his knowledge and get into the wonderful world of books.

He was reading a novel about a detective in the late forties that was chasing a diamond smuggler on the run from exiled Nazis. It had a lot of suspense and intrigue and the setting was New York City, a place he knew well. He was beginning the chapter when the detective finally has the Nazi cornered when a large shadow appeared over him. Red looked up to see a tall man dressed in jeans and a Western wear shirt standing in front of him and carrying a jacket over his arm. "You look like you're deep in that book boy."

It didn't take Red" more than a second or two to recognize the situation he was in. Standing before him was the man they were hunting. Red had now become the game. He folded the book over his lap and contemplated rushing him. His look gave his thoughts away.

"Now I wouldn't try anything rash. I got a .45 under this here jacket, and it's pointed right at your heart. I'd sure as hell hate to waste you, but if I have to, I'll do it."

Red relaxed in his chair. He was in total control of his emotions. He had been in this position before. "So what's the move?"

He pointed to a white Ford in the parking lot. If Red hadn't been too involved in his book he would've heard the car drive up and he wouldn't have been taken by surprise. "You get up off that chair and walk over to the car. I'll follow you and then we're going for a ride."

It was then that Red knew he was marked for murder. He would have to do something to get out of his plight, otherwise he knew he'd never come back. He looked around carefully but couldn't decide on how to act. With a .45 pointed in his back while walking toward the car, he couldn't do much then. An opportunity will come, he thought, then I'll blow his brains out with his gun.

He opened the passenger side door and slid across to take the wheel. "Buffalo Bob" quickly sat next to him, the barrel of his weapon pointing out from his folded jacket. "Where we going?"

His eyes were cold and his voice hardened. "Just drive where I tell you and make sure you obey all the traffic laws."

They drove north, up the Garden State Parkway for about half an hour, then turned off and onto a main route then off to a wide road that led them to a smaller street which turned them onto yet a smaller road. They drove that small road for about twenty minutes. Red had no idea where he was except probably somewhere in northwest Jersey. Once I get this guy how the hell am I going to get home? he asked himself. He was confident he could overcome his foe.

Red was instructed to turn off and onto a dirt road. They drove the road for a mile or so, and then Red made one more turn which took them into a lightly wooded but heavily brushed area.

This is where he's going to kill me, Red thought, *he sure picked an out-of-the-way place.*

He was told to bring the car to a stop. "This is where we get out. The ride's over."

Red acted quickly and decisively. He swung his right hand from the steering wheel and struck his assailant across the forehead with a clenched fist, banging his head against the window and cracking it.

Red was quick, but not quick enough. As he saw the arm swing his way, "Buffalo Bob" pulled the trigger.

The bullet entered under Red's armpit and left through his neck, leaving a hole the size of an apple. It tore out whatever was in its path, splattering blood and flesh all over the front compartment of the car.

An hour went by before the Texan came to. The force of Red's blow had rendered him unconscious for that time. When he woke his head was ringing and the car smelled of gunpowder. His own body was covered with blood that now had become sticky from the heat. He looked across the seat to see Red slumped halfway down and covered in blood. His eyes were still open and they were staring at him. Flies were buzzing around his wounds. He didn't plan it to go this way, but that's the way it happened. He'd have to live with it.

He got out of the car and walked down to a stream that was nearby. He revived himself with some cold water. He had charted his route for days and knew exactly where this stream was. He had planned to take Red down to it, shoot him there, and cover him over with leaves and brush. Now he'd have to drag the huge man all the way down.

When he opened the door the body quickly fell out. Red weighed a solid two hundred and was too heavy for him to pick up. He took hold of both arms and dragged the body down the embankment and near the stream. His own body was exhausted and his head was ready to explode, but he couldn't stop. Grabbing leaves and brush he covered the body until it blended right in with the landscape. Before he left he went into Red's pocket and removed his wallet. He took out the money, about two hundred dollars, and put the wallet in his pocket, then walked back up the bank. When he reached the top, he looked down, and nothing could be noticed. It was as pretty as a picture. He got back into the car and drove away.

At just about the same time that Red was meeting his fate, Roxanne was showering with Vince in preparation for her lunch date with Luellen. The morning had gone by quickly. Too quickly for Roxanne's sake and she took Vince one more time while in the shower.

Vince walked her out and noticed that the lawn chair was empty. Red's book was on the ground next to the chair, pages open, as if not to leave his place. Vince assumed that he had probably grown stiff sitting all morning and was taking a walk around the complex. He shrugged his shoulders and went back inside to take an afternoon nap. His morning tryst had left him tired and a nice rest was just what he needed. He set his alarm for four and fell quickly asleep.

Roxanne arrived on location and quickly found Luellen. Her role in the movie was that of a female executive working for a large brokerage firm on Wall Street, and she was dressed for the part. She wore a sky blue two-piece suit with a light pink scarf and dark blue blouse. The role required her to wear glasses.

She is a very beautiful woman, Roxanne said to herself, admiring the shoulder-length blond hair and olive skin that men all over the world admired, but she'll never have him as long as I can do something about it.

Luellen walked over and with a charming smile extended her hand. "It's so nice of you to come."

"I didn't know you wore glasses," stated Roxanne.

Luellen laughed. "I forget I even have them on. Besides, they're no lenses in them so all I'm doing is looking through plain glass. Come on to my trailer, I've got a couple of corned beefs on rye. I hope you like it."

Roxanne's nose turned up. She was used to better, to eating lunch at a fine mid-town establishment like 21 or Sardi's, but she wasn't there for the food, so it didn't matter. "I've never had it, but if it comes from a cow, I'm sure I'll like it."

"You're my kind of girl."

After some small talk about the movie and the team and about the hot summer weather, Roxanne turned the conversation to her lover.

"Tell me," she said in a manner that a lawyer questions a witness, "do you see much of Vince?"

Luellen's face was puzzled.

Roxanne continued. "I mean you work during the day and most of his work is at night, so when do you find the time to see him? It must be hard."

Luellen acknowledged the fact. "It is very hard. At the end of the day, I'm pooped. I very rarely have time to go to one of the games. When I do have time to relax, I put the game on TV and usually catch the last few innings. That's how I judge about what time he'll be over."

"Come over?" *Surprise* was written all over Roxanne's face.

"He's over every night. After Domenic',s he brings me something from there to eat and stays the night."

"Stays the night!" Her jealousy was apparent.

"Why are you so upset about it?"

Roxanne was taken back for a moment. She searched for words. "Because, uh, doesn't he have a curfew? He surely must break it every night if he's with you. If Tex found out, it would set him off. Their relationship's not that strong now as it is.

Luellen took a bite from her sandwich and studied Roxanne's eyes. They were lying. *She'd make a terrible actress*, Luellen thought. Luellen became very candid. She had learned from Vince that the quickest way to find out an answer to something was to ask a direct question. "You didn't come over here just to have lunch. You have something on your mind concerning Vince and me?"

Roxanne's smile was a confident one, and she slowly nodded her head. When she spoke, her words pierced through Luellen Lee like hot needles. "He may spend the nights with you but he spends his days making love to me, and I'll never let him go! You've been after him for years and haven't hooked him yet. It looks to me like he just keeps you around for some steady lovin' when his wells run dry."

She wanted to thrash her and tear her to bits. Explode on her like Vince had done to so many of his foes, but the lady in her wouldn't allow it. She rose from her seat and walked toward the door. She opened it and said, "Get out of here and don't bother to ever get in touch with me again!"

Roxanne was flaunting now, sure that she had hurt Luellen more than she could have imagined. "Oh, I won't. I have no need to. But remember the next time you feel that hard rock of his that it was in me all day." She slowly walked out and down the steps then turned for one final salvo, "And it tastes awful good too."

Roxanne strutted through the set knowing she had done her damage. She was banking that Luellen's character would not accept the situation as it was and she would force Vince into choosing between the two of them. Roxanne was confident that Vince would choose her.

In the trailer, Luellen was shattered. Tears quickly came to her eyes and ran down her cheeks. It wasn't the fact that Vince was physical with another woman that bothered her. After all, he had told her so from the very beginning, it was which woman that bothered her and how she had just come into her cabin and bragged about her infidelity. She stayed a long while in her trailer, then reappeared, looking as fresh and as beautiful as ever. It was one of the finest acting jobs she had ever done.

At four o'clock, Vince's alarm sounded, and he quickly jumped out of bed and began to get dressed. He had had a nice restful nap, and his thoughts were now beginning to focus on the evening's game. He always started to get his mind into the game a good three or four hours ahead of time. It was part of his dedication to the game.

He temporarily forgot about Red's absence as he ate a bowl of mixed fruit and wheat germ topped with honey. He finally realized that Red was missing when he went out to get him only to find the empty chair and book in the same place they had been long before his nap.

A search of the visitor's parking lot showed Red's car was still there. Vince touched the hood to see if the engine was warm if perhaps Red had taken the car out and had just returned. It was only warmed by the sum, not its engine. His instincts told him that something was wrong. He went back inside and quickly phoned Johnny. He wasn't in but Vince left a message with his wife to meet him at Domenic's after the game and told her the reason why.

The game that night wasn't any help to Vince or any other of the Riders as once again they were badly beaten. To make it worse, Jack Ronan was the second base umpire and called Vince out on a close play at second.

Vince exploded at Ronan and finally did what he had promised to do to him for so many years. Being restrained by Jerry and

Paul Milar, Vince reached out and threw a wild right hand aimed at Ronan's jaw. Fortunately, for Ronan, Hip happened to saunter right in the way of it and took the brunt of the blow right on the side of his head.

Vince was ejected immediately and Ronan said that he'd put him on report with the commissioner. Hop, a little woozy, held no hard feelings at all toward Vince and threatened Ronan that if he put Vince on report, he wouldn't take the next punch aimed in his direction but let it go instead.

Tex finally made an appearance after the game and seemed pleased that Vince had turned on the crowd once again. Tex's promotion that night was "Birthday Night." Those who had a birthday that day were let in free of charge, and smiled when he said, "They all got a great birthday present."

He later addressed the press by saying, "I'll back Vince Donato all the way to the Supreme Court if I have to. Everybody knows that Jack Ronan doesn't like him and never did. Why Ronan should ever be allowed to do any of our games again, I'll never know. It's a crime what he does to Vince. I don't blame my player for taking a poke at him. A man can only take so much before he breaks."

"Where have you been, Tex?" the press asked.

"I just took a little vacation from here for a while. I figured by me not being around it would loosin' them up a little. Guess it did at that, but the results haven't changed."

Hop was also in a talkative mood as the clubhouse was buzzing with quotes from everybody concerned. "I couldn't let poor Ronan take that punch. I didn't want my player brought up on murder charges. Jack Ronan owes me a close call in the next game he works that we're in."

"Gonna have a headache tonight, Hip?"

"Nah, I got nothin' in there to ache."

"Crowd emptied out early tonight."

"Yeah," answered Hip, "it's gettin' so bad around here that they're orderin' hot dogs to go by the fifth inning."

Vince had calmed down a lot from the raging whirlwind that he was on the field, but his anger still showed. He had five or six reporters in his court for over an hour as he recalled every incident throughout the years between himself and Ronan.

“That guy’s a fuckin’ prick. He never cared for me, and I never cared for him. He has to judge a game fair, and he lets his dislike for me stop him from doing that. Now I call that a crime. Why doesn’t anybody bring *him* up on report to the commissioner? Maybe I was wrong to take a swing at him, but what he’s been doing to me for seventeen years is a downright crime. But I’ll get even before I leave this game. As sure as snow is white, I’ll get that prick, and you can all put it in the papers.”

When asked how he intended to get even, Vince refused to comment, but when a reporter jokingly brought up the name of Johnny Midnight, Vince exploded once more. “You got exactly one minute to get out of my sight before I break your nose and splatter it all over your face. I do my own fighting. I don’t need Johnny for anything like that. Now you better get your ass on out of here ’cause I’m mad enough now to tear you apart for saying that.” There was blood in his eyes, and his jugular vein was bulging. His fist was clenched, and his lips were drawn tight. He made an imposing figure when he was mad.

His action was uncharacteristic. It was due largely to the favorable press he received that he had become such a popular player, and now he was quick to strike at one small off-color remark that before the game, he would’ve laughed at or retorted with a funny comment. It was wrong of him to bite the hand that had fed him so well throughout the years.

It was fortunate that Hip was nearby to cool down the situation. “You had trouble hitting the right guy before. What makes you think you can take on”—e stopped to count the reporters standing around his locker—“two, three, four, five reporters. You’re tough, but I can’t see no giant S on your chest, or maybe that’s because my head’s still a little dizzy. Is Jimmy Olsen standing next to him?” he asked one of the scribes, “if he is Clark Kent, I’d sure as hell like to meet Lois Lane.”

Vince looked at the old man standing there in just his shorts, bow-legged as a cowboy, and couldn’t help but feel a deep respect for him. He quickly calmed down and realized just how much of a fool he had made of himself. If only he could learn to keep his temper, but at times it was very hard to do. He shook his head and smiled at the scribe. "Joe, I'm real sorry. I guess I lost my cool. I owe you one."

They shook hands. Hop said, "Good, now that we know you got a heart, let's see if you can fly."

Vince finished dressing and quickly left the stadium to go to Domenic's. He hoped that Johnny had received his message and was anxious to find out what news he had of Red.

He was halfway through his dinner, steak alla Domenic, which was steak sliced through the middle and filled with cheese and Italian ham sauteed in a white wine sauce and mushrooms when Lucy joined him. Her face was full of concern, but it wasn't about Vince's incident on the ballfield, although she started her conversation with it.

"I heard about tonight. Ronan again, uh?"

"I don't worry about it anymore. I lose my temper, then I calm down. Like Luellen said, it's only a little boys game. I'm more upset at the fact that I blew up at a reporter and almost hit him. That would be inexcusable. I shouldn't let it get to me." He paused. "So what's up? You look like something's bothering you."

She sat still. She stared off to the side, but she saw nothing. Her mind was someplace else. She slowly shook her head, then spoke softly. "I should be confiding in Grace and Antionette, but they'd never understand."

"Understand what?" he said as he dunked some bread in the wine sauce and put it in his mouth.

"I think I've fallen in love with someone else."

Vince leaned forward across the table, "Did I hear you right?"

"Yeah, I think I've fallen in love with another man, and I just don't know what to do about it." Her voice was distant.

He leaned back in his chair, refusing to believe what he just heard. "You've got to be joking. You, fooling around?"

"It's not like that at all. Don't draw conclusions."

He interrupted her. "Let's start all over. Who is it?"

"Tex Hardin."

"Now I know you're joking. You better be joking. If you're not, I'll personally break both his legs."

"There you go again, losing your temper and always ready to beat up on somebody." Tears began to form in her eyes. "Will you listen to me please? I've got no one to turn to but you."

Vince immediately reached out and held her hand. He would never allow his sister to face a crisis all alone. He'd take care of Tex in his own way, but for the moment, he'd be the crutch she needed.

"At first, I knew he was a come-on. He threw lines about his great Texas ranch and how beautiful it is, and right away he asked to take me there. I kidded with him about it, but I would never do anything like that, and I told him so. Then his whole attitude started to change. He's always in here early now instead of late. We sit and talk. Never about us. He's serious at times and yet has a very humorous side about him too. He's a very interesting man, more so than I ever thought he'd be. It's gotten to the point where I look for him to come in. I look for him to touch my hand. I look for his kiss on the cheek when he says hello. Vince, the man has grown on me. I think about him more than I know I should. I just can't get him off my mind Vince, I can't."

Vince looked into her face; it was crying for help. He spoke carefully, "I can't believe I'm hearing this from you. You were always the one that was so sharp, so sure of men. You never read a man wrong, and I admired you for that. But, Lucy, you have this guy all wrong. I'm going to tell you what type of guy he is and believe me I know."

"This may come as a surprise to you, and I don't want you to get alarmed because we have everything under control, but there's somebody out there trying to kill me, and I strongly believe that Tex is mixed up in."

"No. He wouldn't."

"Don't assume anything about the man. He's ruthless. He'll do anything for the almighty dollar, and having me stalked like this will sooner or later break out in the papers, and that'll draw the people wherever we play and put money in his pocket. Trust me, I know. It's his style of working.

"You want more? The guy fucks like a bull in heat. He could never ever be faithful to only one woman. Plus I've seen him in action, the man has no morals, and he has no God. His God is the dollar sign. We weren't brought up that way Lucy. That's not our way.

"Now I know he can turn on the charm. He's smooth, real smooth, but Lucy you have to go beyond the cover and into the book. The guy's phony through and through.

"You have a husband that's a good provider and loves you with all his heart. You have a family and children who love you just as much. You've too many good things working in your favor to jeopardize it all by getting involved with a guy like Tex Hardin."

She held his hand tightly. "I know, Vince, I know, but shit, I'm having a hard time fighting my emotions. It's not easy."

"Just remember what's more important to you, a fling with Tex Hardin or the love of a family. There shouldn't be a choice. You just keep fighting it, and you'll win."

She looked at him with admiration and love. She was his older sister, but it was Vince who, throughout their lives, had always kept an eye out for her well-being. This was a severe test for her, but she knew that with his help and guidance, she'd somehow pull through.

She smiled for the first time. "I'll try. I'll really try."

"You'll do it, and if you ever need me, you know I'll be there."

She wiped a tear from her eye and rose from the table to hug him. "I'm so lucky to have a brother like you."

He smiled. "I think you better get back to running this restaurant. Otherwise, the cook will come out of the kitchen and wonder where his hostess has been."

She hugged him again and went off to her hostessing duties. Vince wondered if everything would be all right with his sister and vowed he'd let her try to work it out alone. But if Tex was still an obstacle after a while, he'd take matters into his own hands.

Vince had just finished his cheesecake and espresso when Johnny came in accompanied by a tall, well-built, good-looking young man. The two sat down and ordered coffee.

"This is Tony Torta. We call him 'the cake.'" He'll be taking over for Red until we find out what happened to him."

Vince shook hands. Tony's grip was as strong as a vice, and Vince knew he'd be safe under the young man's protection. "Got any word on Red?"

Johnny's voice was grave. He was all business. "There's only two things that could've happened to him, and neither is good. We haven't been on the best of terms lately with the other families. Drug business. Maybe they got him as a way of getting back at me for something I did to them recently." He paused, stirred his coffee, and continued. "Or your man is in the neighborhood, and he got the drop on Red. If that's the case, then Red's a dead man. He'll kill Red just to make you squirm a little more."

Vince was quick to defend his manhood. "Johnny, I stopped squirming a long time ago. Sure, I was a little upset in the beginning, who wouldn't be, but now I can't wait to meet this guy. When I do, it'll either be me or him."

Johnny smiled. "It's good that you're not afraid. I didn't think you were anyway. We've been through tougher times than this."

Vince nodded in agreement. "Where do we go from here?"

"Tony will stick with you the way Red did. You may think he's young, but I trust him with my life. He's as good as Red. I'll find out soon enough if the other families hit him. If they didn't, we can assume that your man did. We should always keep in touch." Johnny looked at his watch and realized it was late. "I've got to run. I have some business in New York to take care of. You keep cool, and don't worry, we'll get him."

After Johnny left, Vince ordered some veal and a salad for Luellen, and he and Tony were off to her hotel.

Tony escorted Vince to Luellen's door and told him he'd wait outside all night if he had to. Vince laughed. "Come on in. If you wait in the hall, you would have to wait all night."

Tony was humble. "No, really. I'll wait here. It's okay."

"Hey, listen, Red stayed here. You can stay here. You're welcome. Luellen won't mind."

Tony finally conceded and went in with Vince. When Tony met the famous movie star he stuttered and became extremely nervous, shuffling his feet and shoulders. Vince laughed. "Jes, I hope if we ever get into any trouble, you don't act this nervous."

Tony returned the smile. "I'll be all right, Vince. Miss Lee, it's a pleasure to meet you. I've seen all your pictures. You're great."

Luellen was appreciative. "Thank you very much for the kind words. It's always very nice to hear them"

After Vince showed Tony where he'd be staying and took him to the TV room, he and Luellen went to her room. It was an enormous bedroom decorated in light blues and white provincial furniture. Luellen made them a drink, and they sat down at a small table.

Luellen began to eat her meal and started the conversation with what was on her mind the most. "Roxanne Hardin came to have lunch with me today."

Vince was surprised. "Oh?"

"Vince, she told me everything."

Vince looked at her. Even without makeup on, she was as beautiful as a sunset. *Why can't I marry this woman?* he thought, *and then all this type of shit would never go on. She'd be happy, and I'd never hurt her like she is now.* "So now you know."

"So now I know. I was hurt. She came in and flaunted it, sort of rubbed it in my face. I thought about it a lot. It's nothing you never told me, but I never knew who. Now I do. I'm kind of surprised. I can't picture you with a woman like that. You're so up-front and direct. Your cards are always on the table. Her cards are always up her sleeve."

Vince grew angry. He envisioned how Roxanne must've strutted around Luellen and taunted her with their affair, loving every second of it, fully knowing that it was hurting Luellen with every word she said. He'd soon take care of Roxanne Hardin; she'd join her husband on Vince's list. Now he'd have to find some way to rationalize his affair and explain it to Luellen.

"Like I said from the very beginning, it's only physical. I couldn't care if Roxanne Hardin lived or died. She means nothing to me. 'There can never be anything between us.'"

Luellen's voice was firm. "Well, you do what you have to do. Just remember that at the end of the season, you have a decision to make. We'll know, then just what Roxanne Hardin means to you."

That behind her, she then changed the conversation to their days activities. When Vince told her about his mishap concerning Ronan, she scolded him like a mother scolded her child. He agreed. "That's why I need you Luellen. You have a certain way of putting me in my place when I'm bad and making me feel like a fool. Only you can do it and get away with it."

"Well you deserve it," she said as she ate her salad.

"And rightly so."

"By the way," she asked, "it just dawned on me. Why isn't Red here?"

Vince never lied to her, but in this instance, he didn't want to get her unduly alarmed, for fear that it might upset her to learn of Red's disappearance. "Johnny sent him on another job. Tony will be with me for a while."

"That Tony is certaintly a handsome young man."

Vince rose from his seat and walked up behind her. He gently put his arms around her and his hands found their way to her breasts. "And I'm certaintly a handsome young baseball player, aren't I?"

She turned and looked him in the eye. "Oh, Vince, I love you so much."

They made love for hours and finally fell asleep in each other's arms.

When morning came, Vince ate an early breakfast with Luellen, then went back to his place to await the call from Roxanne he knew would come. He had just finished answering some fan mail when the phone rang.

"Hello, stud." Roxanne's voice was sensuous. "Tex flew to Dallas for a couple of days, which means I'll be all yours. You can do to me whatever you want, honey."

Vince smiled, thinking he'd like to blacken her eyes for the way she hurt Luellen, but he was coy. "Good. I've got something to tell you. I'll be right over."

Roxanne beamed with joy. *It worked*, she thought, *I bet she couldn't take it and threw him out, and now he'll be all mine. Oh god, I'm horny just thinking it.*

FIFTY-SIX

Vince told Tony he wouldn't be long as he rode the elevator up to Roxanne's suite. She answered the door wearing a red bra and panties. She greeted him with a long wet kiss. Vince responded. It would be the last time he'd ever have her. He picked her up, and they went to the bedroom. It didn't take him long to reach his heights. He hadn't even taken off his pants all the way. It was the quickest he had ever done it.

Roxanne was hot and wet as soon as he touched her. She reached her height as soon as he entered her. She was always receptive to him and always would be. Vince rose off her and pulled up his pants. Roxanne's eyes opened wide. She was shocked to see him getting dressed rather than taking off all his clothes.

He spit at her. "You're a real fuckin' pig. Did you think you could split us up by telling Luellen all about us? That's just how your mind works, isn't it? It's always in the gutter. You could never break us up. Luellen's too strong for that type of bullshit you threw on her. She's got too much character for that. She's got qualities you never even thought of. And besides, she loves me, not my body or my money, but me. That's something you can't understand. To you, life is sex and money. The more you get, the more you want. I could never love you. What makes you think I could love you?" His voice was screaming now. "You have nothing for me to love. Luellen and I sit and talk. We get into each other's minds. We could spend all night in bed just talking and sharing ideas. You could never understand that.

"All you talk about is sex and all your fuckin' money. Well, you can take all your fuckin' money and shove it up your ass because you're never going to hear from me again."

He turned and left, leaving her shell-shocked. She watched as he slammed her bedroom door. Hate began to fill her. She thought only of one thing, get Luellen Lee. She'd do it anyway she could.

4

It was a small conference room in an office building in Brooklyn. Johnny was the last to enter, and when he did, he immediately thought he would never be allowed to leave, alive. Seated before him were Frank Tempo, Ray "the Pipe" Corriero, Angelo "the Angel" Lombardi, and Salvatore "Tito" Palma, and they all had hate in their eyes directed toward him. The five of them made up the so-called five families, which ruled the underworld of the New York Metropolitan area.

Johnny sat down in his assaigned seat, in front of the others, and listened as Frank Tempo began the proceedings. Tempo was the capo di capo, the head of heads, and being so gave him the right to make the major decisions and preside over major meetings like the one they were in. The old man with white hair and a mustache was noted for being a fair man, and his rule was the law.

When he spoke, he commanded the respect of all.

"I don't like what's been going on. For a man, that never got too heavy in the drug business all of a sudden you're like a kid let loose in a whorehouse. You can't get enough. Your people are seen in Brooklyn, the Bronx, Manhattan, all over. What's the matter? Jersey not big enough for you?

"There are people in this room who are mad, good and mad, and they have a right to be. They keep their business in their own territories and wonder why you can't do the same. They want blood. But I'm a reasonable man, and I believe that some things can be talked out. Hopefully, we can do it here tonight."

Johnny listened to every word that Tempo spoke to him. He knew he was safe by him, but the others showed no such assurance. Johnny looked across the table at Corriero. The Sicilian met him with a stare that could freeze water. Lombardi was no different. Palma had a trusting face but was noted for his backstabbing. Tempo was his friendly port in the storm. He addressed them by standing and talking to the old man.

"Don Tempo. It's true that I have stepped into some territories that maybe I shouldn't have been and if that offends some people here, then I'm sorry for it. The deals that you mentioned were deals that originated in Jersey but came down in New York. In the drug business, nothing is sure. You go with the flow. If the flow says we go to Brooklyn, then we go. If we have to go to the Bronx or Hell's Kitchen in Manhattan, then that's where we go. That's the way it is. We all know that."

"Then why don't the flow ever go to Jersey?" interrupted Lombardi.

Tempo presided. "Let him finish."

Johnny knew he was on the spot and was beginning to feel the heat. His people had brought in close to three million in deals during the past month involving cocaine in Bedford Stuyvesant in Brooklyn, heroin in the South Bronx, and marijuana in Hell's Kitchen in the middle of Manhattan. It was money that the others, by territorial rights, should have had.

Johnny continued, "If I'm a hunter and tracking a big beautiful buck for hours, and all of a sudden, he roams on somebody's private property, am I going to stop tracking him, or am I going after him, making my efforts worth wild? I think I'm going after him. I think you all would." There was no regret in his voice. His people had worked hard for those deals and were richly rewarded for their efforts. Johnny felt he shouldn't give out to the others a piece of the pie that was theirs all along. When he was through, he sat down and waited for Tempo to begin. The old man motioned first to Corriero.

Ray "the Pipe" Corriero was in his middle sixties with a hawk nose and big brown eyes. He earned his nickname years ago by going after people who owed the mob money and breaking their legs with a lead pipe. He had risen up the ranks and had been in control of Brooklyn for the past twelve years. His relationship with Johnny had been cordial in the past, but now it was strained.

"The way I see it is that you owe me from the Bed Sty deal. I don't care where the deal was originated from, it came down in my territory, and I deserve a cut. I'll uphold the law passed by Don Tempo, whatever it may be, but don't ever make a deal again in Brooklyn without my consent, or there'll be trouble."

Johnny knew that "the Pipe" didn't bluff. Men of his upbringing lived by the spoken word. When he threatened someone, they weren't just idle words. They were words to be taken and remembered. Johnny would remember Corriero's words, but they didn't ruffle him. Corriero's organization was strong but not as strong as Johnny's. He'd pose little opposition if it came to war.

Lombardi spoke next. His black curly hair seemed to come alive as he spoke. He had never liked Johnny. Years ago, they had gotten into a fight, and he still wore a scar on his chin from Johnny's fist.

"I've never liked you from the very beginning. You and all your fancy clothes. And the reason I don't like you is because Tony Sasso was a close friend of mine, and we all know what happened to Tony."

"Let's stick to the issues." Tempo ruled again.

"What you did was against all rules. It was wrong. I own the Bronx, and you got no business dealing there without my permission. I'll abide by Don Tempo's ruling, but don't let our paths cross again, or you'll join Tony in hell."

Johnny was a little more leery of Lombardi than of Corriero. Corriero was an old timer and thus played by the rules. Lombardi, on the other hand, had no rules. It was he who started the last war among the families by assassinating Mike Polizzi, the peaceful and fun-loving capo di capo after Don Polizzi had ruled against him in a matter involving police protection. Lombardi was cunning and knew a lot of influential people. He'd prove to be a dangerous foe, but one Johnny knew he could handle.

Palma was the last to speak. The dark skinned man, dressed in a silk suit given to him by Johnny as a birthday present, lacked the anger in his voice that the others had, still his message was the same.

"The word I got is that the take out of Hell's Kitchen was close to a million. Johnny, I figure you owe me at least 30 percent of that if not more. I'd never do that to you, and I can't understand why you'd do it to me. If Don Tempo orders payment, then that's fine with me. If he doesn't, then I'll be a little more careful who I let into my territory."

Palma was the one Johnny feared the most. He was the most cunning of them all, and his organization was almost the equal of his. Johnny would have to keep his mind sharp to compete with him. He knew he could.

Seperately, Johnny could handle all three, but united, as they were now, he'd have no chance. All eyes were on Don Tempo as he rose to give his decision.

"Sometimes we seem to forget that this is America, the land of opportunity. It's a land where a man can go out and make a living the way he wants. We reward aggressiveness. We praise the man who climbs the ladder to make it to the top. We respect the individual who sees an opportunity and goes after it. These transactions were tomatoes growing in your gardens. If you didn't pick them they would've gone bad. I think that Johnny 'Midnight' got to them before they spoiled. I can't find fault in a man for seeing an opportunity that was right under your noses all the time, but I can fault him for trespassing in your gardens. Against my better judgment, I'm going to let him keep his harvest and warn him that he'll face the consequences if it happens again.

"But I will say this on behalf of the offended parties. Johnny Midnight is a very powerful man who pulls a lot of strings. Someday another ripe harvest will grow and I'll expect him to let us all share in his rewards. I'd be very disappointed if he didn't." He looked at Johnny. "Do I make myself clear?"

Johnny nodded. Don Tempo continued, "There'll be no retaliation against Johnny 'Midnight' or any of his people from anybody in this room, and we all expect a little reciprocation from him when the time arises. That's the law."

Johnny's rivals were angry. They had come for his head but were handed their own. The tension was thick, and they all felt it. Johnny had one more thing on his mind that he had to say and that time was the only time he was sure he'd ever have them all together under peaceful terms.

He slowly stood and lit a cigarette. "I have one more thing to say before we leave. You all know my righthand man, Red,"

"The colored boy?" asked Lombardi.

"Yeah, the colored boy," Johnny quickly answered, his voice showing anger. "He's missing, and I know that something has happened to him. Now what I want to know is if anybody in this room had anything to do with it. I want a simple yes or no."

He looked straight into Lombardi's eyes. "Angelo?"

"No."

"Ray?"

"No."

Palma answered him before Johnny asked, "No way."

Johnny focused on the old man. "Don Tempo?"

"No. I know nothing of the man's disappearance."

"Somehow I believe you all. Just don't let me find out that anybody here is lying, then there'll be dues to pay. You can bet on it."

Once the meeting was over, Johnny breathed a sigh of relief. He knew what he did would not only bring the wrath of the others, but he also knew Don Tempo's price. Before he went ahead with his deals, he consulted with Tempo and gave him a healthy share of the profits. Tempo's business judgment was remarkable. That's why he sat at the head of the table. Still, if word ever got back to the others, Tempo and Johnny would be marked men. It was the chance they took.

Johnny left there, knowing he'd have to be very cautious and on his guard at all times. And he also knew that "Buffalo Bob" was in town, and Vince could be murdered at any time.

Pressure

1

Johnny called Vince at Luellen's early the next morning. He warned him that now he knew that Vince's assassin had gotten the drop on Red and that their longtime friend was dead.

"I know all about it, John. He called me this morning." His voice started to crack, and tears filled his eyes. "We lost a good friend. A real good friend."

Johnny's end of the phone was silent. Tears filled his eyes as well, but he couldn't let his sorrow affect his thinking. "Yeah, I know. Red was one in a million. He's made it personal now between me and him. He'll get it in the end, Vince. I swear to God he'll get his. You just be careful. You scared?"

"I told you once before I'm over it. I can't wait to get face to face with this guy."

"That's good. You just leave everything up to us. I got a lot of guys on this, and something has to break sooner or later. In the meantime, you just go out and play ball, do your thing, and keep in touch at all times."

"Okay."

A week went by with no word from Buffalo Bob and no leads to his whereabouts. The Riders went on the road and lost four of six, running into Detroit's Gordon again and striking out sixteen times, making it the fourth straight start that the rookie has struck out more than twelve. He has quickly become the king of baseball's hill. He was a marketable commodity, and the press was following him wherever he went. The world was his, and he deserved everything he got from it, for no pitcher has ever taken the baseball world by the reigns like he had.

He was what Hip called a natural phenomenon.

Tex had returned to his club and had been keeping a low profile throughout the road trip. He no longer was found in the clubhouse after a game, and his remarks to the press were not as severe in the criticism of his club. He had seemed to accept the fact that his club was bad, and his first year would be a financial disaster.

But Vince was still wary of the big cowboy and for three good reasons.

The first one was that Vince still suspected that Tex had something to do with Buffalo Bob, and if that were the case, then Tex Hardin was partly responsible for Red's murder.

The second reason was that Tex had made the move toward Lucy that Vince saw coming as far back as opening day, and that was something that Vince would eventually have to take care of.

Thirdly, if Tex Hardin ever found out about his affair with Roxanne, Vince was sure that even though Tex wasn't faithful to her, Tex would find a way to get back at Vince. Tex Hardin was a very simple man on the surface, yet Vince now could see the cunning character that made him the man he was. Tex Hardin was a man who Vince would have to keep an eye on at all times.

It was an extremely hot day in Baltimore. All summer the country was experiencing a heat wave that had run temperatures way up in the nineties and that day was no exception.

The Riders had come to play two games against an Oriole team that had shown them no mercy thus far, never losing to the expansion club. The Riders' record stood at thirty-six wins and seventy losses. They were a full thirty games out of first place. Despite Vince's tenth home run of the season, they lost for the seventy-first time, and the following day, they made it the seventy-second. They returned home from their road trip losing six of eight. They were destined to set the record for losing games in a year and that negative accomplishment didn't sit well with Vince. He was too proud to accept the loss.

As if Vince didn't face enough problems, he was met with still one more when he returned home.

He arrived at Newark Airport early Thursday morning. It was an off day for him, and as soon as he went home and unpacked, he and Tony went to his mother's house for lunch. He lived close to his parents, only five or six miles away, but he didn't visit as often as he knew he should. He took advantage of that off day to spend some time with the ones he loved most.

His oldest sister, Grace, was there too. She didn't look too well, and after their lunch together, Vince knew there was something wrong and took her out in the back to talk to her.

"I don't see you that much, Grace. I don't know exactly what's going on. Mama says you don't call like you used to. You got problems I can help you with, money? Sal giving you a hard time? What is it? It's not like you to stop calling Mama every day."

Grace wasn't as open to her brother as Lucy was. She found it hard to confide in him. After all, she had changed his diapers many times. She felt more like a mother to him than an elder sister. Being ten years older than him had seemed to put a block between them. She didn't think he'd understand her problems and was hesitant to explain them. "Oh, I don't know."

Vince put his arm around her. "You know, Grace, I'll always love you for the way you looked after me when I was a kid. You always had an eye on me. Never wanted me to get into trouble. I remember one day, Red and I were playing in the projects, and I fell off the monkey bars and cut my knee. Blood was running all down my leg, and I ran across the street to Mama only Mama wasn't there. You were the only one home. Remember that?"

Grace smiled and nodded.

"And you wiped off the cut and put ice on it, then applied pressure and finally stopped the bleeding. Then you wiped the tears from my eyes, gave me a cookie, bandaged up the knee, and sent me off to play." He turned and kissed her on the cheek. "I never thanked you for that. I never appreciated you then. I do now."

She started to cry. Only at that moment did she start to realize that her little brother had now grown up to be a man and she needed his strength and help in her family crisis. "We found out that Sal has cancer. It's in his stomach. The doctors are optimistic that they can cure it, but I know they'll never cure it. They never stop it." Her crying was becoming more constant.

Vince knew she was right. He had seen three members of his family, two uncles and an aunt, fall to the dreaded disease and knew that once it put it's bite on someone, more than likely that was the end.

"How's Sal taking it?"

"You know him. He's an iron man. He says he'll lick it, but that's not what bothers me. I can't control that. It's Sal Jr."

"Sal Jr.?"

"He's bad Vince, real bad. He hangs around with a bad crowd. He doesn't have a job. He leaves the house early in the morning and comes home only to eat dinner, then he goes out again till all hours of the night. He doesn't listen to me or Sal. He just doesn't listen to anybody. In a way, he reminds me of you when you were his age, but you were always a leader. You knew right from wrong. Sal's a follower, and I'm afraid he's going to be led into trouble." She turned and looked at her brother. "Sal would never ask, but I need your help with him."

Vince tightened his lips and held her hand. He was steaming inside at the fact that his own flesh and blood would turn out so wrong, but he held back his anger and said, "No problem. I'll take care of the boy, and you take care of Sal."

That night, Vince and Tony went looking for his nephew. They found him standing in a corner with three other young boys. All four of them were in dirty jeans and wore their hair long. They wore boots, and all were tattoed. "Looks like they let the animals out of the zoo," Vince said to Tony. Tony laughed and agreed.

Vince pulled up to them in his Cadillac and motioned the boy over.

"Hey, it's my Uncle Vince!" exclaimed Sal Jr., as he approached the car. He leaned into the window. His hair was long and oily and wrapped in a red bandana. He had a cigarette behind his ear and a straggly untrimmed mustache. His fingernails were dirty, and he wore a tattoo of an Italian flag on his forearm.

"Look, we were in the neighborhood, and I knew I'd find you around here somewhere. We're going for a bite to eat at a place that Tony knows in Staten Island. Why don't you join us? I don't see you that much. I'd like to know what your up to."

The boy jumped at the opportunity to ride in his uncle's Cadillac and be seen out with him. He quickly opened the door and jumped in the back.

Vince wasn't sure if his idea would get his nephew back on the right track, but he knew the street and it's ways. Might was right, and if that was ever true, then what he had in mind would work. If it wasn't, Sal would be lost.

The talk in the car was congenial. Although Vince didn't see him that much, he did know a few things about him. The boy loved the movies and knew all the actors and actresses. He constantly read the fan magazines and was forever asking Vince about Luellen. Vince remembered that he was a good athlete in school and asked if he was playing any summer ball.

"No. It doesn't interest me like it used to."

Vince asked him how he was doing with his girlfriend.

He knew that he had been seeing the daughter of an old friend of his and knew that the two were pretty serious.

"Linda's all right. Maybe we'll get married in a year or two."

The talk then focused on Vince's parents and how good they had always been to him. Vince was glad to see that he appreciated that fact. After telling him about their most recent road trip and adding in a story about Darnell Taylor and a girl he had met in Baltimore, they finally crossed the Gothels Bridge and, in a few minutes, were turning down a small side street and parking in the front of Cafe Italiano.

"Would you look at those old-timers?" said Vince as they gazed at four small dark and aged men sitting on wooden chairs in front of the club.

One man had a day-old white beard growing on his cheeks and wore a little cap slanted toward the side of his head. He was frail in a white tee shirt, and Vince knew that the man had seen many a hard day's work. "Kinda looks like Grandpa, doesn't he?"

Sal nodded. The three got out of the car and after shaking hands with the men out front, walked in. Tony introduced Vince and Sal to a man he called Uncle Joe and the three of them sat down to eat what Uncle Joe called "the best dinner you'll ever have this side of the bridge."

Uncle Joe wasn't wrong. For appetizers, he served them a cold scungilli salad with oil and garlic and clams baked with bread crumbs and flavored with lemon juice. For the second course, he served green and white noodles covered with a cream sauce and sprinkled with sage leaves. The main meal consisted of chicken sauteed in white wine with hot cherry peppers. Black coffee and anisette complimented the dinner to a tee.

The old men from out front had come inside and started a conversation with Vince and Tony. After many drinks and a few card games, it was time for Vince to teach his nephew what they had taken him there to learn.

"Ready, Tony?"

Tony nodded. Vince looked at the others, and their faces told him that they knew what was about to happen.

"We'll go out the back," said Tony, as he paid Uncle Joe.

The three got up from the table and walked down the little club and through the back into a small room that had no windows and only the one door. Tony locked the door behind him. There was no way out for Sal. He saw that Tony and Vince were staring at him. "What gives?"

"Sit down," ordered his uncle.

"Why?"

Vince hit him with a short quick punch to the boy's ribs that made him keel over. "Because I said so and because you're going to learn a few things in this room from me tonight."

Sal was folded over, holding his side. Vince picked him up by his shirt and threw him into one of the wooden chairs that the old men had been sitting in, then smacked him with the back of his hand. It was a smack that made the old men in the other room wince. "Now we're gonna' talk."

"About what." He was defiant, and Vince was proud, but he had a job to do and that job was to break down the courage that Sal was showing and turn it into a fear of him that would never leave.

"About you and what you're doing."

"What am I doing?"

Vince smacked him again and came back one more time with the back of his hand. The boy raised a fist, and Vince grabbed it with his left hand and smacked him two more times with his right. "Don't you ever raise a fist to me again? I'll break your arm if you ever do that again." Vince put on the craziest, meanest, angriest, face he could. He saw that Sal was beginning to break. The boy seemed genuinely afraid that his uncle, his crazy uncle who went after the Yankees in their own locker room, was about to beat him to death.

"You're doing nothing. That's what you're doing. You're fuckin' around with a bunch a lowlifes and losers, getting into trouble, and headed nowhere and you know what?"

"What?"

Vince smacked him two more times, forcing Tony to look away. "It's killing my sister that her boy is heading for no good. Your father has cancer, and that's a big enough problem, and my sister." He smacked him still one more time with the back of his hand. "Shouldn't have to." Still, once more, he smacked him. "Worry about her son getting in trouble."

Sal's face had quickly swollen, and he felt nauseous. Vince grabbed his hair and pushed his head back. Sal vomitted all over himself, the noodles running down his front. Vince looked him face to face. "So what's it gonna be Sal? You gonna straighten up and start acting like a man or do I have to beat your ass blue every day 'cause so help me mighty God I'll do it. You give my sweet sister," he struck him one more time, "any more hard times and I'll fly in here from wherever I am and pound my foot up your ass. Boy, you don't know what trouble is till you have Vince Donato on your back. You got that clear?"

Sal nodded. He was so scared he was shaking. "Uncle Vince, I'll do anything you say. Just don't hit me no more."

"It's not that easy. You gotta show me you want to do better."

Sal screamed in quick and rushed words. "What do you want me to do?"

"What do you want to do?"

His lips were puffed, and his eyes were almost shut, but he knew what he wanted to do. "I want to be in the film business. Can Luellen help me?"

"She can get you in, but you have to hold your own. There'll be no turning back. Now tell me what you do all day."

Sal thought they were through. He underestimated his uncle. "Hang."

Vince stepped hard on his foot and smacked him once more. Tony quickly opened the door and left, feeling nauseous himself. "Hang shit. Tell me what you do all day."

Sal was leaning in the chair and was having dizzy spells. He had never experienced such a beating in his life. He was past the pain. It was the agony of it that he was feeling now. Vince raised his hand one more time.

"No, please. No more." Vince knew he had finally broken him.

Vince's voice turned more civilized. "Then tell me what you do."

"Cop a little weed. Some shakedowns. Get laid."

"Starting tomorrow, I'm taking you down to where Luellen's filming, and she'll get you a job there. The rest is up to you. You fuck up, and you answer to me, so you have nowhere to go but up. Do I make myself clear?"

The boy nodded. "Say it."

"I won't fuck up. I don't want any part of this again."

"And from now on, you treat your mother and father with a little respect. They're two beautiful people and don't deserve the shit you've been giving them. Do I make that clear?"

"Yes, sir."

"Shake on it." Sal stood and quickly fell back in the chair.

Vince picked him up and embraced him; there were tears in his eyes. "Don't make me do this again Sal, but if I have to, I will."

"I won't, Uncle Vince, I swear to God I won't."

The next morning, Vince was at Grace's house at seven o'clock in the morning to pick up Sal Jr. and take him to the set where Luellen would get him a job as an errand boy.

Grace had the coffee on and Vince and Sal, who looked bad to Vince, talked about Sal's favorite team, the Yankees. When his son came down to join them, his father exclaimed, “What the hell happened to you? You get in a fight again?”

Sal Jr. looked at his uncle, then at his father. “I think I finally met my match last night. From now on, I’m going to stay clean. No more trouble. I’m going to take this job that Uncle Vince got me and go straight to the top.”

“Talk is cheap. You have to show us,” said Vince.

“I will.”

“My god, how will you explain how your face looks?” asked Grace.

“I’ll tell whoever asks that I was mugged. Nobody will question it. They’ll all feel sorry for me.”

Vince smiled. The boy was quick in the mind, always was. If he was serious about this, Vince was sure he’d do all right. If he wasn’t and went back to his old ways, then Vince would have to back up his threat. It was something he wished he would never have to do.

Vince dropped him off at Luellen’s trailer and wished him luck as he and Tony went off to make a personal appearance with Jerry, Hip, and Ishito, for one of the hospitals that Vince was helping raise money for.

Luellen had no trouble getting Sal a job. She was the star’s star and anything she wanted she got. She never took advantage of her status, she was too humble for that, but every now and then, she did go a little out of her way to request a small favor. To the director, this was the smallest. Sal started as a helper to the assistant director’s assistant director. It was the most menial of jobs and paid the minimum wage, but Sal was as happy as a duck in the rain. He smiled all day and stayed at the set long after he was told he could leave. He was hooked, and he owed it all to his uncle. He’d never forget him.

Luellen couldn’t wait for Vince to visit her that night so she could tell him all about Sal. She seemed genuinely happy for the boy. “Vin, he’s like a fish in water. He knew everything about the set there was to know. He knew who the whole staff was and each of their functions. He got along well with the actors, and everybody seemed to like him right off the bat. Of course, they all felt a little sorry for him about being mugged. Did you have to do that?”

"He's a street kid. That's the only language they understand. I hope this works out, and he doesn't go back to that motley crew of his."

"You didn't go back once you found your niche in life."

"And I thank God for it too."

The Riders lost the next three games to Chicago before a sparse three-day total of only ten thousand, then took off for Toronto. At the airport, Tex returned to his old ways, lambasting the players once more in front of the press as their pens were busy quoting every word. Vince's mind was not on what Tex was saying. It was on Roxanne.

While leaving the team bus that dropped them off at the airport, he happened to bump into her as she was leaving her limousine. Tex always traveled in style. She was dressed in a light-brown suit and blue blouse. In Vince's eyes, she was as attractive as ever, but he didn't look at her anymore with the lust that he once did, although it did cross his mind.

"Least you could call once in a while just to say hello," she said.

Vince was quick to answer. "Phone works both ways." He was surprised that she seemed to hold no ill feelings for the way he walked out on her.

"How's your movie queen?" she asked. Her look was piercing yet seductive. She wanted him more ever since he slammed the door on her. She ached even more for what she knew she couldn't have. Every time Tex made love to her she'd fantasize and think it was Vince. When Tex wasn't around, she'd fondle herself just thinking of the ballplayer that she had had hundreds of times and now could have no more.

"She's fine."

She approached him only to be stopped by Tex, who grabbed her arm and ushered her into the terminal, walking right past Vince without even noticing him. As she was swept away, her eyes never left him.

I have a feeling she could be trouble, he said to himself, *real trouble*.

The three games north of the border proved fruitful to Vince even though the Riders lost two of them.

In the first game, he doubled in the winning run in a four-to-three victory. He followed that up with his eleventh homer the next day. He was seeing the ball the best he had all year and his swing was becoming systematic. It was level, and for the past five or six games was producing solid line drives.

After the brief road trip, the first thing Vince did when he came home that night after the last game was call his nephew. The boy was very enthusiastic and beamed with confidence. He was sure he could make it in show business, and Luellen had enrolled him in a New York acting class and would help him every chance she could. He couldn't thank Vince enough.

Grace got on the phone next and told her brother that she couldn't get over the change in Sal in just one week. "Vince, I don't know what you did to Sal, although I can take a good guess, but whatever it was, it sure worked. It's like he's a whole new boy. He does everything for us. I'll never forget it, Vince, never."

Vince brushed it aside. It was his duty to take care of the family, and he didn't look at it as anything special. "So how's Sal? Put him on."

"He can't right now; he's resting. He always gets tired at night after work, more so now than before." Her voice seemed to trail away. "We got results back today from another test. Doesn't look too good."

"What do you mean?"

She was evasive, not wanting to say out loud what they both knew. "You know."

"Grace, nothing in life is easy. God gave nobody any assurances on anything. You have to be strong with him. He needs you now."

"I know."

"I'll be around. I love you."

"I love you too."

After he hung up with Grace, he called Lucy. As he was dialing the restaurant, he was thinking to himself, *What's next? I have a guy trying to kill me, the murder of one of my best friends still fresh on my mind, Tex on my back, Roxanne after me, a nephew that I hope is going to go straight, a brother-in-law dying of cancer, and Lucy falling for Tex. God, help me.*

"Domenic's." The voice was Lucy's.

"It's me. How's it going?"

She was silent for a second. She knew what he meant but tried to evade the question. "Business?"

"You know what I mean. He left Toronto and came back after the first night which means he was around for three days. So what's up? Was he in?"

"Listen," her voice was rushed, "I'll see you tomorrow, and we'll talk about it. I'm too busy now."

Vince knew something was wrong, and he knew he would get no answers on the phone. "Sure. Anything you say. I'll be in for an early dinner tomorrow."

Soon he hung up the phone rang. "Who's this at eleven-thirty at night?" he asked Tony. He picked up the receiver and answered.

"On the phone a while. You shouldn't tie up the line important calls can't come through."

Vince recognized the voice immediately, it was Buffalo Bob. "Hello, prick. I missed you for a while. I hoped you didn't leave before we had a chance to meet again."

There was a laugh on the other end. "No, I didn't go. I called to ask if you checked your mail?"

Vince hadn't. He motioned Tony to the mailbox out front. "No, why?"

"I sent you your friend's wallet, just for memories. I know you two were good friends."

Vince was quiet. He immediately thought of how he died trying to protect him and it hurt him very deeply that Red would have to lose his life the way he did.

"Yeah, thanks," he said. His voice turned grave and his eyes were in another world as Tony handed him the package. He spoke with controlled violence, "I'm going to kill you. I'm going to put a gun in your mouth and blow out the back of your head. You understand what I'm saying? I'm going to put you in hell mister. You and the devil are going to be good friends."

Once again, the voice laughed. "My, my, such horrid thoughts. I should be shaking."

"You should be," he seemed to come out of his trance. "Anything else you have to say? It's late and I'd like to go to bed."

"Only that it's nearing your time my friend." Vince heard the dial tone as he hung up.

Vince took a deep breath and started biting the nail on his thumb. He looked at Tony, and to Tony, he seemed shaken by the phone call he had just received. "I was beginning to think that maybe he forgot all about it. I guess he didn't. How'd he get my number? How'd he know where I live?" He was becoming excited. "How's he know when I'm home to call, where I go? Why can't we get this fuckin' guy?"

Tony held his arm tightly. "Relax, Vince. He's got to go through a lot to get you. We'll get him before anything happens."

"That's all I've been hearing from Johnny, Red and now you. Did Red get him? No." He held up the envelope that contained Red's wallet. "Now this is all we have of Red." He threw the envelope across the room and walked away, going into his room, leaving Tony standing there with no answer to his questions.

Vince walked into the kitchen the next morning and smelled the fresh coffee that Tony had made. He had a restful night as he fell asleep talking to Marie, asking her to help him with the situations he had found himself in. As always, whenever he thought of her it relaxed him, and that made it much easier to wipe his mind off the problems he had and allow him to relax.

"I'm sorry for the way I blew up last night," he said to Tony.

"Can't blame you a bit. You don't have to apologize for anything."

"Well, I did. Now sit down and I'll make you some sausage and eggs, okay?"

"Sounds good to me." Tony smiled, and Vince hugged him as a big brother would hug his younger brother after they had made up after a family squabble.

They were each reading the paper, Tony the sports and Vince the gossip column, when Vince said, "Will you listen to this? Luellen Lee, here on location shooting the movie 'Opening Bid,' is at the end of her rope with a hunk of a ball player Vince Donato after many years of trying to rope the outfielder and bring him to the altar. She's been seen the past two nights with old friend and Broadway director Palmer Brooks. Somebody better tell Vince that if he lets Luellen go, it'll be the biggest error of his career.

"Well, I think we better go down to the set and just find out what's going on between Luellen and this Palmer guy," he continued, amused at the story.

He met Luellen for lunch just as she had finished a very dramatic scene in the picture. Everyone on hand gave her a rousing applause when she finished. When Luellen acted, it was like DaVinci with a brush in his hand, Sinatra on stage, or DiMaggio in center field. It was the very best.

She came off the set and greeted her man with a kiss. "That was tough."

Vince smiled. He was proud of her in the way that she could make people believe that she was an entirely different character. "If I didn't know you any better I'd swear that you're really like that. I could easily hate you for the way you just talked to that guy. Does he come back and kill you? If you talked to me like that that's what I'd do."

She laughed. Her smile was pure white. "No. He just lost a five-million-dollar account because he was out boozing with the boys and had a hangover. He couldn't make the big deal because his mind wasn't sharp so I had to fire him. He comes back, with another firm, and we do battle one more time."

"Speaking of doing battle," Vince said in a nonchalant manner, "We might have to go at it if I find out that you and this Palmer Brooks guy were keeping steady company while I was on the road." He was half kidding. It was a minor irritation to him to read about Luellen and another man in the papers, only because he was sure of her love. Nevertheless, it did strike up a small jealousy in him.

"Oh, that," she said as she waved her hand, "I met Palmer Tuesday for an early dinner. We go back a long way together. He directed my first picture. Since he's shifted to the stage and is here in New York, I thought it'd be nice to see him again."

Vince seemed irritated at her casual manner. He had given up great sex with Roxanne on account of her and now Luellen's name was being linked with someone else. The small jealousy in him was starting to grow, "What do you mean you thought it'd be nice to see him again?"

She scolded him like she had done hundreds of times before whenever he started to lose his temper. "You're not going to get all hot and flustered over this are you? Palmer and I are nothing more than friends, that's all. You know I love you. I shouldn't even have to say it. I swear, sometimes you act like a little boy."

He blushed. He knew she was right, but he had to ask one more question. "Where did you go after dinner?"

She was getting irritated. "Really, what is this? The third degree? After dinner, I went back to the hotel, alone. I even saw your home run on TV. I don't know how this thing ever got in the papes, because Palmer and I were the only ones in the restaurant, but you have nothing to worry about but making a decision at the end of the season."

Going over all the recent pressures put on him in his mind, he sarcastically answered back, "Yeah, that's all I have to worry about."

He glanced at his watch. It was almost one, and he promised Johnny he'd do a public appearance for him at one of his stores in a local mall. He kissed her and said, "I'm sorry, honey. Guess I have a little jealous streak in me. I've got to make an appearance for Johnny. I'll see you later."

"Be careful," she warned.

He joked back to her, "Oh, I'll be around a long time. I want to see this picture you're making win you an Academy Award."

She smiled with pride as he walked away. She knew the pressures he was facing and he still had time to joke and smile about them. She said in a silent whisper, "God bless you, my love. God bless you."

For Vince, it was a long but enjoyable afternoon. He was signing autographs and was surrounded by hundreds of fans, most of them young women. He was cherishing every minute of it. This was his time. To him, this was part of the fringe benefits of being a major league baseball player. In his younger days, when he was more of a free spirit, he'd pick out three or four of the best-looking girls and line them up for the night. But now he was just satisfied to look until a tall, lightly-skinned black woman with a huge bust approached him.

She wasn't the common everyday groupie. She was well-dressed in expensive clothes and seemed more mature than the others. Vince immediately felt the passion flow between them. "Hello," she said. Her lips were colored with a bright-red lipstick. "My name is Portia. I work in the boutique right next store. My little brother loves you and would love to have an autographed picture."

Her eyes told more than she had just said. Vince smiled. It was a smile that said I see exactly what you're driving at. "Why don't I bring it to you next door as soon as I'm finished here."

"That'd be fine."

He signed autographs for another hour, all the time thinking of Portia in the tiny boutique next door. When four o'clock came, he went into the back room with Johnny to discuss another appearance he'd make soon, and receive his pay for the day.

"What gives with the tall black girl next door?" he asked.

"One of my salesmen is hitting on her. Best head he ever had." Johnny knew Vince like a book. "Go easy on her. She's just a kid, about nineteen or twenty."

"The thought never entered my mind."

Johnny's eyebrows rose. "Help yourself, but do it later. Let's discuss the plans for the next appearance."

They talked for close to an hour before Vince finally shook hands, and he and Tony walked away. Vince immediately went to where Portia was working. He couldn't get his mind off her. Her long legs and huge bust were just the remedy he needed to ease the pressures of the day that had been building up. He told Tony to wait outside and walked in.

She met him with a warm hello. "I was beginning to think you forgot me."

"No. I was just a little tied up next door. Here's your picture. How do you want me to sign it?"

"To Charles, a good boy, from Vince Donato."

"No problem." He scribbled quickly and handed her the picture. Their hands met, and Vince felt a charge go through his body. "Is it always this slow at this time?"

"Dinnertime. No customers ever come around at this time."

His look was inviting. His mouth was sensuously half open, and his lips were moist. He was tall, and she noticed a bulge in his pants. He began to nod his head as she looked down on him. He reached out and stroked her arm softly, then firmly grabbed it and reeled her into him. She understood immediately. "There's a couch in the back-room. We have to hurry."

She led him back to a small stockroom loaded with racks of dresses and sweaters. She quickly made the first move, and in a short while, their clothes were off, and her legs were wrapped around him like a pretzel. He was in her quickly, and it was tight and moist. She loved every minute of it and pleaded with him not to stop.

Their lovemaking was interrupted by a voice calling in from the store, "Is anybody here?"

"Shit," she said. "We can't do it here. Come back later, about ten. I'll be off from work then."

Vince assured her he'd be back, but he knew he wouldn't. She was a temporary plaything for him, and the time of her existence quickly had run its course.

When they were leaving the mall, Tony pointed out a woman wheeling a small boy in a wheelchair. "Now there's a crime," he said. "Poor kid can't even walk. Look at the braces on his legs, and just a kid."

Vince walked over to the boy and introduced himself to him and his mother. "You like baseball?"

He wore a Yankee cap and had a face full of freckles. His hair was short and white. "Sure."

"What's your name?"

"My name's Mickey, but my friends call me Whitey."

"Okay, Whitey. How would you and your friends and mother and father like to go see the Yankees play?"

"Sure. That'd be great." He was excited.

"Well, even though I don't play for the Yankees, I have a friend there who can see about getting you the best seats in the house." He looked at the boy's mother She was smiling appreciatively. He took her aside and reached into his picket. "I'd appreciate it if you bought the boy a nice uniform or something, as a present from me."

She was humble, "Oh no. I couldn't take it."

"Look. I have no kids of my own to spend my money on. He'd like it, and so would I."

She took the money from his hand and kept it in hers. "Thank you so much. God bless you."

"Now just give me your address so I can have the Yankees send you some tickets."

She gave him the address and kissed him on the cheek before they walked away. When they were gone, she opened her hand and saw how much he had given her. In her hand were five one hundred dollar bills. It was the money he had earned from the day's promotional work. She stood there and cried.

Domenic's was crowded for a Thursday night. Word had circulated that it was a frequent stop for Tex Hardin and that, along with Vince always being there, brought out many a sports fan for an evening meal.

Lucy was busy, but she found time to join her brother and Tony at their table. She looked at Tony. "Tony, Lucy, and I have some family business to discuss. It's kind of personal."

Tony nodded and walked away to the bar. He would never let Vince out of his sight.

"Vince, it's hard, real hard. I know what I have to do, but I just can't tell him to leave and not come in. I can't tell him to leave me alone because I don't want him to leave me alone. I want him here. I want him to come in every night."

Vince's patience was running thin. "Jesus Christ, Lucy, if you don't know right from wrong, then what am I supposed to do? You want me to tell him to leave you alone? If I do that, I'll wind up giving him a beating."

"No," she quickly answered, "they'll be none of that. Please."

"Do me one small favor. When you go to bed tonight I want you to look at your kids. What do you think they'd think of their mother carrying on with a fellow like Tex Hardin? Look at your husband in that kitchen. He sweats his ass off every night just so he can make you happy and you want to throw it all away because one good-looking rich cowboy comes along and puts a move on you. You disappoint me, Lucy, you really do.

"Grace might lose her husband at any time with this cancer thing, and you're ready to trade yours in. I just don't understand it."

She was silent. Her lips were tightly shut and her eyes were looking down. Her brother had just belittled her like he had never done before and she knew everything he had just said was true. *If only I could get away from Tex,* she thought, *then it'd be so much easier, but it couldn't be.* She'd have to wash him off her mind with sheer determination. She'd have to do it if she wanted to keep the things in life she loved the most.

She looked away and said, "I'll take care of things, and don't you start any trouble."

"Well, you better take care of things," he answered and said to her as she left, "because if you don't then I will."

Vince was as troubled as she was. His sisters' problems weighed heavy on his mind. Sal's illness was something he had no control over and his job was to see that Grace was strong and prepared when the moment of death arrived. That would be the easiest of his two tasks.

Lucy's situation was much different. She was once a strong hard headed woman who would go her way and do what she wanted and never allow herself to be led. Now Vince was seeing a whole different woman. She was weak and vulnerable, and he'd have to be around at all times to see that Tex never took advantage of her when she was most vulnerable. Lucy's problem was most paramount in his mind. It took preference over Luellen, Roxanne, Buffalo Bob, Grace, and all else. In times like this, Vince knew that the strength of the family would have to pull her through, and he swore that it would.

Baltimore was a hot club when they came into Jersey Stadium to begin a four-game weekend series, but not as hot as the weather. For the sixth straight day, the temperature had hovered near the one-hundred-degree mark. The heat had taken its toll on everyone. The Rider team looked slower than normal, and they were all dragging. Even Vince, who had been the catalyst in motivating them, seemed to be slowed down by the heat.

The series didn't go well for the Riders as Baltimore won all four games. They had now lost eleven of their last twelve and the stadium had begun to be called, "the ghost town on Route Three." Nobody was showing up. Friday night Tex had planned Rider balloon night, where every fan received a helium balloon with the Rider logo imprinted on it. The game drew only six thousand and Tex was stuck for fourteen thousand balloons. Between the double-header games on Sunday Tex had planned a home run-hitting contest between fifty fans. The fan that hit the most out, using only five swings, would win a trip for two to the Bahamas. It was a disaster as none of the fifty hit one into the stands prompting Hop to say, "Well, it looks like the cowboy has some future prospects here."

The four games with Baltimore were all close until the final innings when Hop had to go to his bullpen. It was responsible for all four losses by issuing walks and wild pitches every time one of the relief pitchers was summoned.

"My bullpen would be great, the best in baseball if only the plate was low and outside," Hop told reporters.

Vince may have been slowed by the heat, but his batting eye was as sharp as it ever had been. He hit safely in each one of the four games and, on Saturday, hit a massive home run, his twelfth of the season, deep into the left field seats. His swing was smooth, and he made contact on almost every swing he made.

"I can't remember a time I was swinging this smooth in the middle of August," he told the beat writers, "maybe the heat is doing something to me."

The sweet-swinging continued. On an eight-game road trip to the coast, Vince hit in every game and ran his hitting streak up to twenty games, a career-high. During his streak, the Riders were four and sixteen but Vince wasn't responsible for any of it. He was playing the best ball of his career and under the most pressing of conditions. It was a credit to his concentration on the game that he could be as successful as he was.

Vince returned from the road trip to find a letter waiting for him in his mailbox. It was from Buffalo Bob.

Congratulations on your twenty-game hitting streak. How long can you go? When it stops, that's when I'm going to kill you.

Vince showed the letter to Tony and said, "Guy has a way about him, doesn't he?"

Tony nodded. "Haven't heard from Johnny in a couple of days. Let's call him and see what's up with this guy."

Johnny had encouraging news for once. "We think we have a guy that may be our man. We know that this guy's from Texas and he's a loner, always out by himself. He's living in a rooming house on Long Island. We have a couple of tails on him, but nothing is happening yet. If you want to stay alive, just keep on getting hits."

Vince grew angry. "Cut the shit, John. How far do you think I can keep it going? It's going to stop sometime, and if you haven't gotten him when it does, then I'm a dead man."

"So don't make it stop. Look, we're doing the best we can. I'll call you if anything breaks with this guy. Be cool."

Vince hung up. "Be cool. It's a hundred degrees out and he tells me to be cool."

It was an exciting Thursday night game with the California Angels for the seven thousand fans that showed up on Free Hot Dog Night. First, Vince doubled in the first inning to turn his streak of consecutive hit games to twenty-one. The message board flashed his achievement. Vince thought, *Well, I'll at least have another day not to worry about.* Secondly, they went out of the park on a happy note for once as the Riders, once again behind a Vince Donato double, pulled one out in the ninth inning.

The clubhouse was in a festive spirit. It was about time that they won a game in their last at bat after giving so many away in the same fashion. It was a well-deserved win for a club that needed one.

Tex walked in wearing a wide smile. Free Hot Dog night had brought in a few more fans than he had expected, although many came because both the Yankees and Mets were playing out of town and off local TV. He was also smiling because he saw what Vince's streak had done to the crowd. They had come alive when they read the information on the scoreboard, and Tex envisioned even bigger days ahead if Vince could keep the streak going.

The cowboy walked up to Vince and patted him on the back. "Nice going. I've been waiting a long time for some excitement from you. Now it looks like I'm finally getting it."

It was a perfect opening line for Vince to bring up what had been bothering him most. "You keep on going to my sister's, you'll get more excitement from me than you bargained for."

Tex's face showed surprise. "What's that supposed to mean?"

"I mean that I want you to stay away from Lucy, and if you don't, I'll kick your ass in so far you'll be shittin' out of your mouth."

The conversation had been a quiet one just between the two of them, not a shouting match like after the game that Gordon had pitched, but nevertheless, it managed to blanket the clubhouse with silence. Whenever the two strongest personalities on the team came face-to-face they always took center stage.

Tex kept his smile. He finally had Vince hooked and now he was ready to reel him in. The time was right. Vince was a hot player and the team would be home for the next nine games. Tex saw the turnstiles spinning from what was about to come.

His voice grew loud. "I've let you say a lot of things to me that I normally wouldn't let go, but don't press your luck with me, Vince. You'll find I just might be more than you can handle."

Vince's famous temper was starting to appear. "You think that I can't handle you? Well, let me tell you something, Mr. Tex Hardin, I've always been one step ahead of you. You think I don't know that you've been trying to bait me all year? You think I'm a fool? You want headlines? I'll give you headlines that'll make your head swim."

Vince had just baited Tex. The hunted had become the hunter. "Just what do you mean by that?"

For a brief second, Vince thought about what he was about to say. He thought about the consequences and repercussions that would follow. He decided to go ahead. "I mean I've been fuckin' your wife all summer long, and you didn't even know it."

Tex exploded. He lunged toward Vince and pushed him back into his locker. The big Texan hit him with a glancing blow to the face, then was backed off by a knee to his groin. Vince managed to strike a blow himself before Jerry, Darnell, and Marty Milar all interceded and held him back.

2

The clubhouse brawl was the biggest news story to hit the Metropolitan area in years. Every newspaper featured it not only on the sports pages but also on the front page, sharing billing with the world news.

Reporters came from every major newspaper in the country and hundreds of TV crews suddenly appeared from nowhere. They all had one thing in mind, to interview any witness and get a lead story. If they found one of the combatants that would be better.

Vince made himself available to the press as readily as he always had. Over twenty reporters were waiting in Luellen's hotel lobby early the next morning when he escorted Luellen out of the elevator and to her ride.

As soon as the elevator door opened, they mobbed him. "Not right now, fellas," he said, as he held up his hand, "let me walk Luellen to her car first, then I'll talk all you want."

He walked Luellen through the lobby and out to where a limousine was waiting for her. He put her in the car, leaned over and kissed her, then turned and walked back into the lobby.

The questions came immediately. "How long was it going on?"

"Quite some time. She was getting too much to handle so I called it off."

"Doesn't your conscience bother you?"

"She was cheating, not me. I have no wife."

"Did Tex hurt you in the fight?"

"Not really. For a guy that big I thought he'd do a little more damage than he did."

"Are you still with the club?"

"As far as I know, I am. I play hard every day, and Tex knows that. He's got no baseball-playing reason to suspend me."

"What does Luellen think of all this?"

"What goes on between Luellen and me is our business and not yours. Let's keep her out of this."

"Have you talked to Hop about it?"

"Not yet, but I'm sure he'll come up with something to say."

Vince answered questions for close to an hour and then excused himself while he and Tony went to Long Island to meet Johnny. They had closed in on the man that Johnny thought was Buffalo Bob and Johnny needed Vince there to make proper identification.

The assembled press at Tex's hotel lobby was as heavy as it was in Luellen's. They were all mingling around waiting for the rich cowboy to come down and face them.

Up in his suite, Tex was as calm as a country lake. He had finally had the moment that he had been dreaming about ever since he made Vince an offer to join the club. Vince had the area alive as only he could and now, finally, Tex was confident that he'd start to draw the fans and turn a profit.

As far as the affair between Vince and his wife, Tex knew from the outset. He knew his wife well enough to know that when she first said hello to Vince when Tex introduced them, she was plotting when to get him alone. Tex chose to have Roxanne with him not out of love, but out of his dependence on a good, steady bed partner, and woman who played the role of the loving wife when he needed her to be. In one sense, Tex and Vince were alike. They could never be a one-woman man. The affair didn't bother Tex at all.

Roxanne was in the middle and had little power to do anything about it. Still hurt over Vince's rejection, her hurt was made more severe when Tex told her, "You can do what you want. I don't care. Just be in bed when I need you and at my side when I need you to be there."

She once had the best of both worlds, now she belonged to neither. Despite losing the greatest lover she had ever known and the confidence of Tex, she held her composure well.

She answered him by saying, "If that's what you want me for, then that's what I'll be around for."

She cared little for Tex. She'd play the role that he wanted and take the fringe benefits for doing it. Her life was now dedicated to Vince Donato and she'd do anything to get him. She was obsessed with him—the only thing she thought of night and day. Once again her thoughts focused on Luellen, and they raged with an evil anger that had to be taken out on her.

The elevator doors opened, and Tex was besieged by a sea of reporters. He handled them as calmly as Vince.

"Will you suspend him?"

"I don't know. He's a hot player now, and we need him and what he can do for the club. Besides, I attacked him."

"Is there a divorce in the works between you and Mrs. Hardin?"

"I'd say that's a personal matter between Mrs. Hardin and myself."

"Is there truth to the rumor the whole thing started over Vince claiming you're after his sister?"

Tex laughed. "Which one? He has three you know." He cared enough for Lucy not to drag her name into it.

"The one that has the restaurant where you eat every night."

Tex extended his finger, making a point. "This is the truth, boys. I eat there every night because I like the food. Lucy's a great gal, but I would never go after her. Too many complications." He was adept at lying with a straight face. It worked. The reporters quickly changed their questions back to Vince.

"Is there a meeting planned between you two?"

"I think we should sit down and talk. It appears to be the mature thing to do."

Tex finally ushered himself out and went to the stadium to have a meeting with his baseball people, leaving the reporters to call in their stories for the afternoon papers.

3

It was a big old Victorian home that so often appears in a horror movie. It had well over twenty rooms and had recently been converted into a boarding house. Tony noticed Johnny sitting in his car as they pulled up across the street from the house. They got out of their car and into Johnny's.

"You at it again?" was Johnny's opening statement, in reference to Vince's fight with Tex.

"The prick had it coming. Besides, it's good for the team. We'll draw thirty-thousand tonight."

"Let's stick to business. We have the place surrounded. I have men on every corner of the house, and I even have a guy in the next room from him.

"Now we know that the guy's from Texas and he fits the general description that you gave us. He has no set schedule and comes and goes as he pleases, so he's had plenty of time to stalk you. Now I don't want to kill an innocent man because I'm the one pulling the trigger, so I need you with me to make proper identification."

"You're going to do it?" asked Vince.

"I owe it to Red"."

Vince's adrenalin was flowing. He had waited a long time for this moment and now it finally had arrived. All the frightful anticipation that this man had caused Vince to have was now about to be taken care of. The sorrow and pain that he had put on all of them by killing Red was now about to be avenged. Vince licked his lips; he couldn't wait for it to happen. "So how do I properly identify him?"

"We go up and knock on the door. When he answers, we'll know."

Vince nodded. They crossed the street and walked up on the porch and into the house. All the while Vince was thinking of his friend who had died for him, of all the good times they had shared together. It was now payback time.

They walked up two flights of dimly lit stairs and down a long hallway. As they walked Vince noticed how old and yellowed the wallpaper was. It was a flowered pattern that was peeling at the seams.

Johnny nodded to his man who was standing in the doorway of his room. "Anything?"

"Quiet as a church."

Johnny held his jacket over his hand. Under the jacket, he carried a .38 short-nosed pistol with a silencer attached. Vince hoped he wouldn't get splattered with blood.

Johnny knocked. The door was oak, and it made a solid sound. There was no answer. He knocked again. "Yeah, I'm coming," said a voice from the other side of the door.

The voice sounded familiar to Vince, and all of a sudden, his heart started pumping quickly. His palms were wet and sweat was forming all over his face. He found himself biting his bottom lip as he heard the sound of the lock being taken off on the other side of the door.

He was shaking now. In the time it takes to unlatch a door lock, Vince had grown extremely nervous. The doorknob turned, and he hurled himself through the open door and onto the man, pinning him down on his bed.

Vince's eyes were crazy, and the man pleaded, "No, leave me alone."

It wasn't him. "Shit!" yelled Vince and quickly got off the man and walked out, Johnny following.

He felt an empty sensation in the pit of his stomach. He became frightened and started to yell at Johnny as they ran down the staircase. "When are you going to find this fuckin' guy, John? When I'm dead?"

Johnny showed his frustration. For the first time in his life, he went after the only man he could trust. When they reached the porch, he turned and grabbed Vince by his shirt and threw him up against the house. "Listen to me, you cryin' fuck. It's too hot for me to listen to your bullshit about me not gettin' this fuckin' guy. Nobody wants him more than me for what he did to Red, and I don't want to hear you askin' me when we gonna' get him because I don't know when we will. But I can tell you this, and God be my judge, I'm gonna get that guy if it's the last thing I ever do on this earth."

Vince had no fight in him; he was emotionally drained. His energy had all been let out on the poor man who was still shaking upstairs in his bed.

"I'm sorry, John. I know you're trying. I just get frustrated when I think about it."

Sweat was pouring off Johnny's forehead. It was another day in the nineties, and his shirt was soaked with perspiration. We're all frustrated. It's times like these when we have to keep our heads on. Let's go have a cold beer."

"Sounds good."

Over forty thousand fans came to the game that night to either boo or cheer Vince. Their opinion was swayed by any number of newspaper articles that appeared in the daily papers.

The Daily News focused their story on the affair between Roxanne and Vince, saying, "It had been a hot and torrid summer for Vince Donato in more ways than one." It went on to say that Vince was the one in the wrong and should apologize to Tex in any way possible.

The Post's lead story concerned the clubhouse brawl. "In a mad rush of jealous anger, Tex Hardin charged across a crowded clubhouse filled with reporters and wrestled Vince Donato down to the ground when he found out that the ballplayer was having an affair with his wife."

The Jersey Journal had an exclusive interview from Vince in which he said, "It's all over between Roxanne and me. I wish she'd realized it. The only girl in my life now is Luellen."

Other stories focused on Vince's past loves, going back to Chicago newswoman Pat Best, and even a famous Miss America.

The *Newark Star Ledger*, in a four-page special, covered Vince's career on the field, off the field, and his life with Luellen. The back page of the story was an exclusive interview with the actress in which she said, "To love Vince is to put up with this sort of thing. It comes with the property, but I'm hoping that one day it all will change."

All the five o'clock new shows had TV crews at the stadium to interview either one of the combatants. Vince was once again making news as only he could, and he said, "I put out for my teammates and my manager, but not for Tex Hardin. He's one man I don't trust and never did. This isn't the end of this. You can mark my words on that."

"Is there something else in the works?"

"I won't say here. But in due time, it'll all come out in the wash." Vince was enjoying putting the public in suspense. He knew that it was playing into Tex's hand, but he also knew the power of the press and what it could do to stir up the public. Vince imagined packed houses every night and that would be good for the team.

Vince's first time to the plate created a loud grumbling of noise from the crowd. He heard many boos and just as many cheers. He stepped out of the batter's box and tipped his hat to Tex, who was seated in his private box near the dugout. This was what Tex had wanted all year, and Vince had finally delivered. By no means was it a sign of peace between the two, only a recognition from Vince that he had done the job asked of him, and the team and Tex were better off for it.

Vince turned the boos to cheers as he brought in a run with a single to left center and quickly went to second as the throw to the plate failed to get the runner sliding in. It was the twenty-second straight game in which he got a hit and helped the Riders win their second in a row.

There was no meeting between Tex and Vince before the game, but all eyes and camera lenses were focused on the owner when he walked into the clubhouse after the game and straight to Vince.

"It was like two heavyweight boxers in a championship fight," wrote Brian Corcoran of the *Chicago Sun Times*, Vince's old friend there on special assignment, "They just looked at each other, trying to stare each other down."

Tex was the first to break the silence. "I'd like to talk to you in Hop's office."

Dressed in only his uniform pants, Vince nodded in agreement and followed Tex into Hop's little managerial office. The reporters followed and quickly had their ears to the door.

"Let's get a few things straight. Put everything up front, I know that's how you like it," started Tex. "I knew about you and Roxanne all along. Roxanne is only company to me. She's a great bed partner, as you found out, and good company at social affairs. I could never give my love to only one woman, so your affair didn't tick me off as much as I let it on to.

"But isn't it wonderful the way the media has put us on the front pages? The place is alive, it's pumping, it's excited. And all because you and me, the two most dominating figures on the team, are at each other's throats. This is what I imagined ever since the first day, and it's going to stay this way as long as they think you, and I are going to kill each other at any time.

"Vince, it's real, and it's happening here in Jersey Stadium. We're beating the Yankees and the Mets in their backyard, and it's all because of you. I owe you a lot. You're finally going to make this club start turning a profit.

"You keep on staying hot like you are now, and I'll even make it worth your wild at the end of the year."

Vince finally interrupted. He couldn't believe what he was hearing. "Let me tell you something right to your ugly face. Number 1, any man that tells me it's all right to fuck his wife is no man at all. Number 2, I want you to stay away from Lucy. If I ever find out you go there again, I'll break your legs with a bat, and number 3, I couldn't care less how much money you make on this club. You have some real good kids here who have been busting their asses every day, and you never once said a kind word about them all year. So they don't have the best talent in the world, at least I could say that they've given it all they had and you can't ask more than that. But all you care about is your fuckin' money. Well, you can take all your fuckin' money and shove it up your ass."

He turned and opened the door. Five reporters fell into the room. "Get up and out of here. I'm not done yet," he ordered. The reporters saw that he was not in the mood to argue so they quickly got up and left, feeling the wind of the closing door behind them.

"One more thing," Vince continued, "I still think that you're involved with the guy that's after me and Lord help you if you are because Johnny wants revenge for Red, and believe me, he's going to get it. So just don't cross my path anymore because right now, you're walking on a fine line." Vince gave him a final stare, hoping Tex would once again attack, then left when he didn't.

The reporters flocked to him like vultures on fresh meat. He was still at an emotional high as he answered their questions. "I told him exactly what I thought of him and that he was walking on a fine line with me."

"What's that supposed to mean?"

Not wanting to drag Lucy into it again, he answered, "It's between Tex and me, but if he acts up again, I'll break his legs with a bat."

In Hop's office, Tex was equally as open. "I wanted to talk about it with him in a calm and mature manner, but it seems that we can't do that. Maybe it's too hard for him."

The Yankees would be taking a back seat for a while as long as Vince and Tex were carrying on their feud. Even Gelford Gordon's no-hitter with seventeen strikeouts couldn't put the Riders off the front pages.

Vince stayed away from Lucy that night. He knew that her temper was almost on a par with his and that she'd be furious about his explosion with Tex. He decided he'd wait until she cooled down to see her and discuss it. He spent the night at Luellen's, eating the drab hotel food instead of Domenic's delights.

More than forty-five thousand came the next day to see Vince "break his legs" as the headlines said. The New York teams have had their hot-tempered, controversial players in the past, but none of them ever had the area turned on as Vince had. People came as far away as Maine and Kentucky to see exactly what, if anything, would happen between Vince and Tex that day.

They left the park disappointed. The game was a rout as California beat Dailey and the Riders ten to two. Vince singled, getting his streak up to twenty-three, but there was no post game arguments or threats. Tex was absent from the clubhouse and Vince had little to say about him that all ready hadn't been said.

"Hey, Vince!" yelled Hop, "I'm going to take a shower. If you're going to beat up anybody, wait until I'm through, I want to see it."

Vince spent the night away from Luellen and any other friends or family, except Tony. Tony was always there. He just wanted to be away from it all for a night, away from the microphones, pads, and cameras. For years, he relished being in the limelight, but this night, he needed to be alone.

Luellen was very understanding of it all. Being a star and in the limelight herself, she knew too well the moments that one wants to spend by themselves. The thing that worried her most about all the publicity was that Lucy was somehow involved in it all and that it would lead to some very special people in her life getting hurt. She saw how much it bothered Vince when he mentioned it to her and she was afraid that it would separate a brother from a sister he loved very much.

Vince wanted to call Lucy and explain to her that he did what he did out of love for her, but he knew that she wouldn't talk to him. She carried the Donato temper with her like Vince carried it with him. He planned to see her late Sunday afternoon after the game, at his mothers, where the family ate dinner every Sunday. He didn't know what he'd say to Domenic if he brought it up, but he knew he'd have to protect Lucy at all costs until she straightened herself out, even if it meant being at odds with her.

Thinking about Lucy and the good times they always had, then thinking about Grace and her problems, made him lonesome for them. He picked up the phone and called Grace. She was happy to hear from him. Her husband wasn't getting any better, but Sal Jr. was great. Vince felt proud at the fact that he set the boy straight, regardless of the method he used. He told her he'd see her Sunday then called his other sister, Antionette.

It was good to hear her voice. Vince wasn't as close to her as he was to Lucy and Grace, yet his love and devotion for her could never be questioned. She did not give him any news to be happy about. She and her husband had been arguing constantly and not getting along. He had even threatened to leave. He could tell in her voice that she was upset, and it bothered him that he couldn't help her right there. He told her that he'd have a talk with his brother-in-law and that he'd see her Sunday with the rest of his sisters. "Sit tight. I'll do all I can to help you, you know that."

Vince felt that the weight of the world was on his shoulders. *Why had all this happened now, at this time,* he asked himself. *It's one problem after another and each one needs all my attention. Good Lord, please help me with it all. I can't do it without help.*

After he hung up the phone with Antionette, it quickly rang. There was a familiar voice on the other end.

"How long you think you can keep this streak going?"

"Long enough till I hang your ass out to dry," he answered back, knowing it was his assasin on the other end.

There was a laugh, and it irked Vince to no end that he couldn't meet him face-to-face. "We'll see who gets who. Just remember that when the streak stops that's when you die."

"Fuck you." Vince lost all patience and threw the phone, knocking a picture off the wall. The pressure was starting to take it's toll on him. As strong a man as Vince was, too many things were happening in his life too quickly for him to get a firm grip.

He leaned over on the end of a coffee table and yelled, "Shit, shit, shit!"

Tony quickly came to his side. "Easy, man, easy."

Vince asked for a shot of brandy. He quickly took one, then another, then eased back on the sofa, apparently calmed down. "How much can one man take before it gets to him?"

"You've got a strong backbone, Vince. You've gone this far, you'll get through."

He took another shot and waved his hand through his hair. He was still. His hands stopped shaking, and his voice was firm and strong. "One day I guess, we'll look back on all of this and laugh about it."

Tony nodded. "See, you're calm now. You'll get through it."

He rose from the sofa and said, "With the help of the good Lord, I hope you're right. I'm tired now. I'm going to bed."

Vince showed no sign of easing up on the American League pitchers as he hit a home run, single, and double the next day to disappoint Buffalo Bob once more. California pitchers were the easiest thing he had to face that day. Later in the afternoon, he'd have to face Lucy and explain to her his tirade against the man she had fallen in love with.

He and Luellen walked into the house only to see his three sisters and mother alone in the front room crying. His immediate thought was that Sal had taken a turn for the worst.

He asked his niece, Grace's daughter, "Where's your father?"

"He's in the back with Uncle Dom and Grampa."

He quickly walked through the house and out the back to see his father and two brothers-in-law sitting peacefully in lounge chairs, drinking wine and eating fruit.

"You okay?"

"Yeah, why?" answered Sal.

It was then that Vince realized that his other brother-in-law, Antionette's husband, wasn't there. He turned and went back in the house to where the women were.

Luellen quickly met him, tears in her eyes. "Marvin left her this morning."

"That fuck." There was fire in his eyes.

"Calm down," Luellen warned, "Antionette needs you now."

Vince looked at Antionette. She was pathetic. Her face was red and wet with tears. Her hair was out of place and he noticed that an earring had fallen out. She wasn't the beautiful woman he had known and loved, instead she was hurt and shaken, by a man he had never liked in the first place.

I'll make him pay for this, he thought to himself.

He looked at Lucy. She stared at him defiantly. He knew what he had to do. "Lucy, I want to talk to you out on the front porch."

She didn't move as he walked out. He turned and said, "Now."

Reluctantly she got up and walked out to meet him. Her eyes never left him, and they were filled with hate. "You just had to do it, didn't you?" she started, "You couldn't let me do it my way. You had to be the big bad Vince Donato and start a fight with him. Now I have everybody in the world wondering if Tex and I have something going. Even Domenic asked questions, and all because you couldn't keep your big mouth shut. You never could keep your big mouth shut. You always went looking for trouble, and you always found it. It's a wonder you're still in one piece."

Vince was angry. His face was fixed, and his lips were tight. If it wasn't his sister talking, he'd have settled it by now, but he chose to wait until she was finished.

"If looks could kill," she went on. "So what have you got to say for yourself?"

"You through?"

"With you? Yes." Those words hurt him more than he was ever hurt in his life. They told him that she didn't want anything to do with him again, but he had to say what was on his mind.

"You listen to me, and you listen to me good." She turned her back on him. He grabbed her by her shoulders and turned her around, forcing her to look at him. "What I did I did because I love you and this family. I don't want any pain or hurt to come into it, and if you ever got involved with that guy, that's just what'll happen. Can't you see that? You're all crying and upset now over what happened between Antionette and Marvin, but it could just as easily be you, and we don't need that.

"We don't need the grandchildren of Vince and Rosetta Donato growing up in a broken home. I don't want that for any of them, and I don't want it for you.

His eyes began to fill with tears. "I may not have the most subtle way of doing things but Lucy it's the only way I know how. I did it, and I'd do it again if I knew it would keep you away from him."

Tears were rolling down his cheeks now. "Sal is going to die. Mama and Papa are old, and their time will come soon. Antionette's going to need our help and Grace and her children too. Lucy, I can't do it all alone. I need you with me, by my side, to hold this family together."

It was a sight that made Lucy feel two feet tall. He protected her from what he thought was evil by doing the only thing he knew how, and she was belittling him for it. She reached out and hugged him tightly, crying freely.

"Oh, Vince, please help me, please help me."

He stroked her hair. "I will, Lucy. I will." They composed themselves and started to chart their plan for Antionette. "Now the first thing we have to do is pull Antionette through some hard times. But first I'd like to know exactly what happened. I talked to her last night on the phone, and she was saying that they weren't getting along."

"He just told her that he was leaving. He said that he was through being under her thumb all these years and that he wanted some freedom."

That prick finally stood up. I didn't think he had it in him. He silently thought to himself, *I'll talk to him.*

"Not like you talked to Tex."

"I'll be easy. I promise. As for you, he won't be around anymore. I made that clear. So it's out of sight out of mind."

"It won't be that easy."

"You can do it. We can do anything that our minds tell us we can. Now let's go inside and care for our sister."

Vince walked back in and sat down next to Antionette and held her hand. "Things will work out. I'll talk to Marvin. You two have to talk it out."

She continued to cry and put her head on his shoulder. "Crying is not going to bring him back, but if it does you any good, then let it all out."

After he sat with the women for a while and helped compose them, he went downstairs and played with the kids, holding Lucy's youngest daughter high over his head and flying her around like an airplane. He ended it all by wrestling with all five of the little ones and being pinned by all of them.

Next, he went outside and immediately started an argument with Sal over the Yankees. Sal's beloved Yankees were in a torrid pennant race with Detroit and a good old-fashioned baseball argument was just what Sal needed to perk him up. When the argument was over, the four of them played bocce ball in a pit built long ago by the senior Donato. The kids came out in the yard to play, and Vince let each one of them throw the *paline*. He was in heaven. He'd rather be nowhere else than with his family.

Luellen watched him intently. She had seen this side of Vince many times before, and she loved him even more for it. Under the tough exterior, there lived a warm gentlehearted man. Watching him hug and console his sister, argue with his brother-in-law, and play with the kids made her want him even more. She said a silent prayer for him to a statue of the Blessed Virgin Mary that was in the yard, then went in to join the others for coffee and cake.

The Streak

1

The Oakland As came into town for a three-game series, and Vince easily ran his streak to twenty-seven, despite the Riders losing all three games. The short series drew in excess of thirty thousand each night and Tex was smiling that attendance seemed to be picking up and publicly said that it was because Vince and he were at ends with each other, and Vince was a hot ballplayer. “I don’t know if the fans come to see Vince hit me or the ball.”

After the As left town, Vince saw two articles in the paper that caught his eye. He knew that he shouldn’t take either one of them seriously, but in some small way, they stuck in his mind.

The first was another report in Trudy Giles’ gossip column about Luellen and Palmer Brooke. The paragraph said that Palmer was a frequent visitor to the set of “Opening Bid” and often lunched with Luellen in her trailer. It closed by asking the question, “Could a romance be brewing?”

Vince immediately called Luellen at the set to find out if there was any truth to the latest rumor. She assured him that nothing was going on between her and Brooke and that once again he was acting like a little boy. “All we did was have a cup of coffee together and it was out on the set and not in the trailer. I don’t care what you read in the gossips, it isn’t true. Now I don’t want to hear any more about Palmer and me.”

Vince was embarrassed. *I must look like a real jerk*, he said to himself. *I know she loves me. What am I worried about?*

“I think we better go see Trudy Giles and find out where she’s getting her information from,” he said to Tony. “But I’ve got a hunch I know where.”

The second story that caught his eye was in the sports section. For the first time since his hitting streak began, it was getting some national attention. He was currently at twenty-seven games and almost half way to the great DiMaggio's record of fifty-six.

"Imagine comparing me with the greatest player of all time," he said as he resumed his morning coffee. "I couldn't even shine his shoes. I wouldn't have been a pimple on his ass if I played when he did. The guy was in another world when it came to playing ball. Who wrote this article?" he asked as he scanned the byline. "Peter Huggs. He's a good writer, but he should know better than stir up this sort of stuff."

"You're hot now, Vince, you've got to admit that, and you know that when you're hot you can go on and on. How many more games left? Who knows, maybe you can pull it off."

Vince reached for a schedule. He knew that he was swinging the bat as well as he ever had, and he knew that when he was as hot as he was, there was no telling how far it could last, but fifty-six?

"Nah. Don't be silly. Let me see," he scanned the schedule and began counting the games left. "We have exactly twenty-nine games left. That means if I ever take it all the way, I'll have to do it on the last day of the season. Can you see Tex's face if that ever happened? We'd be a million games out of first place, yet the park would be loaded with people. Wouldn't that be something?"

"Sure would."

Vince paused a moment and thought, *Every game I hit keeps me alive one more day. Maybe I do need this streak or until Johnny gets our man—Tony.*

"Yeah."

"I'm going after it. If I stay hot, maybe I'll have a decent shot of doing it. Besides, I've got to do it to stay alive."

Tony lifted a cup of coffee, "Here's to fifty-six."

Trudy Giles had been the city's premier gossip columnist for the past twenty years. She had started as a copywriter for a small paper in Georgia and migrated to New York only after failing in Hollywood. She was the ex-wife of three of the richest men in New York City and was noted for her sexual adventures with young actors on the way up.

FIFTY-SIX

To be mentioned in Trudy Giles' column was a feather in anyone's cap. Unfortunately, Vince didn't see it quite that way.

Vince walked right into her office and sat down. She was on the phone and motioned him to wait one minute. She was a pale woman with bright orangey-red hair. Her face was painted with heavy rouge and makeup, and her eyes were outlined with a big, thick, black line. Vince wondered how three men could be stupid enough to marry a woman as ugly as Trudy Giles.

She hung up and sang out, "Well, hello there. How are you, love?"

Vince smiled a boyish grim. He had warded her off him a few years ago and didn't relish striking up acquaintances with her again, but it was something he had to do.

"How have you been, Trudy?"

"Lovely, simply lovely. What brings you here to see me? Taking in my offer five years late?" She smiled to show yellowed teeth.

Vince squirmed in his chair. He'd rather be alone than spend the night with a woman as repulsive to him as Trudy Giles. "I want to know who's telling you about Luellen and Palmer Brooke?"

"Vince," she scolded, "you know I can't reveal my sources." He put on his boyish grin again. "Not once?"

She got up from her chair and walked around the desk and closed her office door.

"Is it true?"

"I'm asking you," he answered.

She sat near him in another chair and caressed his face, stroking it with her fingers.

He shooed her away. "Trudy, please."

She jumped on him and her lips reached for his. He threw her off. "Make love to me here, now." She reached down between her legs and rubbed herself hard. "Oh, Vince, I'm wet and hot and I want you now, please." She was in a sexual trance.

Vince saw it as a way to get the information he had come there for. He took her in his arms and his finger found her home. She moaned. "Tell me who told you about Luellen and this thing is all yours."

She reached and found a bulge in his crotch. "Oh god, it's so hard," she moaned. "Put it in me."

"Not so fast. Who told you about Luellen and Brooke?"

She dropped to her knees, ignoring his question, and started to unzip him. He stopped her. "Who was it Trudy?"

"Roxanne Hardin. She said I could have anything I wanted if I printed what she told me. She sent over some young actors from an actor's studio that she's sponsoring with their money. Now let me have it."

She reached inside Vince's pants, but he pulled away. "Wait. I have to go to the bathroom. I'll be right back. You wouldn't want me to pee at the same time that you're on it, would you?"

"Hurry back."

He opened the door and found Tony waiting outside. "Let's get out of here, quick."

They left her office and quickly drove out of the city and over to the Hilton hotel where Roxanne was. Vince knew that Tex would not be there. He always spent his mornings at the stadium with his baseball committee. He only hoped that Roxanne would be in.

He didn't bother to ask for her at the front desk, fearing it would cause a scene, so he indiscretely walked up the stairs to her floor.

The look on her face told her emotion. Her eyes and mouth were wide open. "Vince!"

He rushed in. "Is he here?"

Her thoughts immediately were of pleasure. *He's back*, she said to herself and quickly answered, "No."

"I just want you to know that I know what you're doing."

"Doing?"

Vince was angry. "Come on Roxanne. You're feeding Trudy Giles all that shit about Luellen and Palmer Brooke so you'll make me jealous and I'll leave her. It won't work. Why don't you forget about me like I forgot about you."

She proclaimed her innocence. "I don't know what you're talking about."

He wanted to hit her. He raised his hand but wisely took it back. "Up your ass," he yelled in her face and left, slamming the door behind him.

It won't work, she said to herself. I've somehow got to get to her even if it kills me.

The Seattle Mariners proved no match for the hottest player in baseball as he dominated them in a three-game series, collecting six hits to run his streak to thirty.

As the team prepared to go on a brief road trip that would take them to Cleveland and Detroit, Hop called Vince into his office for a man-to-man talk.

The old man was serious, with no jokes or laughs, and it made Vince a little nervous to see him that way. "Vince, I've got a gut feeling that you're going to give this thing a long ride, and I want you to know exactly what you'll be up against.

"I was breaking into baseball in '41 when DiMaggio had his streak. Baseball in those days was the only game in town. Nobody gave a shit about football or basketball like they do now. People ate, slept, and shit baseball twelve months a year. It was their game, and DiMaggio was their player.

"As the streak went on, it attracted media attention like yours is now. When it got into the forties, you couldn't walk the street of any city in the country without somebody asking if Joe got a hit in the day's game.

"He was in the newsreels every night and hundreds of papers throughout the country put the Yankee boxscore on the front page. The country was about four months away from war, but nobody cared about Roosevelt, Hitler, or the rest of those guys, all they cared about was Joe DiMaggio and his consecutive game-hitting streak. They wanted it to go on forever.

"When it got into the fifties the national press followed him wherever he went. He couldn't take a shit without them knowing how many pieces of toilet paper he used. He couldn't show his face in the public because he'd be swarmed by thousands of fans. And it went on and on until it came to an end.

"Now it's over forty years later, and you're gonna make a run at a record that baseball people have said will never be broken. There are a hundred times more newspapers. They'll be a hundred times more reporters. TV cameras will be looking at you every step you take. You'll pour your breakfast cereal in the morning, and reporters will come out of the box. They'll be everywhere because it's a reflection of the time we live in.

"And there'll be people who'll be for you and people who'll root against you. There'll be articles denouncing you to even be put in the same sentence as Joe, and there'll be articles praising you. As the streak goes on, the pressure will get heavier every day. You'll have more pressure on you than any man has ever had in any professional sport. I'll do my best to take it off you, but I can only do so much.

"Now I know that you're a hell of a man. A man's man. You don't back away from anything, but this is something you can't fight. I pray to God you can handle it because if you let it get the best of you it'll break you and show no mercy."

The words sank deep into Vince's mind. He had never looked at it the way that Hip had just described. His stomach turned when he remembered Hip's saying, "You're gonna' make a run at a record they say will never be broken."

"Hip, if it's gonna be, then it's gonna' be. I'm swinging at the good pitches and letting the bad ones go by. If I get a hit I get a hit, if I don't, then the streak stops. I've been through more pressure recently than any man has a right to, and it hasn't broken me yet. I think I'll be all right, and I thank you for your concern."

It was a quiet and matter of fact conversation, but Vince left Hip's office knowing that the man cared for him and would do all he could to help him out when the going got tough. Vince smiled and somehow knew that with Hip's help and his talent he'd surely give it a run for it's money.

The Cleveland Indians were almost as bad as the Riders. If it weren't for the expansion team, the Indians would've found themselves firmly entrenched in last place. Their pitching was horrendous and the hitting was feeble. When they played in the spacious Municipal Stadium, the crowds appeared lost against the backdrop of the huge ballpark. In a stadium that could seat well over seventy-thousand, the daily attendance was a little over five thousand. The baseball world was dead on Lake Erie until Vince Donato came to town to resurrect it.

That morning the Cleveland Plain Dealer ran a story about DiMaggio's streak and how it was stopped one night in the same park that Vince would be playing in. The story stirred up some interest in the dormant fans as eighteen-thousand showed up for the first game of the series.

Vince quickly put an end to the Cleveland jinx for that night as he singled his first time up to run his streak to thirty-one.

After he got his hit, the entire stadium emptied like a dam that had suddenly sprung a leak. By the third inning there were only about five-thousand people left. The others had come to see what they wanted and quickly went on to better things.

After the game, Hip told reporters, "I'd of left too. Who wants to see the two shittiest teams in baseball play a meaningless game? Besides, tonight is Monday, and that means Monday night football. If I were a fan, I'd much rather be watching that."

The morning papers were headlined with stories about Vince's continuing streak. It was good copy, and it was selling papers and creating interest, just what a good story is supposed to do. That night's game drew in excess of twenty-five thousand. This time, Vince waited until the sixth inning to get his hit, and once again, the mass exodus occurred, leaving the die-hards to watch the Indians win in the ninth.

Interest in the streak was beginning to hit national attention. *Sports Weekly*, the most widely read sports magazine in the country, sent its best reporter and photographer to Cleveland to do a cover story on Vince and the streak.

For his last game in Cleveland, he played in front of a crowd that was close to forty thousand. He routinely got hits his first two times up and proclaimed to reporters after the game, "I can only remember one other time when I swung this good and that was the spring training when I made the White Sox. I had a little help from somebody up there, maybe she's with me now too."

On Friday night Tiger Stadium was a confused ball of madness. It overflowed with fans as they came to see the hottest pitcher in baseball, Gelford Gordon, pitch to the hottest hitter in the game. A Hollywood writer couldn't have written a better script. It was no contest as the cagey veteran got good wood on Gordon's lightning fastball and singled his first time up. His next time up, he lined one of Gordon's fastballs down the left-field line for a double. Gordon struck him out his last two times up, on slow curves, but Vince had proved that he was in charge on that particular night.

Gordon handled the other Rider batters with ease as once again, he struck out in double figures and finished with a shutout to put the Tigers in a dead tie with the Yankees. But the tight pennant race was taking a back seat to Vince and his streak. At least fifteen new reporters were on hand for the game, besides the beat writers for each club, and every one of them wanted a piece of Vince. Even Gordon, the press' darling for the past month, was put on the second page. Vince was front-page material, and he made the best of it.

He showed no sign of the strain he was under as he handled each question in a confident manner. "The way I'm swinging now is unreal. If I keep my swing, who knows, maybe I can hit fifty-six. But a streak that long, even this long, needs a lot of luck. I can hit the ball on the head four times and have four line drive-outs and the fifth time gets jammed and has it bloop in for a single. But that's what makes this game so great, and that's why I love it so much."

The next day, the papers were full of his quotes, and Detroit was buzzing like never before. Long lines were formed outside the stadium for Saturday's games as a ticket to the game became the hottest item to get since the Tigers played in the World Series. Tickets were scalped for as much as one hundred dollars and fans were seated in the aisles. A dozen more reporters flew into Detroit for that Saturday afternoon game and the major networks all had T.V. crews there. The game was selected for the national TV game of the week and Vince gave a lengthy interview before playing on his feelings about all the turmoil with the team and what the streak meant to him.

"It's unfortunate that Tex Hardin turned out the way he did. I trusted him in the beginning, but now it's hard to trust the man.

He's sneaky. People might say that I'm the one who can't be trusted, being that I had that affair with his wife, but as I said before, she was cheating, not me. Besides, he only uses her like he uses everything else, for his own satisfaction.

"As for the team, Tex was the only one that expected great things from us and that's what happens when you have a non baseball man involved. Frank Gilroy and I told him way back last October that it would take five years to be competitive but it went in one ear and out the other. We've got some talented players here, Cedeno, Taylor, and Ishito, but we're at least five years away from being competitive. Hop's been the greatest. I wish I played my whole career for him. I love the guy.

"As for the streak, well, I go to the plate looking for a good pitch to hit, and when I see one, I swing. If it's a hit, it's a hit. If not, the world will still turn. I don't want anybody to compare me to DiMaggio. He was the best of all time. All I'm doing is playing hard, trying to win a game, that's what baseball's all about."

After the announcer thanked him for a very candid interview, Vince took the microphone and spoke one more time to the camera. "I'd like to say hello to all my family back home, Lucy, Gracie, Antionette, Mama, and Papa, Sal and all the kids. I love you all, and I'll be home soon."

His family's affairs were still the most important thing to him. Every night he was on the phone to Lucy, who was still in turmoil over her situation, giving her an outlet to cry to. He also called Grace and Antionette, listening to their problems and giving a helping word of advice whenever he could.

Antionette's problem bothered him more recently because now his sister was becoming chronically depressed because her husband had refused to talk to her.

"I'll settle with him when I come home," he told her. "Leave it to me."

The game seemed to have a flair for the dramatic. It was perfect scheduling that the country should have such a game to view on national TV. The Yankees were winning and the Riders were beating Detroit easily, which would mean the Yankees would move back into first place, yet it was Vince that had millions in suspense. It was the seventh inning. He hadn't gotten the ball out of the infield, lining out to third, popping out, and grounding out, and this was possibly his last time up. His last time to keep the streak, and him—alive.

He was nervous as he stepped in the batter's box. He looked around and saw thousands of faces all looking at him. They were silent as each one knew they were witnessing a special event.

So this is what Hip meant by the pressure, he said to himself, as he dug in and prepared to face the pitcher.

"Good luck, Vince," said the catcher, but Vince didn't hear him, his concentration deep on the man on the mound. The windup was quick, and Vince picked the ball up immediately as it left the pitcher's hand. It came in low and away, and Vince reached across the plate and made solid contact. It flew off his bat and quickly over the second baseman's head and into right centerfield for a single. The crowd quickly came back to life and gave a thunderous ovation. Vince took his cap off and raised it in appreciation. He had met the first challenge and won.

The Riders won the game, but nobody seemed to care. The clubhouse was stuffed with reporters from all over the country, and they all asked the same questions. They held him up for more than two hours after the game, but Vince didn't mind one bit. He was proud of himself. For once, he was being interviewed for something he accomplished on the field as a professional baseball player and not for fighting, boozing, or balling. He was at the top of his game, and for him, there was no coming down.

Sunday's game, once again played before a packed house, was a duplicate of Saturday's. For the second day in a row, Vince came up for the last time needing a hit to keep it alive, and for the second day in a row, he met the challenge and won.

It was the same atmosphere again in the clubhouse, reporters were everywhere, prompting Hop to bellow, "If all you guys come on over here, I'll tell you what we feed the guy."

It was a quiet plane ride back to Newark Airport. Vince, Jerry, and Darnell Taylor played cards in the back while Hip kept the reporters at bay by telling them about the streakiest players that he ever managed.

"Remember Nate Frazier?" he began. "Played first base my first year with the Tigers. Nate was something like oh for the month of July one year. I think he went about eighty or eighty-five times up without a hit. That's got to be a record. It was the worst slump I ever saw, and I saw hundreds of them.

"Come August, and the poor guy is really going batty. I mean he's hangin' the walls. He lost all his hair worrying about it, couldn't sleep, had the shits, didn't eat. Had eye bags under his eyes the size of suitcases.

"Charlie Brown was in our club then, and Charlie said he knew a guy that could get a hold of a genuine African witch doctor and get him to come over to our clubhouse and do his thing for Nate and get him out of the slump. Nate was all for it. When you're in a slump like he was, you try anything to get out of it. So Charlie went ahead and made the contacts.

"The next night, this black guy comes walking into the clubhouse decked out to the tee. He had hundred-dollar shoes on and a big wide-brim hat. He wore diamonds on every finger and a big gold watch. With him was another tall black guy dressed in an overcoat. Now I started to wonder who the guy was. Hell, it was August. You don't wear an overcoat in August. Charlie introduces the two to Nate and Nate coughs up a hundred dollars to the flashy dresser. He turns and says something to the other guy in mumbo jumbo, and the guy strips his coat. Well, wouldn't you know it? The guy was dressed in a loincloth and had bones and beads hanging from his neck. He sure looked like a real witch doctor.

"The flashy dressed guy gathers everybody around and says that the doctor is a genuine African and can't speak any English. He just arrived and was working strictly for him. He told everybody to be quiet and turned out the lights and told the doctor to get started.

"Well, the first thing this guy did was light a small candle right in front of Nate. Next, he sprinkled some powder in the air, took out a rattle, and started singing and dancing all around Nate. It was right out of the movies. We were all caught up in it.

"Remember Bobby Martin? Outfielder with a good arm? Bobby was a great one for a joke, one of the best I ever had. Well, Bobby just happened to have a box of tacks in his locker. Now don't ask me what he was doing with a box of tacks in his locker, but he had them. He started to throw them out to where the good doctor was dancing around in his bare feet. Naturally, he stepped on them and started yelling out. We didn't know if it was part of the ritual or what. Finally, he yells out. Now remember this guy is right from Africa, can't speak English, and he yells, 'Who the fuck put the mother fuckin' tacks on the floor?'"

"We all busted up. I mean it was the funniest thing you ever saw. Nate and Charlie Brown grabbed the guy and got Nate's hundred dollars back and kicked the two of them out of the clubhouse. Maybe that's what he needed because he went out that night and got three hits and returned to being himself again. But that was one hell of a funny scene."

Hip continued his stories, keeping the press well entertained until they landed at the airport. To Vince's surprise, there were about two hundred fans at the terminal ready to mob him. Naturally, the TV crews were there and once again Vince had to answer the same questions one more time. It was very late when he finally reached home, and the comfort of his bed was just the thing that he needed to rest his body and mind.

Monday was to be a busy day. He rose early and had breakfast with Luellen at her hotel. The talk was cordial, and she showed genuine concern that the streak and the mounting publicity it was causing, would cause him to get tight. "All they talk about on the set is this streak. Everybody asks me about it. I don't know what to tell them. Can you do it? Can you get to fifty-six?"

"What do you tell them when they ask you about it?"

"I tell them if you do it you do it, if you don't, then you don't. But, honey I worry about you. I really do. It's not enough with the family and all, but you're on every front page in the country and on every newscast."

"And don't forget you. I still have that decision to make at the end of the year."

She blushed. She didn't want that to be an extra cross he had to carry and didn't bring it up because of that, but she was glad he mentioned it. It showed her he hadn't forgotten. "In due time. In due time."

His next stop was to visit his brother-in-law Marvin and see what, if anything, he could do to help the situation out. On the way over, he remembered his promise to Lucy that there would be no rough stuff. He intended to keep his word.

The secretary was a cute little dark haried Italian girl with a beauty mark under her lip. She recognized Vince immediately and asked for an autograph: Vince wondered if maybe his brother-in-law had left his sister for her.

Marvin leaned out of his office. He was pale and nervous. Vince quickly surmised that he was afraid that Vince was there to get him. "Don't be scared. I've just come to talk about it."

Marvin knew very well that Vince could be playing a game with him, pretending to win his confidence than pouncing on him when the moment was right, but he had no alternative. He told him to come into his office.

Vince looked at him. He was a tall man with sinewy features. His hairline was receding, and he wore big black-rimmed glasses. He hadn't shaved that morning, and his hair was ungroomed. Vince wondered what his sister saw in him but realized that beauty was skin deep. "So what's the story?" Vince towered over him like an oak to a blade of grass.

"Sit down."

Vince quickly answered back, "I'll stand. I said what's the story."

"I've just fallen out of love. I don't think your sister has any respect for me as a man. How could she? All she does is boss me around like I'm a slave or something. I've finally had it. How could I love a woman that treats me like I'm shit?"

"There're other ways to do it. You just don't walk out on a wife and kids. Did you talk about it?"

"Was no use. Your sister never listened to me anyway."

Vince was starting to grow angry. "My sister has a name. Call her by it. So what you're telling me is that you don't want to go back, is that it?" He was to the point.

"I don't know. I just don't know."

"Well, you better find out quick enough because I have a sister that cries every night on account of this, and it's got to come to a head one way or the other."

Marvin leaned back in his chair and shook his head. "It'll never change. We're too old to change now. She'll always be the way she is, and I'll always be the way I am. The thing that's changed is that I won't accept being pushed around anymore. I guess this is the only way."

Vince would never plead, it wasn't his way. "So be it then, but don't ever neglect those kids because if you do you'll have to answer to me. You're no man Marvin, you're a mouse. If you were a man, you'd go to Antionette, grab her, tell her you love her, and listen to what you had to say. If she didn't, the marriage would be over. You can make it work if you both give in a little. Shit, it worked all this time. With some changes, it can still go on."

"Just once in your life take the bull by the horns and stand on your own two feet. You can do that can't you?"

"We'll see."

"We'll see? We'll see?" He held up a hand. "Don't even bother. Stay home and wax your cane every night because that's just what you'll be doing. Look at you. You look like a piece of shit. Who's going to want you? You should consider yourself lucky you have a wife like Antionette."

Marvin paused. Vince could see he was deep in thought. He thought that maybe if he embarrassed him enough maybe Marvin would take the bull by the horns and do something about it. "Maybe you're right afterall. I'll talk to her."

"Don't do me any favors, just do what you have to do. At least try to make it work. You know, I never cared much for you. I could never understand how you allowed Antionette to boss you around so much. In a way, I'm glad you finally stood up. Maybe you've both learned a lesson from this. Maybe things will be different and maybe they won't, but a man has to try. A man never runs from his problems." Vince extended his hand and smiled. "Good luck."

From the pharmaceutical company, Vince and Tony went to Sal's butcher shop. Vince knew that Sal wasn't getting any better and, in fact, was growing progressively worse, and wanted to see a man he genuinely loved and cared about.

Sal had lost weight since the last time Vince had seen him and his face was shallow. The illness was taking its toll on him quickly. His body may have been sick, but his spirits were as fiery as ever. Vince instructed Tony to start an argument about how the Tigers were going to pull away from the Yankees and that the Yankees would eventually fold. On cue, Tony started his argument, and it kept Sal running his mouth for well over an hour about the virtue of wearing the Yankee pinstripes and the pride involved in playing in Yankee Stadium. Finally, he had to stop to take a rest. It was tiring him.

He sat down on an empty crate and said, "Why don't you go to the house for lunch. Antionette's there too. They'd like to see you. You cheer them up."

Vince nodded. He shook Sal's hand, and Sal held it firmly and looked up at Vince with tears in his eyes. "Thanks for coming over. Thanks for everything."

Vince pounded his shoulder. "Just stopped by to tell you the Yanks are going to fold."

Sal shooed them away. "Get out of here. Don't get me started again."

In the car on his way over to Grace's, Tony said, "It's not fair. It's just not fair."

Vince agreed but answered, "We've got to play with the cards we're dealt. Sal's a good man. When he goes, the good Lord will take care of him. That I'm sure of."

When Vince walked into the house, he immediately saw that both his sisters had been crying. They each had their own reasons to cry, but Vince had to pick them up any way he could. "Sal's spirits are high, but when's he going to realize that the Yanks are going to lose the pennant?"

Grace smiled. "You saw him?"

"Sure. You'd think I'd miss a chance to needle him about the Yanks?" It was Vince's way of telling her that he'd be there. "And I saw another brother-in-law of mine too."

Antionette looked up. "You saw Marvin?"

"We had a nice talk. I think things will be okay if you both give in a little. You have to understand that he's a man and wants to be treated like a man. No man likes to be constantly hounded. Know what I mean?"

She nodded. "I know what you mean."

"Good. Now let's have some lunch."

They ate a full lunch of fresh Italian cold cuts, tomatoes, white onions, provolone cheese, black olives, fresh Italian bread and all topped off by a homemade apple pie. Full, Vince left to meet Johnny to see what progress, if any, he had made in discovering the whereabouts of Buffalo Bob.

When they walked into Johnny's store, Johnny had just finished fitting a customer in a double-breasted white suit that Vince had modeled when the summer line was exhibited at the winter shows.

"Fits like a glove, uh, Vince?" asked Johnny. He didn't have to mingle with the customers, but it was something that Johnny liked to do.

Vince eyed it over, feeling the fit across the back. "Like a rubber on a prick."

They all laughed. "Let's go in my office and talk. It'll be quieter in there." Johnny led the way as the five or six customers that were browsing all patted Vince on the back and wished him luck in the streak.

"Christ. That's all people talk about now is you and that fuckin' streak," Johnny said. "Can you take it that far?"

"I've got to go all the way, remember? When it stops, I die. That's when he pulls the trigger. Which is why we're here. Got any leads?"

Johnny lit a cigarette and shook his head. "Not a fuckin' thing. When's the last time you heard from him?"

"It's been almost two weeks. He's due."

"Yeah. You know somehow I have the feeling that that fuck Hardin has something to do with it. I know the fag denies it, but just maybe the fag doesn't know about it. Hardin's a ruthless man. He'll stop at nothing for the publicity that he thinks this can get."

"Then why hasn't he broken it to the papers yet?" asked Tony.

"Probably because he doesn't need to. Vince's streak is getting all the publicity he needs. My guess is if things hadn't turned out the way they did, he'd have probably told the press by now."

"So what's the plan?"

"I have a tap on his phones, and if it turns out that he's involved, then we'll get him too."

"If he's in it, I'll get him, not you," answered Vince.

"Just sit tight and keep it going. What else can I say?"

"Not much, John, not much at all."

2

Over forty-five thousand packed the stadium to see the two worst teams in baseball play. The only reason they flocked to the park that night was to see if Vince Donato could hit for the thirty-seventh straight game. There was no other reason to go.

Sports Weekly appeared on the newsstands that day and it fed the growing fire that Vince had started by challenging the great DiMaggio. On its cover, it had a picture of Vince in action with the headline, "Can he take it all the way?"

Vince put all doubts aside as he singled his first time up and the fans, who now were 100 percent behind him, gave him a standing ovation that lasted over five minutes. In what had become a normal ritual, Vince turned to the crowd and tipped his cap.

Tex thought that it'd be a good idea if Vince met the press before and after each game in the pressroom rather than the clubhouse. So many reporters were assigned to cover Vince's streak that it was becoming impossible to fit them all in the clubhouse. It was a good idea, and Vince consented.

Before the game, he met with more than forty-five reporters to answer the same questions that he had been answering the past ten games. After the game, it continued. He explained how his philosophy on hitting had changed since the streak had reached thirty games. "I know that they'll be pitching me more carefully now. I'll see fewer good pitches to hit, so I have to swing at the first good one I see and hope I hit it."

The postgame interview lasted an hour before Vince turned it over to Hip, who naturally entertained the press by describing Vince and DiMaggio in the way that he saw the two. "From the chest on down, Vince Donato is the strongest ballplayer I've ever managed, and that included legs too. Of course, his feet and toes are weak, but then he doesn't walk much either, strikes out a lot, but never walks. But now about this batting streak here and the great Joe DiMaggio. They're both Italian you know, and if Vince ever gets to fifty-six, then I'll instruct all my players to eat pasta every day 'cause that's the food that Vince and Joe were raised on, and if it works for them then, it's got to work for the rest of my players too. Then I suppose that we'd all be drinking wine instead of beer.

"Now if he don't get to fifty-six, then I guess that we won't be eating all that pasta unless you want to anyhow, but then it won't make a difference 'cause the streak will have been stopped. Does everybody follow me?"

He should have been a comedian. He had the assembled press laughing like they were being entertained by a top-named star in a Las Vegas nightclub, and he was doing it for nothing. Hip was doing his best to take some of the pressure off Vince in the only way he knew how, and it was a sheer pleasure to watch and listen to the man who had seen many a player come and go, but never one who had the press as excited as Vince had.

Vince was seeing firsthand what Hip meant when he told him "that everywhere you go, you'll have people hounding you, trying to get a piece of you at every turn." It seemed true even in Domenic's. A quiet, small, neighborly place had suddenly turned into the headquarters for a dozen or so reporters and their parties.

When Vince walked in with Jerry and Tony, he was immediately mobbed by all the reporters, six or seven friends, and five high school girls who screamed frantically.

Tony shooed off most of them as he would a gnat buzzing in his ear, but they constantly returned throughout dinner, forcing Lucy to put them in the kitchen.

After dinner, he talked with Lucy about Tex and her dilemma with him. She told him he had stopped coming in for dinner. He mailed in the check for the postgame meals they supplied, never coming in person like he used to. He did call once to say he was sorry he hadn't come in a while, but that business forced him to other places.

Vince nodded. “So how you holding up?” he asked, deciding then that when the season was over he’d take a bat to Tex’s legs for the phone call.

Her voice was remorseful, as if she wanted to say I wish I had done it and got it over with, but she answered back with encouraging words. “I think the worst is over now. It’s still hard, but I realize now that I could never hurt Dom and the kids.”

“You’d hurt me too.”

“I know. And Mama and Papa, Grace and Antionette too. I’ll make it, and I thank God I have a brother that cares.”

He hugged her and held her tightly against him. He released her and smiled. “Piece of cake. Now if you still want me to eat here every night, we’ve got to do something about this crowd that gathers here waiting for me.”

“I’ve got a good idea.”

“What?”

“We’ll feed them. What else is a restaurant for?”

They laughed and embraced each other again.

Vince’s first day home had proved to be a happy one. He was confident that Antionette would get back with her husband and work out their problems. Grace’s situation had not changed, but now she knew that he’d be there to give her support when the time came and that would help ease the sorrow. Lucy was pulling out of it, and that couldn’t have made him happier, and to top it all off, he kept the streak alive. He couldn’t have asked for a better day.

His second day home was not as pleasing. The morning papers quoted Larry Midas, the Cleveland pitcher for the night’s game, as saying, “I never liked the guy all these years. He’ll never see a good pitch from me tonight. Even if I have to walk him all four times, he’ll never get a pitch to hit.”

At the press conference, before the game, the comment was quickly mentioned, and it lit a fire in Vince’s competitive nature. “I’ll tell Midas to his face that I always thought he was shit. I’m not the greatest player in the world, but Larry Midas never got the best of me, and you could look it up. He’d have to throw the ball a foot over my head or a foot outside for me not to hit him. Larry Midas? He's small potatoes, let's talk about something else."

Once again, over forty-five thousand fans turned out to root for their man against the man who said he wouldn't play the game fair. Banners rooting for Vince to take the proper action against Midas were everywhere, and even some obscene ones had to be taken down from the left-field upper deck. Midas' comments had turned on the crowd, and they were electric when Vince came up for the first time in the game.

True to his word that he gave the press in the pregame meeting, Vince took a few steps toward Midas and started screaming at him. The Cleveland catcher, a rookie who was much bigger than Vince, stepped in front of him, thinking that the roughhouse ballplayer was going out to the mound to do battle. It stirred the crowd to no end. Their boy was at it again. Every fan was standing and cheering at the top of their lungs. They were all waiting for the action to happen.

"I've got no quarrel with you," Vince said to the catcher, then pointing to Midas he yelled again, "you fuckin' asshole! You couldn't get me out if your life depended on it. You're so shit you should be flushed down the bowl."

Order was restored by the home plate umpire, as he ran out from behind the plate and grabbed a hold of Vince. "I'm calm. I'm calm," he said, "I just wanted him to know that I think he's shit and he's always been shit."

"Okay, I think he's got the message. Now let's play ball."

Vince dug in as the crowd became as noisy as Times Square when the ball dropped on New Year's Eve. It was impossible for anyone to concentrate with all the noise going on, but Vince heard nothing. He wanted Midas bad, and his concentration on him was immense. He'd hit anything that Midas pitched, high, low, outside, or inside, it didn't matter. He was challenged, and he'd have to meet it.

The tall righthander wound up and came overhand with a pitch that was at least two feet outside. The crowd booed in a rhythmic unity and started to chant, "Mi-das sucks. Mi-das sucks."

The second pitch was a foot over Vince's head and way wide. The pitcher was smiling at Vince. Vince returned the smile with hate in his eyes. Midas knew he had him riled and quickly dropped a curve ball on the inside corner for a strike. Vince was surprised. He didn't expect a hittable pitch. He'd have to be aware of Midas from that moment on.

The third pitch was coming in high and wide, like the second one, and Vince went for it. He reached way out and made solid contact with the ball. He immediately laughed at Midas at the crack of the bat and started running. With youthful speed he slid into second base with a double as he lined the pitch down the right field line.

The crowd went wild. Vince was pumped up like never before. He stood at second base jumping and clapping his hands and yelling at Midas, "You asshole. You never got me out. You never got me out."

Midas dropped his glove and went after him. Vince met him halfway and dropped the tall pitcher with a flurry of punches as both benches emptied and met in the middle of the infield. Players were grappling with each other all over. Vince left Midas and went after a Cleveland player who was on Jerry. Darnell Taylor had an Indian in one arm and was swinging at another with his free arm. Vince hadn't been in a good old-fashioned brawl in over two years, but the way he acted showed everyone at the stadium that it was still in his blood.

When calm was restored, Midas was ejected from the game for going after Vince, and the Riders held on to win the game on a Taylor home run in the ninth inning.

The postgame press conference and the clubhouse atmosphere were as frantic and exciting as the game had been. Hop was at his best, and Vince was as open and candid as ever when he said, "I'd kick Midas' ass seven days a week and twice on Sundays. He has a lot of nerve going after me. He's lucky I didn't seriously injure him. Shit," he said as he threw a towel down, "I'm still pissed at that jerk off." He hadn't calmed down at Midas' antics and kept up his quick-paced chatter.

At that moment, Tex entered the press room, and Vince quickly remembered the phone call to Lucy that the cowboy had made. It riled him to no end. "Don't come near me unless you want your head bashed in." Tony and Jerry quickly held him back. "You didn't listen to what I told you. You couldn't stay out of it. Your day will come. I swear to God your day will come."

Tex gave a sly smile then backed out. It was Vince's center stage that he was in, but it was Tex who was reaping the profits. He'd let Vince have his way as long as the fans were flocking to the park.

To the press, it seemed like they all had died and gone to reporters heaven. Vince Donato was to a newsman what thrills are to a daredevil. The more they got, the more exciting it became. Without Vince, there was no story, no excitement, and no anticipation of what might happen next. They needed him, and he wasn't disappointing them one bit.

The next day's game saw the first sellout at Jersey Stadium since opening day, and Tex could thank Vince for every fan filling it. He homered to run his streak to thirty-nine, and then it was off to Yankee Stadium for a series with the Yanks.

It was a sellout crowd at the big ballyard in the South Bronx. The tight pennant race between Detroit and New York was on every fan's mind. It was their Yankees against the team from the other side of the river, and they all envisioned a Yankee sweep.

The streak was just as prevalent in their minds as the pennant race. Emotions had been running higher each day it grew as it received more and more publicity. Many fans were questioning the judgment of the papers to compare Vince Donato with Joe DiMaggio. Said one man on a radio call-in show, "That guy couldn't shine Joe Ds shoes. All's he's good for is fightin'. He's been an average ballplayer all his career, and now all of a sudden, the papers are tryin' to make him into another DiMaggio? Give me a break. He should be embarrassed. The only thing the two have in common is that they're both Italian."

But Vince had his followers too, and they made their voices seem just as loud. On the same program, a man called Sammy said, "As dedicated a player as the game has ever had. I've been watching baseball a long time, over thirty years, and I can't recall a player that played the game any harder than Donato does. He uses the talent that God gave him and that's all we can ask for. Sure, he's no DiMaggio, but then again who else is? Besides, what's everybody excited about, he's still got a long way to go to break the streak."

Thus the mood was set as Vince batted against the Yankees that hot Thursday night. Every at bat he had was filled with suspended silence, and once again he was coming up for the last time in the game needing a hit to keep the streak alive.

All eyes were on him as he slowly came to bat in the eighth inning and took his stance in the batters' box. Tex looked at the huge crowd and privately thought that forty percent of the gate, and 60 percent of the future home gates would all be his, and that would finally put him in the black. He stood and openly rooted for Vince to "hit a rope" somewhere to keep the streak alive and the flow of people coming.

Roxanne, sitting next to Tex with the Yankee owner and his wife, saw the strain on her ex-lover's face and felt for him. She wanted to hold him, to caress him, to make love to him, anything to ease him of the mental anguish and pressure that he was going through. She sat silently with clenched fists as the pitcher began his throw.

Luellen sat in a box above the Rider dugout with the rest of his family and Johnny, Frankie, and Tommy. She closed her eyes and silently said a prayer that he'd get a hit. She knew it was important to him to keep it going. He had told her many times how important it was to him to finally be recognized for a baseball achievement and not a fight.

"This is what the game's all about," he said, "and now I finally, after seventeen years, really feel part of it."

Way up in the mezzanine, Buffalo Bob sat silently still. He had waited weeks for it to come to an end so he could perform his devilish deed, and now he realized the time might be just before him. He found himself yelling, "Pop-up, pop-up!"

But there was no pop-up in Vince's bat. On a two-strike pitch, he made solid contact and pulled the ball deep down the left-field line. It fell in the stands for a home run. The streak had now reached forty.

It reached forty-one on Friday and forty-two on Saturday, once again before sold-out crowds that cheered with every swing of the bat.

On Sunday, Vince found his picture on the front of every major newspaper in the country. He was as big as any major figure, sports or political, of the day. He went two for four on Sunday, and there was no end to the media blitz that followed. Reporters even followed him to the shower to ask their questions.

Newark Airport was jammed with Vince Donato fans when the team arrived there to fly to Milwaukee for a three-game series. The terminal where they were departing from had to be blocked off because the crowd had become too big to handle. The media had also become too much to accommodate, and Tex rented a charter flight exclusively for the members of the press, which now numbered over one hundred fifty.

Thirty thousand feet in the air, Vince played cards with Jerry, Darnell, and Hip and reflected on what had become his journey into no man's land. No man other than DiMaggio himself had ever gone this far on a streak, and with every game, Vince was getting closer and closer to the final destination.

"I'm just sitting here thinking how it is that a whole country can get caught up over a game that little boys play every day. Yet I'm getting just as excited as everybody else. I'm wrapped up in it too. I want this thing. I want to be remembered as a player that traveled the same road with DiMaggio.

"It's a challenge. Sometimes I wonder what he thought when he was doing it. I mean, pressure is pressure, whether it was '41 or now. I wonder how his stomach felt every time he went up to the plate needing a hit, but he did it. He handled it good. That's 'cause the guy was great.

"Shit, I don't want anybody to forget DiMaggio, just remember me for what I'm doing now. That's all."

Jerry patted his legs. "You've done a lot with this thing. Nobody is going to forget you. Nobody but DiMaggio has even been where you are now. No, I don't think you'll be forgotten."

"Not by me anyway," said Darnell Taylor. "I may not be big on words, but I'd like to thank you for putting me in my place back in Texas at the beginning of the year. I had a big chip on my shoulder that I thought couldn't be knocked off, but in your way you did it, and I've been a better player for it. I want you to know that we're all for you, and we'll do anything to help you get this streak."

Vince nodded appreciatively. It meant a lot to him to know that the players he had stuck up for so many times in his battles with Tex were behind him. It gave him a good feeling.

"So tell me," asked the manager, "is it startin' to get to you?"

Vince leaned back in his seat and put his cards down. "Yeah, it's getting to me. I don't eat like I used to. I guess I lost eight or nine pounds already. I can't get a good night's sleep. It's always on my mind, along with other things. I find myself taking pills even though I know it's no good for me. I get the shits, go five or six times a day, guess it's nerves. I comb my hair and I find the comb full of hair, that's nerves too."

"When we were in Detroit I happened to pick up a nice-looking head in the lounge, and I couldn't even get it up with her, and that's a sign of nerves. Everywhere I turn, I find a microphone in my face. If I stay at home, they wait for me when I come out in the morning. If I stay at Luellen's, they wait in the lobby. I got no free time alone, they won't let me."

"So far I'd have to say you're holding up as good as can be expected, but it'll get a lot tougher as it goes on, a lot tougher."

3

Once again, Vince seemed to have a flair for the dramatic as he singled in his last time at bat in a hot and humid Milwaukee County Stadium. After the hit in the ninth, the sellout crowd rose and gave him a standing ovation. He tipped his hat, and play resumed.

It was that same way for games forty-five and forty-six as Vince had Milwaukee in the palm of his hand. The fans cheered him endlessly and hundreds waited every day in the hotel lobby just to get a glimpse of the man that was on the threshold of baseball history. The hotel had to assign a special security force just to keep wayward fans from wandering up to his room.

That week, Vince was privileged to grace the covers of all the national news magazines, and in an address to his cabinet in Washington, the President said, "I know that most of the country is worrying if Vince Donato will get a hit tonight, but let's see if we can't take care of some business anyway."

Vince had reached the top, and his streak had made the tight pennant race between Detroit and the Yankees seem a minor thing. All the eyes and ears of the country would now be focused on the ballplayer playing for a last-place team for the final ten games of the year.

The team flew into Newark late Wednesday night after their game with Milwaukee and landed at two-thirty in the morning. Even at that time, there were well over five hundred fans waiting to greet their player. There was no end to it.

He finally arrived home well after four, after addressing the mob at the airport for close to an hour. His bed felt good to him and he quickly fell asleep. He took advantage of Thursday's off day to get away from it all, and he and Luellen, accompanied by Tony, took a ride south to the Jersey shore where Vince had bought a house for his family.

Vince was on the verge of going off the edge. His family problems had more or less straightened themselves out, at least where Lucy was concerned. Grace seemed to be a lot stronger in going through her ordeal. Antionette and Marvin had opened lines of communication and were confident that the problems could be worked out. Vince was happy for them but now he had his problems. He never imagined that the pressure of his streak would affect him so much. He needed the comforting touch and feel of Luellen. It was at this time that he realized that he loved her and needed her as much as he ever loved or needed Marie.

The summer season at the shore was over and the crowds had all left. The weather was a warm seventy degrees and Vince and Luellen walked the beach for hours, hand in hand, just talking about things in general and nothing in particular. The press, with all its microphones, pads, pencils, and inquiring reporters was a thing of the past, today belonged to them.

They sat on the beach and watched the waves roll to shore. A little boy came by and threw bread up to the passing seagulls who caught the small pieces at their height and quickly swallowed them down. Vince and Luellen joined him. It was a happy time for both of them. When the boy left the two sat down and Vince revealed to her many of his deepest feelings. Feelings that only she could understand coming from him.

"This all happened so suddenly for me, everything. My sisters' coming to me for help, Tex and his nut of a wife, the guy that's out to kill me, Red's death."

"Red's death?"

"I never told you because I didn't want you to get alarmed, but the guy killed Red. Tony's been with me ever since."

"You said Johnny sent him away on business."

"I didn't want to get you alarmed."

She paused and looked at him. Her eyes were full of sorrow for the man she loved. Vince continued, "Then this streak starts up, and the guy says he's going to kill me when it stops. Imagine, I've got to get a hit to stay alive."

"Oh my god."

"Luellen, I'm scared as shit. Scared because I just can't take it anymore, I can't. Look at me," he said as he stuck out a shaking hand. "I got the shakes. I never had them before in my life. Why me? Why did God have to do this to me? I've always tried to be a good person. Why is he putting the weight of the world on my shoulders?"

She reached out and touched his face. The tears were dripping down her cheeks. Before her was a brave man who never had known fear. A man who had always faced his problems and never ran from them, but now he seemed beaten. There was too much against him to fight back. He was drained, and she knew that he was coming to her for the support that he needed.

"God would never give you anything more than you could handle. He's got reasons for doing what he does. In our minds, our human minds, we can't rationalize them, but they must be good reasons. Whatever happens and whatever you do, I'll be there. Through the thick and thin of it. Don't feel like the weight is only on your shoulders because I'm always here to help you carry the load."

He looked at her and realized how lucky he was. Her blonde hair was blowing in the wind, and he marveled at her natural beauty.

"You know, you belong with all of this."

"What do you mean?"

"I mean look around. The sea, the beach, the sky, birds flying, they're all nature, and nature is beautiful, and you're beautiful."

Luellen blushed. He had never spoken to her in this way before, and it made her feel a little uneasy, yet she loved the way he expressed himself.

"You know I'm a lucky man. I've been blessed with two women in my life who love me with all their hearts, and now I love both of them with all my heart. I'm not going to wait for the end of the season to tell you this because my season, my life, could be over any day. But I love you, Luellen, and I want you to spend the rest of your life with me as my wife and the mother of my children."

She hugged him as her tears of sorrow changed to tears of joy. "I want you to know that I'll make the best wife and mother in the world."

Vince needed no convincing. "I know."

They walked back to the house and made love all afternoon.

When Vince arrived at Jersey Stadium for the Friday night game with the Yankees, among his hundreds of letters and telegrams, he found one that was marked urgent. He wondered what was so urgent about it so he quickly opened it.

> Can't call you anymore since you disconnected your phone. This will be the last time you hear from me until I kill you. Good luck with the streak. I'm enjoying it.

Vince crumpled the telegram in his hand and threw it down.

"Something wrong?" asked Jerry.

"That guy just won't give up. He wants me."

Jerry knew exactly what Vince was talking about and picked up the crumpled ball of paper and read the telegram. "Man, I hope you did the right thing by going to Johnny instead of the police."

Vince started to wonder himself, "So do I Jerry. So do I."

For the first time in his streak, Vince went five times up in a game without getting a hit. Fortunately for him, the game went into extra innings, and hopefully he'd have another chance to keep it alive. But being the last player to hit in the ninth inning meant he'd have to go at least three more innings to get up again, and anything could happen in three innings. The Riders could win it with a home run or a single run at any time. The powerful Yankees could easily score a single run, hold the Riders scoreless in their half of the inning, and win the game just as easily. Vince's future was placed in the hands of the other players until he had a moment to take hold of it himself.

In the bottom of the tenth Stallings led off with a double down the right-field line. The fifty-six thousand fans booed. They didn't want to see the Riders win until Vince got another chance to hit, and if Stallings scored the game would be over. Designated hitter Jim

Blake grounded to second which moved Stallings to third where he had six different ways of scoring. He could score on a hit, a walk, a passed ball, a wild pitch, an error, or a long fly.

The Rider dugout was silent. Due to managerial moves that Hip had made in the seventh and eighth innings, the designated hitter had been removed from the game and the Rider pitcher was now up. Hip could pitch hit for him and go for the win, or he could take his chances on the pitcher hitting and leave it up to Cedeno. All eyes were on the old man as he leaned on the top step in the corner of the dugout. The game meant nothing to the Riders, but it did have relevance in the pennant race, and the old man was dedicated to playing the game the way it was meant to be played. He knew that his players wanted him to let the pitcher hit for himself. It would probably be an automatic out, and it would make the Yankee task that much easier to get out of the inning and force the game to go on, to give Vince another chance.

He answered the looks by saying, "We're ballplayers. We get paid to try our best to win games."

Vince looked at him and nodded in agreement.

Hip sent up a young rookie fresh up from the minor leagues to pitch hit. The kid popped up as the fans cheered wildly. It was up to Cedeno. He looked at Vince for direction. They all loved Vince. He had become the one man on the team that they all looked up to and admired. Cedeno was waiting for Vince to give him the sign to dive, but Vince would have none of it.

He walked to the top of the dugout and yelled out to the little shortstop, "Get good wood on it, Hector. Put the Yanks in second place. Fuck the streak."

Hector nodded and went in to hit. He hit the first pitch on the fat part of the bat, and the ball sailed through the infield as fast as a sound. The Yankee's shortstop made an all-or-nothing dive to his left and speared the ball from its flight, saving the game for the Yankees and giving Vince another life.

The Riders held once more in the top of the eleventh and Darnell Taylor almost broke the hearts of everyone in the park when his long fly ball just missed going out of the park by an inch. He wound up on second with a double.

Vince joined Jerry on the on-deck circle as Jerry was preparing to hit. “Whoever said it was a game of inches wasn’t lying,” he said.

“What do you want me to do?” Jerry asked. “I can easily strike out.”

“If I’m going to get it I’m going to get it legitimately. Go up there and take your chances.”

Jerry worked his way on with a walk, leaving it up to Vince to do it for himself. Vince knew that he’d have no more chances. The Yankees were too good a team to keep scoreless. Soon they’d score, and the game would be over. Now was his time. He’d have to meet the challenge once more.

The first pitch was a fast ball on the outside corner of the plate for a strike. The crowd was so quiet that the sound of the ball hitting the mitt could be heard way up in the upper deck. Vince fouled off the next pitch and was now in the hole with two strikes on him and facing a pitcher that he never had much success against. The third pitch was too close to take so he swung and popped up foul behind home plate. The catcher threw off his mask and ran for it. Vince watched the ball sail back and watched the catcher running. He’s got it, he said to himself as he eyed the flight of the ball to where the catcher was running.

With every step he took, the crowd remained in silence until the catcher finally dove into the stands and came up empty, missing the ball by an inch. Vince uttered to himself one more time, a game of inches.

Vince took a deep breath. His stomach was twisted and in knots. He felt like he had to vomit. He stepped out of the batter’s box and took another deep breath. The nervousness wouldn’t go away. He looked down each foul line and saw hundreds of cameras and reporters all focusing on him. He turned away and looked to the sky. “Marie, good Lord, please help me.” He stepped back into the box but stepped out once more. The mugginess of the night was making him sweat like a waterfall, and his hands were wet as rain. He dried them against his uniform shirt.

"Come on, Vince. I know it's tough. I wish you luck, but the games' got to be played. We need you in the box to hit."

Vince looked at the umpire and nodded. He found that he couldn't swallow. He made up his mind to swing at the next pitch wherever it was, just to get it over with. It was a fastball, high and inside, a pitch that he normally would've taken for a ball, but instead he swung. The ball jammed him, and he hit it on the handle of the bat. It blooped out toward third base. The third baseman stepped back and tried to catch it but it eluded his dive. Taylor scored, the Riders won, and Vince was up to forty-seven.

The press swarmed him like a horde of locusts. For what seemed like the millionth time, he answered the same questions. He was holding up to it, but just barely. His voice cracked at times, and at others, he seemed irritable and even got vulgar.

After an hour of their questions, he abruptly excused himself, leaving the floor for Hip and a few of his stories, and ran into the confines of the trainer's room, where no members of the press were allowed.

He came out over two hours later to still see over two dozen reporters waiting for him at his locker. They wouldn't let him go without asking a few more questions. He answered them quickly, dressed, then he and Tony were quickly out.

The players parking lot was filled with fans. They had waited since the game was over for Vince to come out to his car. In unison they started to chant "Vin-ee, Vin-ee" as he walked through them on his way to the car. They parted to let him walk as the Red Sea parted for Moses. He smiled and waved, shaking hands all the way.

A wild young female fan ran up to him and hugged him, wrapping her legs around him, "I want to fuck you so bad. Fuck me, Vince, fuck me!" she yelled.

The crowd roared with laughter as Tony pulled her off him.

A young man in his early twenties yelled out to him, "Donato, you suck! You couldn't shine DiMaggio's shoes." The boy was quickly mobbed, and a brawl ensued.

Vince and Tony ran away from it and into the car. They sped out and were on their way to Luellen's. Vince was shaking in the car and had no control of himself. He started to bang the dashboard with his fist and swearing at the top of his lungs. Tony reached over and grabbed him with one arm. Steering the car with the other, "Easy man, easy."

"Easy. You say easy!" Vince yelled. "Look at me. I'm a fuckin' nut. I'm crackin' up! I can't take it anymore, Tony. I can't fuckin' take it anymore. They want too much of me. I can't give it to them. Why should I? I'm going to be murdered when it's over anyway. Fuck. Why can't Johnny find that fuckin' guy? Why can't he find him?"

Tony pulled the car over and parked. With a powerful swing, he smacked Vince hard across the face. It cut his lip. Vince tried to fight back but had lost all his desire. Tony smacked him once more, grabbed him by his jacket collar, and brought him close to his face. "Cut the tears and act like a fuckin' man. So you're under the gun. It's nothin' none of us ever had before. I've come to respect you and love you so much these past few months. You got ice water in your veins. Don't ruin it now man. They're just people after a story. Your news and that's their job. They'll all go away once it's over. As for the other thing, I'll fuckin' die for you before he gets you. But don't ever doubt Johnny Midnight.' You more than anybody should know that, he'll get him first. Now straighten up and act like the man I know you are."

Vince wiped the blood from his lip with the back of his hand. His senses had quickly come back to him and a killer stare was in his eyes. He looked down at a cream-colored blazer that was stained with blood. Tony didn't know what to expect. "This is a five hundred dollar blazer that you had me bleed on," he said in a threatening voice that scared even Tony. His face broke out into a wide smile, "but it was blood that I'm glad was spilled. I got some tension out. I needed that. I'll be okay from here on out. Thanks."

Luellen was waiting for him with the tender loving care that only she could provide. He fell asleep in her arms as she prayed for his safety and well-being.

4

Ever since he had dumped her, Roxanne had lived with a vengence to get Luellen. It was an obsession that ate away at her everytime she thought about Vince and how Luellen would make love to him.

Trudy Giles had stopped printing the information she had obtained and subsequently exaggerated and that irritated her even more. Luellen Lee had the man she loved, the man she ached for, and Luellen Lee would pay for it.

Roxanne hadn't gone to the game that Saturday night. Instead, she stayed at her suite and watched it on TV. She was drinking heavily, trying to drown the lust that lived in her body when Vince came up in the fourth inning. She toasted him with a drink, and at that very moment, he drove a ball deep off the wall in centerfield and slid safely into second for a double. The streak had just reached forty-eight, eight from the record. She yelled with joy and guzzled down another as the camera showed a close-up of Vince's smiling, handsome, face as he waved to the cheering and wild crowd.

Suddenly she became excited. Her senses were alive, and she wanted Vince to touch her, to make love to her as only he could. She reached down and caressed her home where Vince once hung his hat. She worked hard at it, and it finally shot its warm, wet juices. She let out a moan and started again and became wet once more.

Thoughts of Luellen and Vince crossed her mind as she envisioned them making love. "That fuckin' whore!" she yelled and rushed into her room and then out the door, down the elevator and into a cab.

Luellen also opted to stay in that night and watch the game on TV. She knew that whatever happened at the game, whether he continued the streak or not, he'd be detained for hours after the game, and she didn't want to wait around that long for him to be through. Vince understood. Luellen invited his nephew Sal over for the night, and he brought his girlfriend with him.

The game was in the eighth inning, and the Yankees were way ahead. The three of them were enjoying some turkey club sandwiches that the hotel made when her bell rang.

Sal jumped to get it. Luellen told him to wait, that she'd answer the door. To her surprise, she found a staggering drunk Roxanne Hardin.

"Roxanne!" exclaimed Luellen.

She wobbled on uneasy legs. "You fuckin' whore! You'll never fuck him again." She reached into her handbag and drew a .38 snub nose that Tex had given her for protection.

She fired three shots at the beautiful actress, who stood motionless in total shock. She watched as Luellen fell back and down to the floor. She then put the muzzle of the gun in her mouth and pulled the trigger on herself, blowing out the back of her head.

Blood was everywhere as Sal came to Luellen's side. Her beautiful blond hair was now a bright red as she lay silently still. She was shot through her shoulder, across her head, and in her chest. His girlfriend screamed frantically. She was in total panic. Sal kept his cool. He quickly called the police, then the hotel desk. In a matter of minutes, help had arrived.

Vince was notified just as the game had entered the bottom of the ninth. He and Tony ran from the dugout, through the clubhouse, out into the parking lot to his car, and drove as fast as they could to the hospital.

He arrived in half hour's time, fighting Saturday night traffic all the way. Luellen was in the operating room, and he was told, the prognosis wasn't good.

As soon as the press found out, they stormed the hospital like the Mexicans stormed the Alamo. There were hundreds of them. The hospital staff showed great concern for Vince's feelings as they ushered him away from the scribes and into a doctor's private office, where he'd have to wait for the operation to be concluded.

The seconds turned into minutes and the minutes into hours. The air-conditioner wasn't working in the doctor's office, and the heat and mugginess were beginning to grow as unbearable as the anticipation. He was joined by his sisters and by Johnny, Frankie, and Tommy, his three closest friends. They sat for hours, waiting to see if Luellen would live or die.

At a little after 6:00 a.m., a doctor walked into the office. His gown was completely wet with perspiration, and the strain of all night surgery was written on his face. He walked up to Vince and held his arm. Vince braced for the worst. He spoke in a slow southern drawl. There was a strain in his voice. "I'd like to think she'll pull through, at least I'm fairly optimistic that she will. If she does they'll be a lot of complications."

Vince was quick to answer. "What kind of complications?"

"You have to realize that a bullet went into her head and grazed her brain. We don't know exactly what damage it caused, but it had to cause something to go astray. My guess is she'll have partial paralysis somewhere on her body, as to where we can't determine that yet. She'll have speech and hearing deficiencies, and we don't know exactly how coherent she'll be.

"The bullet in the shoulder shattered her collarbone. We had to do a lot of work to try to put it together again, but that was easy compared to the head wound.

"The chest wound was fortunate in that it went through the body very cleanly without touching the lungs or heart. That in itself was a major miracle. She's lost a lot of blood, and she's very, very critical.

"I'd say right now her chances are 40/60 that she'll pull through. But she should be dead, so maybe the fact that she's still alive means that she's got a strong will to live."

Vince stood in shock. He couldn't believe that his beautiful lovely angel was torn apart by bullets fired by a maniacal woman. His three closest friends surrounded him.

He turned and said to Frankie, "It's Marie all over."

"Pray, Vince. Pray that she pulls through."

"Is there a chapel here?" Vince asked the doctor.

He told them where it was, and they all went and prayed that Luellen Lee, the sweet, beautiful, and innocent Luellen Lee, would come out alive.

They stayed in the chapel for an hour before Johnny got them together to leave. "There's nothing we can do here. We all could use some rest. Leave the hospital your number, and they'll get in touch with you."

"I disconnected the phone," Vince reminded Johnny.

"That's right, I forgot. Look, the press is going to be all over your place, your father's and your sister's. They can't come close to mine, the security. So why don't you all wait it out at my house. It'll be a lot more quieter there."

They agreed, and they all went to Johnny's twenty-five-room mansion nestled away behind fifteen-foot walls and a security force of twelve men and six doberman pincher dogs. No reporter would ever get past the front gate.

Johnny's wife and Vince's sisters cooked a breakfast of eggs and pancakes, but Vince had no appetite. He called the hospital every half hour to see what the diagnosis was. The hardest phone call he had to make was to Luellen's parents. He cried so hard that Lucy had to take the phone from him and explain to them what had happened. They'd be on a plane as soon as they could. They'd have to drive a long way, to Omaha, to even get close to an airport.

They waited. Vince paced endlessly. Johnny sat and stared. Frankie, Tommy, and Tony played cards. The women held their rosaries. It was one in the afternoon when Frankie said to Vince, "You playin' today or what?"

Vince had the look of a worn tire. He hadn't had any sleep. A scrubbly beard grew on his cheeks and he was still in his uniform. "I'm staying right here until we get word on her."

"I wonder what prompted her to do a thing like that?" asked Johnny to no one in particular.

"Tex wanted headlines all year. I guess now he got more than he asked for." Vince looked at Lucy as he mentioned Tex's name. "You all right now?"

She knew what he meant. "Very good. Like I used to be."

Vince smiled. It was the first time he smiled since he slid into second base the night before. "And how are you and Marvin doing?" he asked Antionette.

"We can make it. We're both going to try."

Vince's smile widened. "And how's my oldest sister holding up?"

She smiled back. "As good as could be expected. God will take care of us all."

"God will take care of everybody. You'll see. Luellen will pull through and be as good as new, you'll see." Just at that moment, the phone rang. It was the hospital. All eyes were on Vince as he held the receiver tightly in his hand.

He hung the phone up and yelled, "Yahoo! Thank you, good God. She'll pull through."

The room was alive with joy and wet with happy tears. It's not going to be easy by a long shot, but the doctor said the chances are good she'll be almost normal. Shit, I wouldn't care if she was a cripple for the rest of her life. I love that woman!" he yelled, "God, I love her!"

"We better hurry if we're going to make the game," said Tony.

"It makes you wonder just how small a game that little boys play can be compared to a life." Vince got serious and for a moment they all reflected on his words. "But fifty-six, here I come."

Jersey Stadium was stuffed with fifty-six thousand fans who didn't know what to expect when they arrived. They were filled with the attempted murder or murder of Luellen, depending on which paper they read, and suicide of Roxanne. They didn't know if Vince would be there or not, but they all came to find out.

Hip had made the line-up without Vince's name in it. He wasn't sure himself if Vince would show up for the game. When he did show up, it was ten minutes before the game was to start. When the press found out, he was in the clubhouse they swarmed to him.

"I'll say this just once, then let me go play. Luellen will pull through, but it'll be a grind. The important thing is that she'll make it. I've got no remorse whatsoever for Tex or Roxanne. If you knew them like I know them, then you'd know why. That's it for now. I'll talk to you all after the game."

The crowd was in a hushed silence as Vince came to the plate in the first inning. Luellen Lee was theirs just as much as she was Vince's. She was voted most popular actress three years running, and the beautiful, down-to-earth woman was as much an idol to them as any American sports or movie star. They had no way of knowing that Luellen was going to pull through. Many of them had tears in their eyes when they saw Vince come to the plate, for seeing him reminded them of her and her tragic fate.

He stepped out from the batter's box and slowly looked at the crowd; up the first base line, behind the plate, and then up the third base line. The faces he saw were faces of concern. They were quiet and sad faces. They were his to have. If he wanted their sympathy for the love he lost, they were his. They'd be his strength to carry on.

His face suddenly showed a wide smile, and he gave the thumbs-up sign while nodding his head. They immediately got the message. Luellen would make it. They stood and cheered endlessly. Vince finally had to quiet them down to get the game going.

He dug in and eyed the pitcher. *Somebody's going to pay for me missing a night's sleep*, he said to himself, *it might as well be here and now.*

Vince hit the first pitch right back through the box for a single. The streak hit forty-nine, and the fans in Jersey Stadium never stopped cheering.

All week Vince spent his days in the hospital at Luellen's side. His family had opened their doors to her parents, and every afternoon, they would all go to sit by the fallen star.

Thousands of telegrams and get-well cards came to her from all over the world. Vince filtered all the flowers to other rooms in the city's hospitals and personally wrote thank yous to every person who had taken the time to send a card.

She was still in intensive care and very serious, but she'd survive, and that's all that Vince cared about. He wouldn't leave her side, except to go to the bathroom and the game. He'd sleep there every night, and every morning, he and the hospital priest would say a rosary for her. She couldn't answer back when he talked to her, but she did show signs that she understood what was happening around her. At times, she'd show tears in her eyes when Vince talked and that would make him cry too.

He'd stroke her hair and say, "You'll pull through, honey, and I'll always love you with all my might." That would bring more tears to her eyes, and Vince would gently wipe them. There was no doubting his love for her now; she had finally won him.

The media had a field day with it all. Vince was made out to be a saint for his constant vigil at Luellen's side. Stories appeared in every major newspaper in the country about Vince and Luellen; their trials and tribulations throughout the years together.

Roxanne had also drawn her share of publicity. In her death, she had become a martyr to every woman who felt the pains of a love she could not have. Circulation of all Metropolitan papers doubled because of the shooting. There could be no bigger news, except for Vince's streak.

Vince had reached fifty-three that Thursday night against Milwaukee by banging out four hits. It was the first time in a week that he had had more than one hit in a game, and it left him three games short of the record, the three that were left in the season.

After the game, he told the press, "I was in a little slump the past six or seven games. I guess you can understand why. But tonight, I hit the ball on the fat part of the bat all four times, and I feel hot as a pepper. I know I can stay hot for three more games. I just know it."

5

It was a little after one in the morning when Vince was awakened by the phone ringing. He had a private number installed and gave it to his family, Johnny and the hospital. He had decided to stay at home that night and not the hospital because he needed a good night's sleep in his own bed. The cot that the hospital provided was too stiff and hard for him to take night after night. His first thought was that something was wrong with Luellen. He raced to the phone.

"Hello."

It was Johnny. "We got him. We finally got the fuckin' prick. You and Tony get dressed and meet me at the club in Orange."

"You sure you got him this time?"

"I'm sure. In a little while, we're going to get even for Red."

"We'll be there in ten minutes."

Vince was there quickly. He told the reporters that were camped out in front of his home. They were constantly around even at 1:00 a.m., that he had to go to the hospital. "Nothing's wrong. It's just that it's my turn to sit with her. My sister's getting a little tired and wants me there to relieve her. Why don't you all go over there, and I'll meet you? We'll chew the fat a little."

They quickly jumped in their cars and were off to the hospital with visions of an exclusive story from the man that was three games away from breaking the most cherished record in professional sports.

Johnny and three of his men were waiting. He had murder in his eyes when Vince and Tony walked in. "Tonight's the night," he said as he took a tape recorder out of his desk.

"So where is he? What are we waiting for?" asked Vince.

"Relax. He's not going anywhere. I've got two guys where he is right now. If he leaves, they have instructions to pick him up. I want you to hear this first."

"What is it?"

"Remember I told you that I thought that Hardin still had a hand in it?"

"Yeah."

"And that we put a tap on all his phones?"

"Yeah."

"He finally made a bad move. He made this call yesterday, and it took us all day to trace down the number of where he was calling, but we did it. Here, listen."

Johnny turned the tape on, and Vince sat down to listen.

"Yeah," answered the voice that Vince recognized as Buffalo Bob's.

"I think we can call it off now." The voice was unmistakeably Tex Hardin's.

"What do you mean?"

"With the streak and the shooting, I don't need the publicity anymore. I'm in the black. We were only going to break the death threats if the season got out of control, but he saved it at the last minute. You can go home. I don't need your services anymore."

"Are you kidding or what? I'm in deep, and I won't get out until I kill him and Midnight, You seem to forget that I killed Midnight's ace man, and he won't rest until he gets even. They won't rest until they get me. So I have to get them first. I can't go back."

"Well, I'm washing my hands of the whole affair."

"You can't. You're in as much as me. If they ever find me, they have to trace me to you."

There was a very long pause on the phone. "He's thinking," moderated Johnny, "the wheels are turning,"

Tex continued. "Okay, wait until the streak stops, then get him. I'll take care of the other guy."

"How?"

"I've got ways. You just get, Vince, and plug him once for me."

The phone hung up, and Vince's face was red with rage. He pounded his fist hard against Johnny's table. "That fuck. I knew all along he was behind it. Let's get him too, tonight, with the other guy."

Johnny remained calm. He had been through these situations before. "Relax. There's plenty of time to get him, but I've got to admit. He had all the angles covered. If you didn't produce, he was going to break the death threats to the papers. He was determined to draw one way or the other."

"I kind of like it the way it turned out rather than him breaking it to the press," said Tony, "all except for Luellen."

"I'm sure he doesn't care one way or the other, as long as he turned a profit. Too bad he won't be around long enough to spend it all. Let's go."

The six men piled into Johnny's long black Cadilac and drove up the mountain to neighboring West Orange and a garden apartment. It was a short ride, only ten minutes, and Vince remembered how many times they took the same ride up the mountain to get in fights with a guy from West Orange Mountain High School. Tonight there would be violence too and certain death.

They pulled up with the lights off. Johnny quickly spotted his men, and they came to his car. "He's all alone in there."

"Good. You all know what to do."

They immediately broke up and off into their assigned spots. One was under his bedroom window, another was seated in the white Ford that he used for Red's ride, and still another was on the stair landing between the second and third floors. Johnny and a short older-looking man with a thin moustache talked privately away from Vince and then both drew small handguns. "You stay in the car. I don't want you around if there's shooting," Johnny said to Vince.

"What am I a Boy Scout? I have a stake in this too. He was my friend too."

"Okay, but just go along with the program. Whatever you do, when we get inside his apartment, don't go nuts on him. They'll be plenty of time later for that."

Vince nodded in agreement, and the three of them walked toward the apartment. They opened the glass door and walked up to the second floor and apartment 2a. Johnny knocked softly. There was no answer. He knocked again.

"Who's there?"

The older-looking man with the thin mustache answered quickly, "Tex."

Vince's eyes opened. He'd have sworn that Tex Hardin was standing there with them. The voice was perfect.

The door opened, and they quickly rushed in. The older man grabbed his arm and thrust it behind him, and Johnny put his gun under his throat. "One yell and I'll put a bullet through the top of your head. We're taking you for a ride. Let's go."

Still in his shorts, they led him out and quickly down the stairs and into the car, where Tony had it waiting near the front door. It was all done very smoothly and professionally, in a matter of minutes.

Buffalo Bob sat in the middle of the back seat with Johnny and his hitman on either side of him. In the front seat were Tony and Vince. The others had vanished as quickly as they came.

"I suppose there's no way to get out of it," he said to Johnny.

"Are you joking? You're a dead man, mister, and I'm pulling the trigger."

Vince turned and looked at him. Their eyes met and Vince felt his anger grow. "You fuck." He lost control and threw a punch that landed on the bridge of his nose.

"None of that. I told you!" yelled Johnny as he pushed Vince back.

"I want you before he pulls the trigger. I want to beat you until my knuckles bleed."

"Buffalo Bob" leaned his head back on the seat and closed his eyes. He was shaking with fright and he urinated through his shorts.

Tony got on the Garden State Parkway and drove south until they reached exit ninety-three, almost sixty miles from where they had gotten on. There, between the north and south lanes, was a stretch of trees and heavy woods that acted as a divider between the two directions. It was about ninety feet wide, enough for Johnny's purpose. It was well past 3:00 a.m., and the parkway traffic was very light. Tony cut the lights and pulled over to the divider.

They got out and ran into the wooded area while Tony pulled away.

"Where's he going?" Vince asked.

"He'll pick us up on the other side." He turned and faced Red's murderer. "I'm goin' to turn him loose on you. You give him a good fight, and maybe I'll let you live, minus your prick. At least you'll be alive. Go get him."

In the moonlight that filtered through the trees, Vince saw his initial rush and stepped aside. Vince followed after him with a hard kick to his kidneys and a solid punch to the back of his neck. He let out a loud yell and fell up against a tree. Vince rushed him and hit him with a left hook to the face and followed with a kick to his groin, which put him down to the ground. He kicked him repeatedly, all the time yelling Red's name. Finally, he stopped and leaned back on a tree, emotionally drained and out of breath.

"You're a whirlwind tonight aren't you?" said Johnny as they viewed their victim as he tried to rise. "You through?"

"Yeah," answered Vince.

At that moment, Tony pulled over on the northern side and waited for them to finish. Johnny bent down and grabbed the man by his hair and brought his face close to his own.

"Meet your maker, my friend." With that, he put the gun under his throat and pulled the trigger.

Blood flew everywhere, splattering their clothes. Johnny fired one more shot into his head and quickly covered him in leaves and fallen brush. They hopped into the car, and Tony drove off, leaving behind a murder victim who would never be found simply because nobody ever strolled the dividers of the parkway. Johnny had thought of everything.

With the threat of being murdered off his back, Vince was now ready to face the final three games of the season with a trouble-free mind. It was a challenge he looked forward to.

The Last Day

1

"Uncle Vinnie. Daddy wants to know if you're getting up now."

Vince rose and looked young Johnny Mezzanotte in the face. "Wipe off that jelly from your mouth. Here." He leaned across to his night table and pulled a Kleenex from the box.

The little boy took it and wiped his mouth of the purple jelly. He was five and had jet-black hair and big brown eyes, just like his father. His sister quickly joined him. She was two years older and had the Mezzanotte features.

She jumped on the bed and hugged up to Vince. "Are you going to be famous today Uncle Vinnie?"

He smiled and brushed back her hair. "I'm already famous honey. You know me don't you?"

She nodded. He turned to the boy. "And you know me too, right?" The boy nodded in agreement. "Well, if you two know me, then I'm as famous as anybody."

The little girl giggled, and Vince tickled her to make the giggling turn into laughter. Little Johnny jumped on the bed and joined them and Vince quickly wrapped the two of them up in his sheets and threw them over his back as if he was Santa Claus carrying a sack of toys. All the while the sack contained endless laughter. He put on his robe and walked from his room into the kitchen.

"Johnny, I found two little kids here and wrapped them up for you to have." He gently placed the sack down on the kitchen floor and opened it. "Here they are, John, you want them?"

The senior Mezzanotte burst out in laughter and the kids jumped out and hugged Vince. There was a lot of love in them for him and he loved them as if they were his own family, to him they were.

"Okay, kids, go in the den and watch TV. Uncle Vince and I have to talk," ordered the father. They left without protest. They were disciplined in a way to show respect when their father spoke.

It was Sunday morning and the last day of the season. Vince had carried the streak to fifty-five during the weekend series against the first-place Detroit Tigers by remaining as hot as he ever was all year.

In the Friday night game, played in front of such a packed house that the aisles were even filled, he had four hits in four at bats. The Tigers won the game, which put them in first place because the Yankees lost that night, but it was Vince that the crowd came to see.

As long as the streak remained alive, every game was to be broadcast on national TV. Every major and most of the minor papers in the country had writers there to cover it. Every major magazine from *Life* to *Time* and *Playboy* to *Playgirl* had their representatives there. Even TV crews and reporters from as far away as Japan and Central America, where baseball is as big as any sport, had members of their press in attendance. It was summed up very neatly by Brian Corcoran. Vince's old friend with the *Chicago Herald*, when he wrote, "Vince Donato and his streak has become as big as the Super Bowl, World Series, Kentucky Derby, and any Heavyweight Championship fight that ever was all rolled in one. Right now he is bigger than professional sport itself."

It didn't stop on Saturday, despite a potential problem when Jack Ronan worked behind the plate. Before the game, Hop told Ronan, "Jack, you make one bad call against my man, and I'll come running out of the dugout and take a bat to your head. If you don't believe me, then just go ahead and call a ball a strike, and you'll have Louisville Slugger tattooed across your forehead."

The old man wasn't bluffing and Ronan knew it. He'd put the grudge aside for one day. He'd call the game fair when it concerned Vince. But Vince was so hot it wouldn't have mattered anyway. He doubled in the second and again in the fourth. In the seventh, he hit a gigantic home run over the left-field fence. His six runs batted in beat the Tigers and with the Yankees winning, made first place a dead heat tie with only one game left and set up the classic confrontation for the last game, Gordon vs. Donato. The fireball pitcher against the hottest batter. To escape the hundreds of reporters that followed him like a shadow, Vince stayed in the guarded confines of Johnny's mansion. He would leave only to see Luellen in the hospital and travel to the game.

Now it was the last day, and Vince was eating breakfast with Johnny and his wife. He had just finished his second cup of coffee when Johnny asked his wife to leave the kitchen. "Vince and I have something to talk about." She left and went into the den to play with her children.

"It's been an interesting summer, hasn't it?"

"Sure has," answered Vince, not fooled by Johnny's statement. "I've known you long enough to know that there's something on your mind. It's written all over your face. Want to talk about it?"

Johnny leaned back and looked away. He lit a cigarette. "What I've got to say is as important to you as anything that's happened this summer." He turned and faced him. "So I suggest you listen and listen well.

"I've never been one to call in a favor, you know that, but I figure you owe me for getting the guy from Texas. I don't want to bring it up, but just keep it in mind. There was a time when I once told you when we both chose our ways of life, that our paths were going to cross, and you'd have a decision to make. Well, that time has arrived.

"Ever since your streak hit fifty games, I've been taking book on whether or not it would continue. It might make you happy to know that no matter how long I set the odds against you making it, they still bet you, and bet you big. Between Vegas, Tahoe, and the local books, I've gone in the hole close to four million. I've got a lot of money, but I don't have four million to dish out like that. So now we come to fifty-six. I'm figuring that they'll be three times as much as that bet on you to hit it. That's one reason why I need you to take a dive."

"What's another?" asked Vince in a defiant tone. He didn't like what he was hearing.

Johnny scratched his chin. His black eyes were fixed on Vince. "I owe the other families. I owe them big. I told them that you'd take a dive and for them to bet that the streak would stop. If that happens, I'd just about break even for the whole thing."

"You told them that?" quickly spoke Vince, his temper was starting to show. "You told them I'd take a dive without even asking me first?"

"There shouldn't be anything to ask. I need you now. I'm the one that's in trouble."

Vince paused. *Is Johnny more important to me than the streak?* he asked himself. "What if I get a hit? What if I don't take the dive?"

"We're both dead men. They want me as it is. That'll just be their excuse to put a hit on me. As for you, they'll think you were in it with me and get your ass too. And when they go after somebody, they get them, not like this cowboy from Texas."

"So what you're saying is if I don't take the dive, then we're as good as dead."

"That's it. It's that simple."

Vince stood up and paced the kitchen floor. "Man, did you put me in the fuckin' hole. You got a lot of fuckin' nerve, John. You had no right to say that without asking me. I've got to say no."

"No?"

"And I'll tell you why. You have to be a ball player to know what this record is all about. All my career all anybody thought of when they mentioned Vince Donato was a crazy fuckin' guy who got in fights and banged broads. For the first time in my career, I'm finally. Finally, after eighteen years of playing baseball for a living, getting attention for something I'm doing on the field. Do you know what that means to me? It means that I've finally become a baseball player. I'll never give it up. It means too much to me. I go look at Luellen every day. I see her sweet innocent face all bandaged up, and I see tubes running in her body, and I see the tears in her eyes, and I know that somehow I'm responsible for what happened to her. If I take a dive, I'm taking a dive on her. I won't do it. I won't."

"I'd figure you'd say that. Then we're dead men…"

Vince didn't give him time to finish. "Johnny, after what I've been through this summer, this will be one more hurdle I'll have to leap. You've toyed with death all your life. It's the business as you once said, this is no different for you."

"But it is. I've never faced the other four families together. Unless I stay holed up here, which I'll never do, I don't hide from anyone, we'll be hit in two days, maybe sooner. I guarantee it."

"The only way you'll collect is if Gordon strikes me out every time up because I'm going for it, no matter what the consequences."

"Then God bless our souls."

"Amen."

2

Vince walked into the hospital room, bent down, and kissed Luellen on the cheek. "Hi, hon. I've come to tell you that today I'm going to make history. Today I'm going to get a hit for the fifty-sixth straight game, and I'm dedicating it to you."

She smiled and tried to speak. Nothing came out. "Don't try to talk. Doctor said it's too early yet for you to talk."

He held her hand and kissed it. "I love you so much." Tears came to his eyes. He was thinking of how he was responsible for her being there."I love you so much, Luellen," he said again, "If it takes forever, I'll make you well."

Her eyes became watery. He wiped them with a Kleenex, then told her of the excitement at the stadium in Saturday's game. He brought a smile to her face when he told her that Hip asked him for his autograph. He stayed for an hour, then it was time to have his date with destiny.

Johnny had his date to meet too. After Vince left to go to the hospital, he called the man who was with him the night they murdered Buffalo Bob. He was Johnny's most experienced and deadly assassin and all the important jobs Johnny gave to him.

"It looks like we're going after the cowboy tonight."

"Oh?"

"Vince won't take a dive. I knew he wouldn't. They'll be out for my blood. We can't beat them all, so what I want to do is this. If he gets a hit, call all our people and start it. At least we'll get some of them before they get us. Leave the cowboy to me, I want him. I'll try to get Vince out before they get him, but he's like me, he won't run. I'll leave it up to you to hit them good."

"I'll take care of everything. Good luck."
"If we ever come out of this, I owe you."
"If we ever come out of it."

3

It was a dark day. The weather was in the low sixties and brought a chilled breeze over the stadium. Vince had met the press for two hours before the game and flatly predicted that Gordon would be the only pitcher, if any, that could stop the streak, but "he's not going to do it."

As he came up for the first time in the second inning, he received a fifteen-minute standing ovation. They wouldn't stop. He had given them a season of thrills that they'd never forget, and now they were showing their appreciation in the only way they knew how.

When they quieted down it seemed like a cemetary. There wasn't a sound to be heard. Each fan was caught up in his anxious moment of anticipation to see if this would be the time when history was made.

Vince dug in and looked at the tall rookie. He wasn't nervous like so many times during the course of the streak. He was so confident that he could hit Gordon that he didn't even think about not getting a hit.

"Nothing but fastballs, Vince!" yelled Gordon from the mound.

"That's the way I like it," he answered.

The first pitch was high and in but caught the corner for a strike. Gordon had struck out two in the first and had his good stuff. The second pitch came roaring in and Vince swung under it, the velocity caused by its speed making the ball rise as it approached the plate. Vince swung and missed on the third pitch and was out on three blazing fastballs.

When he went into the dugout, he told Jerry, "That's the fastest ball I've ever seen in my life. Is that kid human?"

Jerry winked. "Not so human that you can't hit him."

Vince was beginning to doubt that as he struck out again in the fourth, again on three straight fastballs.

Johnny was in the crowd with Frankie, Tommy, and the Donato family and had hoped that Vince had a change of heart. He cares too much for life to throw it away on a game, he thought, but he was proved wrong when Vince got a hold of an inside fastball and lined it deep down the leftfield line in the seventh inning.

It was mass hysteria as the ball took off the bat like a jet. There was no question as to whether or not it was out of the park, the big doubt was whether or not it was going to be a fair ball. Ronan was the third base umpire and it was his job to run down the line and see where the ball entered the stands. It was an upper-deck shot and landed just foul by a foot or so.

"Foul ball!" yelled Ronan and he turned and looked at Vince, who had never left the batter's box, and smiled. He was glad it was foul.

"Up your ass too, Ronan," he silently said.

Play continued and once again Gordon got the best of Vince by striking him out for the third time in the game. Vince had one more chance coming.

The Tigers were in the lead by a score of seven to one when Vince came out of the dugout to kneel in the on-deck circle in the ninth inning.

He looked around the huge park and saw thousands of eyes staring at his every move. They weren't paying any attention to Jerry, who was batting. They had come to see Vince hit, and now they were ready as he came to bat for the last time in the season needing a hit for the record.

His stomach was light and squeezy. The nervousness had returned. He looked down the first baseline and saw two cameras, their red lights on, pointing their lenses in his direction. He looked over to the third baseline and saw two more. His head began to pound and he leaned down and rubbed his temples. Just then a small TV cameraman, carrying a portable camera on his shoulder, came running from the dugout and cemented himself not more than two feet from him.

Vince turned and angrily said, "Get the fuck out of here or I'll shove that camera so far up your ass it'll come out your mouth."

The man sensed Vince wasn't in the mood for close-ups and quickly ran away. Vince continued to kneel. His mouth was dry. He felt like he had to move his bowels. "No. Not the shits here." He started biting his lower lip. Jerry flew out, and now it was time.

He slowly rose and took a deep breath. The nervousness was still there. His mouth was still dry, and his stomach now was heavy. He slowly walked to the plate as the huge overflow crowd became so silent that the only noise heard was that of a baby crying along the first base foul line.

"Good luck," said the Detroit catcher.

"Thanks," answered Vince as he stepped out of the box and took another deep breath.

"Nothing but heat!" yelled Gordon once more from the mound. He had fifteen strikeouts thus far and was looking for sixteen.

Vince nodded. "Fair enough," he said a silent prayer and stepped into the box looking to meet his destiny.

His family were all on the edge of their seats. His sisters and mother all held each other's hands. Frankie, Johnny, and Tommy were quiet as they all sat and watched, hoping that their close friend would give them a reason to stand and cheer. Johnny suddenly yelled out, "Rip it, Vince. We're dead anyway." He knew that Vince's long foul ball had marked them for death and he wanted his friend to go down with the record.

Vince stepped out from the box when he heard what Johnny yelled and looked in his direction. He knew exactly what he meant and nodded to him.

"What's that mean?" asked Frankie.

"It's between Vince and me. You're not involved in this one."

Vince stepped back in the box and waited for Gordon's heat. The first pitch was a flash as it came in so quickly that Vince's hand-eye coordination was no match for it. He swung but was late by a wide margin.

Vince stepped out of the box once more. *I've got to get wood on it*, he said to himself. *I can't strike out one more time. I can't. He choked up an inch on the bat, hoping it would make it easier to swing, and stepped back in.*

Gordon's second pitch was a laser. It came by so fast that Vince didn't even have time to swing. "Strike two," yelled the umpire.

He was down to his last strike. He stepped out and looked down. He was beaten. Gordon was too good for him that day. Too fast. He looked up in the sky. "Marie, just let me get wood on the ball. Let me have a shot at a hit. Please."

He stepped back in and faced Gordon for the last time. The tall right-hander wound up and came overhand. Vince picked the ball up clean and started his swing as soon as it left his hand. It was there in a wink of an eye, and Vince heard the solid crack of the ball meeting bat and felt the dull thud in his hands.

He lined it on a bounce down the third baseline. Vince knew he hit it hard and started running. He was looking as he ran and saw the ball bounce over third base and heard the crowd bring forth a thunderous roar.

I did it, he said to himself. *I fuckin' did it.*

His smile was quickly brought to a frown when he heard the crowd booing. Ronan had called it a foul ball. Vince ran across the infield like a mad dog and accosted the short umpire. Hip and his players had run out first. When Vince got there he heard Ronan telling the Rider's third base coach that it "bounced fair before it reached the bag but crossed the bag in foul territory. It was a foul ball."

Vince would have none of it. He reached for Ronan but was held back by Darnell and Jerry. "I'll kill you, Ronan. I swear to God, I'll kill you." He was wild, ranting like a crazy man. Hip was red in the face arguing with Ronan. The umpire turned his back on him, and Hip just walked around and started again. The players wouldn't let up either. The other umpires had to come over and shoo all of them back into the dugout or face fines.

A fan jumped the fence and went after Ronan. He was quickly wrestled down by the grounds crew and ushered back into the stands. Hip wouldn't give up. He picked up third base and threw it at Ronan, receiving an automatic ejection from the umpire. Hip didn't care. He ran and got second base, and threw it wildly into center field and threw first base high in the air.

The fans were being treated to possibly the most exciting moment in baseball history. Hip wouldn't stop. He flung his cap at Ronan and then his shoes, Ronan dodged everything.

"You know it was fair, and you just won't give the guy a break. I hope you rot in hell," said Hip as he was finally through. Face red and completely out of breath, he finally walked back to the dugout, a tired and worn old man.

Hip was through, but Vince wasn't. All the while that Hip was putting on his show he was trying to break the grasp of his two closest friends on the team. They held him tightly, fearing for Ronan's safety if he ever broke loose. Vince fought so hard and long that he tired them out and their grip became weak. He finally broke loose and went straight for Ronan as the crowd cheered his attack. He flew through the air, wrestled him down to the ground, and began to punch furiously. He was a madman, out of control. Jerry and Darnell quickly recovered and pulled him off the fallen umpire, who lay there in a pool of his own blood.

The crowd was in a hysterical frenzy. They had never seen anything like it before and probably never would see anything like it again.

Johnny said to Frankie, "Look at him. He's crazy. We better go out and calm him down."

The three of them ran down and out to the field. They helped subdue their friend and brought him back into the clubhouse. The game was called and Detroit had won.

The clubhouse doors were locked and closed to the hundreds of reporters who had waited outside. Vince continued his rage in the clubhouse. He picked up a bat and swung at the lockers. "He stole it from me. I saw it clear the bag. It was fair. I know it was fair. He stole it from me."

Johnny, Frankie, and Tommy took him into the trainer's room and away from the other players. "Look it's over. There's nothing that could be done now. Forget it," yelled Johnny.

Vince was slowly calming down. His hands were shaking and Ronan's blood was on his uniform. "Forget it. Just like that. I had it, John. I fuckin' had it. The guy took it away from me."

"Look, man. You got it as far as we're concerned. Calm down. Act like a man, will you? What did Luellen say? It's only a little boys game, right?"

Vince's head was nodding. He breathed a deep breath. "Yeah. Thank God for Luellen." He paused a moment and thought how silly she would make him feel over the whole thing. "I guess it was pretty stupid."

"But shit, it was the most exciting thing I've ever seen," said Tommy.

"I guess they all want their story now. Get them all in the press room, and I'll be there after I take a shower. But first, I want to talk to my teammates."

His three friends left and went into the press room, where they were deluged by the onslaught of reporters.

Vince went back into the clubhouse and addressed the team. "I want to say that I've never played with a bunch of guys that stuck by me as close as you guys did during this whole streak. It's like I had twenty-four brothers looking after me. I'll never forget any of you, and I love all of you like a brother."

He walked up to Hip, who was sitting on a chair. "As for you, my friend. I love you like my father." He hugged him and kissed him on the cheek, "Thanks."

Hip was caught for words. His eyes became watery, and he turned and walked into his office.

"I'm going to take a shower, and then I'd like to be alone, to think about it. I'd appreciate it if you told the reporters that I'll be out in a while. In the meantime, I'll leave from the dugout and out the stadium exit."

Vince managed to evade the reporters and leave the stadium without being mobbed by them or any of the fans. He did bump into a few fans who were still left outside the stadium, but they didn't bother him at all.

After a few remarks, they quickly let him go on his way. A crowd had formed in the player's parking lot however and that would pose a problem.

Fortunately for him, a cab driver was stopped in traffic right in front of where he was standing. The driver recognized him immediately. "Think you can get me out of here quick?", Vince asked.

"Are you kiddin'? Hop in."

Vince opened the door and sat in the passenger's seat.

"It's really you."

"It's really me."

"Where do you want to go, Vince?"

He pondered for a second. "Essex Avenue, Orange, New Jersey."

"What's there?"

"A playground, my friend, where little boys play baseball."

4

Vince got out of the cab and took a long look at the apartment where he grew up. It hadn't changed much throughout the years. It was still old and rundown. None of the tenants still lived there that were in the building when his family lived there. The only family close was Frankie's, who lived down the street on the corner house next to the Polar Star tavern.

Across the street were the projects, and Vince immediately thought of Red. He walked into the project playground, sat down on a bench, and watched as eight little boys were playing baseball on the academ.

As he watched he remembered how they used to play in the same academy when they were children. How Red was the home run champ of Essex Avenue because he was the only one who could hit the ball more than three stories high. He remembered how Frankie and Tommy used to hit the ball foul and it would go across the street and roll into the driveway of Spinelli's chicken yard and how Johnny used to rattle the chicken coops every time he went to get a foul ball.

He remembered the time he fell off the monkey bars and scrubbed his knee. The time his father chased him out of the house for drawing a black eye on a picture of his mother and caught up to him in the playground. He remembered how embarrassed he was that all the black women were looking out the windows when his father took off his belt and whipped his rear. How they all laughed and cheered his father. He remembered the time a young black man threw soda bottles down at them from a fifth-story window and how they all wanted to go get him. Red stopped them and went up himself. He came down with a swollen shut eye but he took care of the man and they never had any more trouble from any of the residents of the projects again.

He was home and he felt a peace within himself. It wasn't Beverly Hills or any rich neighborhoods that he had been in, but it didn't matter to him. This was in his blood, this way of life, this way of living, and he never would want it any other way.

It was well after seven o'clock. Vince had been watching the boys play for over an hour and enjoying every minute of it, for it reminded him so much of a happier time. The thought of danger with Johnny's enemies never crossed his mind, but it was there.

Frankie was the first to find him. He walked into the playground and sat down next to his lifelong friend.

"I had a feeling you'd come here. I just had a feeling."

"Look at them," he said as he pointed to the boys, "they've been playing for hours. Remember when we were young? How we loved to play ball here. Remember how "Red" used to hit the three-story home runs?"

Frankie laughed. "Yeah. You hit a few too."

Vince's voice was lost in a fog. His mind was in another place. "Yeah. I hit a few. I got a hit today too."

Frankie remained silent, lost for words.

Vince continued, speaking from someplace far away, out of line with reality. "They took it away from me, Frankie. Everything I ever wanted in life has been taken away. First Marie, she was taken away from me. Then, Luellen, let's face it, she'll never be the same. Then this streak. Red's gone. There's going to be a war with Johnny's business. He'll be gone. It just isn't fair Frankie. It's just not fair."

Frankie was somber. "Maybe it just wasn't meant to be. Maybe it just wasn't in the cards."

As they were talking, they failed to notice three cars drive up on either side of the two tall housing projects. Two men got out of two cars, and the driver stayed in the third. They were Tony Lombardi's men, and they had come for Vince.

They were stationed on either end of the playground and slowly started walking toward Vince and Frankie and toward the main gate. Their plan was to get Vince, anyway they could, and take him for a one-way ride. If anyone else was there to intercede on Vince's behalf he was a dead man too.

Johnny was Palma's target and his men were out searching the area for him. He eluded them at the stadium, and he and Tommy went looking for Vince. They, too, had the notion that he'd return to the place of his childhood home runs.

They drove up, parked in front of the old apartment, and quickly crossed the street and into the playground. They hadn't noticed Lombardi's men either.

"We've got to get out of here," spoke Johnny, his voice in a rush, "the war's started, and we'll be the first targeted."

Vince was calm. He looked at Johnny and smiled as if to not care at all what was about to happen.

"What are you a jerk or what," continued Johnny, "you've got to get the fuck out of here. So you didn't get a hit, so what? The sun is still going to shine tomorrow, and I want you around to see it. Now get up off the fuckin' bench and let's get out of here."

"What war? What are you talking about?" asked Frankie, concerned for his friends.

"If you were smart you'd get out of here too. This one doesn't concern you. For your own safety, you better go."

Vince finally came to his senses. "You better go, Frankie. There's going to be a lot of shooting going on. We'll see you soon."

At just that moment, Tommy spotted Lombardi's men approaching the playground entrance. "They're here."

"Let's get out of here."

They ran out the gate and practically ran down the four men. They were followed by bullets streaking by them. Johnny ran to his car but a bullet had flattened his front tire.

"Through the chicken yard," yelled Vince. As boys, they had run through the chicken yard and out the back alley, which would put them on the next block and nearer Johnny's club, where'd they be safe.

The four ran down the long driveway, past the hundreds of screaming chickens, and quickly turned into the alley they had run through hundreds of times. Their path was stopped by a ten-foot-high concrete wall. It had never been there when they were young.

"Shit. Who put this fuckin' wall here!" yelled Johnny.

The four men found them. They were trapped. They were like fish in a bowl. Hot lead shot out from their guns and in a matter of seconds, four friends lay mortally shot in the back alley of an old chicken yard.

Vince was propped up against the back wall. Across his legs was Johnny, shot through his head and side. Tommy was motionless in the corner, covered with blood, and Frankie lay face down in his red pond. Vince felt no pain. He was shot in his stomach, groin, and chest. He felt blood oozing from his mouth. He looked up and saw a palatial blue cloud. In the blue cloud was Marie. He reached out to her and yelled, "Marie!" At that moment, Vince Donato was reunited with his first and only true love.

Epilogue

The following story appeared in the *Chicago Herald*, written by Vince's friend Brian Corcoran.

They buried a close friend of mine yesterday along with three of his closest friends, all victims of an apparent mob execution.

Somehow it seems just that Vince Donato met his maker in the manner that he did. It was a result of the way he lived his life and the way he was, a man of action.

He was born, raised, and died in Orange, New Jersey, but his life and legend lived throughout the country.

It started in a small Mexican café in El Paso, Texas, in his minor league days when he was set up, as he told me years later, by a man who was getting revenge for feeling the thunder that Vince's fists carried. Vince was brutally beaten and almost died, but he had enough fight in him to live and carry on.

The reputation lived on, growing with every fight and romance. There was the time the brash young rookie with the Chicago White Sox took on the New York Yankees, all twenty-five of them, in their clubhouse. There was the time he spared with heavyweight champ Ali Shabazz and knocked him down and a night club brawl that put him in jail for the night.

Probably his most famous fight of his many was the one in which he punched out a student who was in the process of burning the American flag on the field of Fenway Park in Boston. Vince put the fire out and marched the flag around the park.

The women in his life were as endless as they were beautiful and numbered in the hundreds. He made Casanova look like a shy teenager with pimples. But there were only two that ever meant anything to him, and they were tragically taken out of his life. One totally, by dying in a car accident, and one partially, the victim of a jealous woman's gunshots who couldn't stand to see Vince giving his love to another.

When Luellen Lee found out about Vince's death she lost her will to live and passed on. Now all three have been reunited.

My friend was a family man who worried more about his family's health and happiness than he had a right to. Much of his recent turmoil stemmed from the fact that members of his family were in trouble and he saw it as his obligation to help them in any way he could. That was the way he was.

I can say that a man could have no better friend. Every Christmas my family would receive gifts from him and when my youngest daughter was ill and in need of special care, it was Vince, through his many connections in the medical world from his volunteer work with Chicago's hospitals, that had a world-famous doctor work on her. When I never received a bill I told him and he said to me, "Don't worry about it. It's been taken care of." That's the way he was.

His teammates swore by him. They gave him all their respect and admiration. The first time the Riders played in Baltimore, one of the Orioles continually joked and made fun of the Rider's Japanese player, Isoruko Ishito. Ballplayers are a vicious breed when they joke but the joking got out of hand, and the racial slurs were becoming too serious to bear. Vince approached the Oriole player and told him in plain English to cut it, or he'd shut him up. The joking stopped.

He lived every day of his life as if it were his last. Vince was never deprived of thrills in life and probably his greatest thrill came when he was challenging the great Joe DiMaggio's fifty-six-game consecutive hitting streak.

It ended in the only way that was fitting for him, in controversy. He assaulted umpire, Jack Ronan, a long-time nemesis, and subsequently, the game was called, the only game ever to be called by umpires for reasons other than weather or darkness. The record still stands at fifty-six.

I'll miss my friend and so will thousands of others. As Tex Hardin, a man whom Vince had numerous run-ins with, said at the funeral, "We'll all miss Vince in one way or another. Some loved him and others hated him. He may be dead, but if ever these words were true, he was a man whose legend will definitely live on."

I couldn't help but think that if Vince could rise from his grave he'd tell Tex, "Cut the bullcrap. You hated me as much as anybody. Go pound salt." That's the way he was.

Printed in the USA
CPSIA information can be obtained
at www.ICGtesting.com
CBHW020312171024
15896CB00027B/64